PR
2348
.N4
1964

37117

NELSON
John Skelton, laureate

John Skelton, Laureate

TITLE PAGE OF *DYUERS BALETTYS AND DYTIES SOLACYOUS*
PUBLISHED BY PYNSON WITHOUT DATE

John Skelton

LAUREATE

By WILLIAM NELSON, 1908 -

NEW YORK

RUSSELL & RUSSELL · INC

1964

PR
2348
. N4
1964

NUMBER 139 OF THE
COLUMBIA UNIVERSITY STUDIES IN
ENGLISH AND COMPARATIVE
LITERATURE

Acknowledgments

To Professor Harry Morgan Ayres, of Columbia University, I owe a great deal more than my first interest in Skelton and invaluable assistance in the research. If I have begun to apprehend the meaning and value of scholarship, it has been largely a consequence of his teaching.

It is a pleasure to acknowledge my debt to Professor Jefferson Butler Fletcher, of Columbia University, whose stimulating criticism and kindly guidance I shall always remember most gratefully. The members of Professor Fletcher's seminar in Renaissance literature have listened patiently to a great part of the work and have assisted me materially in revising it. Dr. Henry W. Wells, of Columbia University, and Dr. William G. Crane, of the College of the City of New York, have also provided new insights and helpful suggestions.

An extended and pleasant correspondence with Dr. H. L. R. Edwards, of Corpus Christi College, Cambridge, England, has fortified me with valuable advice and criticism, which I have recognized only incompletely in the notes. I hope for the early appearance of Dr. Edwards' projected editions of Skelton's poems and the translation of Diodorus Siculus.

I wish to acknowledge the assistance of the officials of the libraries at which I have worked: Columbia University Library, the British Museum, the Public Record Office, the Bodleian, the library of Westminster Abbey, the New York Public Library, the Library of Congress, and the libraries of Trinity College and Corpus Christi College, Cambridge. I am especially grateful to Mr. Percy Bramble,

of Caister-on-Sea, Norfolk, England, without whose aid
I should never have been able to find my way through the
maze of the archives at Norwich Cathedral.

I am deeply grateful for the encouragement and un-
stinted assistance given me by my brother, Saul Nelson,
and by my good friends, Raymond and Florette Henri,
and Eleanor Rosenberg. Of my wife's part in the making
of this book, I can say little here. Far more important than
the material help which she gave me is the fact that
because of her the long labor has brought me, not weariness,
but exhilaration.

January 16, 1939   WILLIAM NELSON
New York, N. Y.

Contents

Illustrations

ERRATA

p. 2, *l.* 22.	*after* Henry VIII *insert,* discovered and edited by F. M. Salter
p. 70, *ll.* 23-6.	*delete* In the latter capacity . . . university.
p. 74, *l.* 14.	*for* Ebra[u]cus *read* Ebrancus
p. 74, *ll.* 15-7.	*for* The modern editor . . . certainly correct *read* "Ebrancus" or "Ebraucus" is the mythical founder of York and Henry became the "new York" in 1494.
p. 77, *l.* 18.	*for* second husband of Lady Margaret *read* one of the King's principal advisers
p. 109, *l.* 7.	*for* 1530 *read* 1529
p. 111, *ll.* 19-20.	*for* whose opposition . . . stamped him *read* who was reputed among Protestants
p. 127, *note* 44.	*for* Pynson *read* R. Faukes
p. 134, *l.* 7.	*for* Pynson *read* Faukes
p. 208, *l.* 19.	*for* Duke *read* Earl

Introduction

THAT this book is an uncomfortable compromise between a collection of scattered papers concerning John Skelton and an orderly "Life and Works" results partly from the nature of the material itself and partly from the manner in which the research was pursued. It was originally inspired by a lecture given about ten years ago by Professor Harry Morgan Ayres, at Columbia University. On the day after that lecture, with the thunder of *Colin Clout* still rumbling in my ears, I chanced upon a copy of Skelton, bought the volumes, and read. There was much that was fascinating, much that I failed to understand, and *Speak, Parrot*, in particular, appeared to me the most artfully compounded conglomeration of gibberish that I had ever encountered. Although I am now sure that *Parrot* is anything but gibberish (despite the fact that many passages remain dark to me), I am more than ever convinced that its author was a genius of high rank.

Study of *Speak, Parrot* led to a consideration of the course of events in Skelton's quarrel with Wolsey, and that in turn to problem after problem, until I had meddled with so many Skeltonic cruxes that it became necessary to call a halt in order to fashion the inchoate mass of material into a semblance of shape.

That shape is this book. It betrays its haphazard development both by what it omits and by what it stresses. For example, *Colin Clout*, generally accepted as the best of Skelton's poems, receives less discussion than the mediocre *Replication*. *Magnificence* and *Elinor Rumming* are allowed less extended treatment than the poems against the Scots. Furthermore, the first (and the longest) chapter of this

book concerns a group of scholars at the court of Henry VII
and leaves Skelton himself out of direct consideration.

But these emphases, which would certainly be distort-
ing were the book a "Life and Works," are not without
justification. Since the learned Dyce published his edition
of Skelton's works in 1843 there has been no attempt to
re-edit the poems or to present a full length biography in
English.[1] Scholarly editions of several of Skelton's works,
a number of German dissertations, a scattering of articles
in the learned periodicals, and a flurry of letters to the
London Times Literary Supplement constitute the sum of
modern scholarly effort. In consequence, there are errors
to be corrected, records to be searched, problems to be
posed and settled. Argument requires more space than
simple exposition; new discoveries must be allotted fuller
discussion than facts long established.

Indeed, the account of Skelton here presented is very
different from that found in the pages of Dyce, and naturally
so in consideration of the new material turned up since
his day. Dyce had read neither Skelton's *Speculum principis*
(the instruction book written for Prince Henry, later
Henry VIII) nor the poet's first extant work, the translation of Diodorus Siculus. After Dyce's monumental edition
was published, Ashton printed an early version of the
Treatise against the Scots, Mullinger identified the young
scholars berated in the *Replication,* Bradley solved Skelton's
cryptograms, Brie pointed out that the *Book of Three Fools,*
attributed to Skelton, was part of Henry Watson's translation of the *Ship of Fools.* A document referring to the administration of Skelton's estate, others linking the poet
with Westminster Abbey, and references to him in Cambridge records have been unearthed. J. M. Berdan, H. L. R.

[1] Mr. L. J. Lloyd's *John Skelton* (Oxford, 1938) reaches me just as this book
goes to press. Since Mr. Lloyd's book is "an introduction to its subject" and since
only the first twenty-four pages are devoted to biographical matters, the need for
a full length biography remains.

Edwards, R. L. Ramsay, L. J. Lloyd, F. M. Salter, Ian Gordon, Mrs. Helen Stearns Sale, and other scholars have contributed largely to our knowledge of Skelton.

My own work, which, I hope, adds something of value to the information accumulated since Dyce's time, has yielded results of several kinds. My researches at the Public Record Office and at Norwich have brought to light a number of new documents. A consideration of the activities of a group of scholars at the court of Henry VII has led me to conclude that Skelton, far from being an antic vulgarian, consciously labored to transmute the learned humanist patterns into his native tongue. I have proposed a theory concerning the origins of the Skeltonic verse form. Examination of Skelton's poems on Flodden Field supports the conclusion that the poet was intimately associated with the court of Henry VIII. I have attempted to define Skelton's position in the grammatical controversies of his day and to point out the relationship between his *Replication against Certain Young Scholars* and More's *Dialogue concerning Heresies*. A study of the course of his reputation and of his influence upon the literature of his time proves, I believe, that his contemporaries accepted him at his own valuation, that is, as a learned and witty scholar of rhetoric who modeled from classical example a powerfully effective means of swaying opinion. However, I feel that the chief contribution of this book to the study of Skelton remains the analysis of the problems with which I began. If I have read *Speak, Parrot* and the story of Skelton's quarrel with Wolsey correctly, I believe that this book has its justification.

It is in no spirit of final accomplishment that I conclude my work, but rather in the hope that it will serve other students as a basis for a better proportioned edifice. Perhaps it may also hasten the preparation of a new edition of Skelton's works and may stimulate further study of a brilliant and original poet.

The Scholars of Henry VII

THE FIRST recorded appraisal of the works of John
Skelton is strangely at variance with the opinions of
his later critics. It appears in the dedication to Caxton's *Boke of Eneydos* (1489). The printer begs Skelton,
"late created Poet Laureate in the University of Oxford,"
to correct any faults he may find in the book,

For hym I knowe for suffycyent to expowne and englysshe euery
dyffyculte that is therin / For he hath late translated the epystlys
of Tulle / and the boke of dyodorus syculus. and diuerse other
werkes oute of latyn in to englysshe not in rude and olde lan-
gage. but in polysshed and ornate termes craftely. as he that
hath redde vyrgyle / ouyde. tullye. and all the other noble poetes
and oratours / to me vnknowen: And also he hath redde the ix.
muses and vnderstande theyr musicalle scyences. and to whom of
theym eche scyence is appropred. I suppose he hath dronken of
Elycons well.[1]

What has this learned scholar of the humanities to do with
the man Puttenham describes as "a rude railing rhymer,"[2]
whose works, according to Pope, consist "almost wholly of
ribaldry, obscenity, and scurrilous language"?[3]

Puttenham and Pope are not wrong in their judgment.
Skelton the rowdy is easy to discover. By modern standards
his language is vulgar, his expression loose, his construc-
tion careless. He is boisterous and ill bred. He rants in-
cessantly, sneers, boasts, attacks dead enemies, and taxes
live ones with the crimes of poverty and physical infirmity.

---

[1] *Prologues and Epilogues of William Caxton*, "Early English Text Society [Pub-
lications]," O.S., CLXXVI, 109.

[2] *The Arte of English Poesie*, ed. by Willcock and Walker (Cambridge, 1936),
p. 84. I have followed the practise of modernizing the spelling of short English
quotations in all cases except those in which such treatment might obscure the
meaning.

[3] Note to l. 38 of *The First Epistle of the Second Book of Horace*.

There is no decency in him. If he is liked today, he is liked because these vices may be interpreted as a counterpart to his poetic virtues. He has enormous vigor, a torrential flow of language and a torrent of rhythm to match it, a genius for caricature, abuse, and belligerent partisanship. Such praise, however, is merely the opposite face of Puttenham's medal.

On the other hand, the learned and elegant Skelton, he who had drunk of "Helicon's well," cannot be wholly a myth. Caxton is not alone in his opinion. Erasmus, the greatest humanist of the day, and Robert Whittinton, most productive of Tudor grammarians, concur enthusiastically.[4] Although these critics may have been excessively exuberant in their praise of Skelton as a humanist scholar, there must have been something of scholarship in him to serve as a basis for exaggeration. It is true that the casual modern reader agrees with Pope and Puttenham rather than with Caxton and Erasmus. But fashions have changed, and the marks by which learning was recognized during the early Renaissance in England are not the marks of scholarship today. In order to do justice to Skelton's claim to the title of learning, in order to see the poet in the academic gown which was visible to his contemporaries, it is necessary to set him against the background of the scholars of his own time and of his own country. With a knowledge of the manners of the learned men of the early Tudor period, of their aspirations, their employments, and their literary accomplishments, it will be possible to judge fairly of Skelton's membership in the family, of the extent to which he conforms to and the extent to which he deviates from their tradition.

It is not an easy task. The period of Skelton's development as a poet lies almost wholly within the reign of Henry VII (1485–1509). Although he lived twenty years

[4] See below, pp. 57, 71-73, and 155-56.

after Henry's death, years during which he produced the greatest of his works, the germ of his accomplishment must be sought in his youth. And the literary history of the reign of Henry VII has been all but ignored by students of the Renaissance in England.

I therefore beg the reader's indulgence for a discussion in which Skelton plays no part. The present chapter will be devoted to an examination of the work of the scholars active during the reign of Henry VII. In the following chapter I shall try to demonstrate Skelton's relationship to the background thus established.

Usually the rise of learning in England is attributed to the powerful influence of the Erasmus circle. It is generally supposed that Henry VII was too niggardly and too busy with matters of administration to patronize scholarship. It is said that the vanguard of the Renaissance, led by Erasmus and his friends Linacre, Colet, Grocyn, and Thomas More, struggled vainly to pass the barrier of Henry's miserliness and lack of interest and that only when the young Henry ascended the throne did the ramparts break and learning conquer England. Historical continuity is established by reference to Duke Humphrey's generous patronage of literature and to the succession of eager scholars, each inspired by his predecessor, who went off to Italy, studied under the famous humanists, and returned bearing weighty codexes to the libraries of Oxford. One of the last of the Duke Humphrey line, William Celling, taught Linacre at Christ Church; Linacre taught More; and More was the flower of the Renaissance in England.

Of the many foreign scholars in England during the reign of Henry VII, the only one, aside from Erasmus, who receives more than the briefest of mention is Cornelio Vitelli. Vitelli's eminence apparently depends upon a remark concerning him in Polydore Vergil's *English History*:[5]

[5] *Historia Anglica* (1603), p. 1566.

"omnium primus Oxonij bonis literis iuuentutem erudiuit." Since the distinguishing mark of the Renaissance is frequently taken to be Greek, it has been assumed that Vergil's "good letters" refers to a course of lectures in that best of languages. From this assumption it has been easy enough to derive the conclusion that Vitelli may have given the first training in Greek to the corps extraordinary of the English revival of learning, Linacre, Grocyn, More, Colet, and Erasmus himself. Actually, Vitelli was not the first humanist to teach at Oxford.[6] He may or may not have taught Greek there. He may or may not have instructed the great English humanists. He created very little stir in England, and with the exception of a single piece,[7] none of his writing seems to be connected with his adopted country.

The rich fruit of English humanism cannot depend on so slender a stem. A rare scholar like Tiptoft, imbued with a passionate love of learning and wealthy enough to travel to Italy in search of the exotic, and a rare Italian like Vitelli, quietly teaching at the English universities, do not constitute a sufficient explanation for the full English harvest. The truth is that the works of More and his friends followed hard upon the works of a crowd of scholars who were subsidized by Henry VII. The great figures of the English Renaissance belong to a tradition established in England by a group of foreigners, chief among whom were Pietro Carmeliano, Giovanni and Silvestro Gigli, and Bernard André.

The usual picture of the development of English humanism, I believe, is out of focus. The center of the movement is to be found neither in the generosity of a disinterested Mæcenas nor in the love of learning for the sake of learning. Scholars followed the humanist discipline

[6] Stephanus Surigonus preceded him. See R. Weiss, in *London Times Literary Supplement*, Jan. 9, 1937, p. 28.
[7] See below, p. 26.

because they hoped for employment at court. And the king fostered and encouraged the humanists because they were needed in the affairs of the nation.

Had the courts of Europe failed to take notice of the rediscovery of classical Latin, the new discipline might have stirred the schools for a time and then died at the birth of a new academic fashion. The ancient language could not compete with the fecundity of medieval Latin in terms for legal concepts or for the ideas traded in religious and philosophical disputation. Renaissance Latin was saved from ineffectiveness by the fact that its first home was, not the school at all, but the court.

The theory behind the political preoccupation of the Renaissance students of classical Latin is obvious enough. The purpose of language is to convince. Language which best carries conviction is that dressed in elaborate and beautiful ornaments. With a sufficiently lovely instrument one can sway, not only stones and running brooks, but antagonistic peoples and hostile rulers. The rhetorician is therefore a servant of great value to the governors of states. Besides furthering the ambitions of princes, he can bring the barbarous multitude to civility; he can persuade kings to virtue. Through him comes the age of Plato's philosopher-prince.

There were other reasons for Henry VII's employment of Renaissance scholars. During the late fifteenth century the course of diplomatic relations brought England into close contact with the humanist courts of Italy and the incipiently humanist courts of France and Spain. The fashion made rhetoric and the new-found Latin of Cicero diplomatic necessities. Speech making was the order of the day. The high point of every embassy was the oration, and its composition and delivery were the subjects of active criticism. The grace of an ambassador consisted, not in the message he carried nor in the gifts he bore, but in his oratorical powers. The papal Curia was profoundly shocked when an emissary of the king of England broke down in the middle of a congratulatory speech and had to retire in confusion.[8] Diplomats without eloquence shed no honor on their country.

The newly rediscovered Latin was also required in diplomatic correspondence. The king was in regular receipt of letters from the pope, from Venice and Genoa, from France and Spain. The pope thought it worthy of comment that letters from England were couched in elegant Latin.[9] The prestige of the nation demanded that the king of England employ secretaries who could write as well as those of other monarchs.

If the men who could speak and write the new Latin filled a national need, so too did those who could teach it. Ambassadors and secretaries required training. Furthermore, it was advisable that the king himself understand the language in which he was being praised and addressed. On one occasion, apparently, it was necessary for Henry VII to draw aside in order to discover from his councilors what the Venetian ambassador had said to him.[10] He determined that his children should not suffer from a similar disability. Teachers had to be employed, therefore, both at the universities and at court.

The princes of Italy had been fed to the strutting point with literature designed to eternize their fame. The perdurability of the written word was the bait offered by every scholar in search of patronage. The most trivial state occasion was excuse for an ode; petty skirmishes provided matter for epics. Annals and histories preserved for future generations the deeds of the Renaissance states. England could not admit a lesser glory.

[8] The ambassador was Cardinal Bainbridge, to whom the misfortune occurred on two occasions. See Jervis Wegg, *Richard Pace* (London, 1932), pp. 22, 28.

[9] *Letters and Papers of the Reign of Henry VIII*, I (ed. 1920), No. 3220.

[10] *Calendar of State Papers (Venetian)*, I, No. 754 (October 11, 1497).

The spread of humanistic learning thus forced the king of England to patronize the fashionable kind of orator, letter writer, historian, occasional poet, and teacher of Latin. Despite a variety of function, position, and emolument, the scholars employed by Henry VII formed an essentially homogeneous group. They were linked by their proficiency in the disciplines of grammar and rhetoric. The Renaissance emphasis on these studies was a consequence of the discovery of the new Latin and of the political use to which it was put. Grammar and rhetoric were no longer merely the first childish steps to accomplishment in higher studies. They were not simply keys to the understanding and expression of valuable ideas. They were ends in themselves, worthy of arduous study. The scholar who had learned the proper rules of word order, of vocabulary, of syntactical structure, and of poetic meter, who could expand and ornament a theme in the classical manner, was a distinguished man. Furthermore, he was especially equipped to serve the king, both in diplomacy and in literature. Symbolic of the identity of these apparently disparate fields of endeavor is the fact that the words "orator" and "poet" were understood as almost synonymous. Although "orator" had the special meaning of "ambassador," and "poet" designated particularly a student of the humanities, the words appear coupled so frequently that it is evident that an ambassador and a humanist were much the same sort of person. Caxton pairs "orator" and "poet" in a passage already cited.[11] Hawes uses the words interchangeably to designate disciples of the school of rhetoric.[12] Skelton dreams of a splendid celebration of his poetic glory attended by Quintilian, Hesiod, Theocritus, Homer, Cicero, Sallust, Ovid, Lucan, Statius, Persius, Vergil,

---

[11] Page 4.
[12] *The Pastime of Pleasure*, "Early English Text Society [Publications]," O. S., CLXXIII, ll. 1212, 1226, 1247, 1260.

Livy, Ennius, Aulus Gellius, Terence, Plautus, Boccaccio, Poggio, Gaguin, and many others, a festival at which

> blessyd Bachus, that bote is of all bale,
> Of clusters engrosyd with his ruddy flotis
> Theis orators and poetis refresshid there throtis[13]

To orators and poets, therefore, Henry VII gave employment and patronage. Individually the scholars of his court have little importance for the student of literature. But in the mass they constitute a factor highly significant in the development of humanism in England. They demonstrated to Englishmen that humanist learning was an effective aid to the attainment of court favor, wealth, and position.

The following sketch of the activity of the scholars of Henry's court will therefore proceed by genres rather than by individual authors. The employment of these humanists as ambassadors and secretaries will be considered first. Next, their pedagogic labors will be reviewed, together with their instruction in methods of government, in grammar and rhetoric, in religion and morals. Finally, the historical and poetic compositions which they produced will be examined. Throughout the discussion the role of the king as prime mover of their activity will be kept in view.

AMBASSADORS AND SECRETARIES

Polydore Vergil, employed by Henry VII as historian, describes the hiring of a humanist for the English diplomatic service. It is useful to present the passage at some length, for it explains why the man came to England, what his qualifications were, what tasks he was set, and what payment he received. The translation is that of the contemporary chronicler, Hall:[14]

[13] *Garland of Laurel*, ll. 323–85. The edition of *The Poetical Works of John Skelton*, by the Rev. Alexander Dyce (London, 1843), is referred to throughout, except when another text is specified.

[14] *Hall's Chronicle* (London, 1809), p. 448 (the abbreviations are expanded silently). See P. Vergil, *Historia Anglica* (1603), pp. 1472–73.

. . Innocent bishop of Rome had sent in legacye Adryan of Castella . . . This Adryan taryed certayne monethes . . in England and was made much of, and highly commended and lawded too the kyng by Ihon Morton bishop of Caunterbury, whiche for the good learnyng, vertue, and humanite, that he sawe and perceaued to be in him shewed to hym all poyntes of humanite and frendshippe, that a frende might do to a frende. And vpon hys commendacion, the kynge thynkynge thys man woorthy to be looked vpon, and mete to do the kynge pleasure, muche phantasied and more fauoured this legate Adryan, in somuche as he was Oratour and solicited his cause, bothe to Innocent and also to Alexander the sixt, Bishops of Rome. And after this, for his diligent seruyce, he so loued and fauoured him that he made him Bishop of Herford, and shortely after, that re- signed and geuen ouer, he promoted hym to the Bishoprike of Welles and Bathe . . . . The manne was of profounde learninge and knowlege, not vulgare, but straunge, newe and difficile, and in especial he was a man of ripe iudgement in electinge and chosynge concinnate termes, and apte and eloquente woordes, whiche firste of our tyme, after that golden worlde of Tully, moued men with his writynge to imitate and foloe the moost approbate, and allowed authours that were of eloquencie, and taught the trade and phrase to speake fyne, pure, freshe and cleane latyn, so that by his example and document, eloquence flourisheth at this houre in all places of Christendome. . .

Adrian is but one of a numerous throng of humanist schol- ars who served Henry VII as diplomats and ambassadors and were paid well for their services. Giovanni and Sil- vestro Gigli, both Latinists of repute, acted as proctors at the Curia, and each became bishop of Worcester. William Celling, one of the few Englishmen who had studied the humanities in Italy, also represented the king at the court of the pope. John Gunthorpe, a pupil of Guarino, was sent to Maximilian and to Ferdinand and Isabella. Silvestro Gigli held the office of Latin secretary; Paul Gigli was em- ployed to make "transumpts" of the king's bulls.[15] Pietro Carmeliano, Polydore Vergil, Pietro Vannes, and, in the

---

[15] Public Record Office, MS E. 101–415–3 (June 20, 1501).

next reign, Erasmus' friend Andrea Ammonio, handled diplomatic correspondence.

A sketch of the career of one of these "orators" will serve to show the richness of the reward for which they could hope. Pietro Carmeliano, of Brescia, was a scholar who was passionately fond of travel.[16] During one of his expeditions, he visited England, intending to continue to Germany. He never reached his destination. Upon his arrival in England, Edward IV seems to have employed him in the Rolls Office. Apparently Richard III ignored him, for the scholar protests that if Richard grant no aid he will be destitute.[17] But under Henry VII and Henry VIII, Carmeliano's fortunes prospered. He became Latin secretary and was entrusted with the safe keeping of copies and replies. In return for these services he received church preferments and gifts from the Privy Purse. For the war loan of 1522 the once poverty-stricken Carmeliano was assessed the magnificent sum of three hundred and thirty three pounds, six shillings, and eight pence[18] (more than twenty thousand dollars in modern equivalent).

The examples of Adrian of Castello, of Gigli, and of Carmeliano created a potent argument for the development of English humanism. Richard Pace, one of the new group of scholarly career men, uses it in an attempt to prove the value of education to a sporting English gentleman:[19]

One of those whom we call gentlemen, who always carry some horn hanging at their backs, as though they would hunt during dinner, said: "I swear by God's body I would rather that my son should hang than study letters. For it becomes the sons of gentlemen to blow the horn nicely, and to hunt skilfully, and elegantly

[16] See Carmeliano's dedication of *De vere* (MS Royal 12 A xxix) to Prince Edward, son of Edward IV, fol. 2.

[17] Dedication of his *Life of St. Mary of Egypt* (MS Laud 501).

[18] *Letters and Papers of the Reign of Henry VIII*, III, No. 2483.

[19] *De Fructu* (Basle, 1517), pp. 15–16; translated by Edith Rickert, *The Babees' Book* (London, 1923), pp. xxiii–xxiv.

carry and train a hawk. But the study of letters should be left to the sons of rustics. . ."

"You do not seem to me to think aright, good man," said I, "for if any foreigner were to come to the king, such as are ambassadors of princes, and an answer had to be given to him, your son if he were educated as you wish, could only blow his horn, and the learned sons of rustics would be called to answer, and they would be far preferred to your hunter or fowler son."

The fact that during the reign of Henry VIII, Englishmen began to replace foreigners as ambassadors and Latin secretaries is proof of the effectiveness of the argument.

EDUCATION

Henry VII supported the universities financially, visited them on several occasions, and took an active interest in their functions and ceremonies. The account books of the King's household include such academically pleasant items as the following:[20]

Item to the iiij mastres that kepte the disputaciouns at Cambrige in the scoles affore the kinges grace xx li and to the hole uniuersite to drinke with certen buckes for their recreacioun xx li.

Fr. Filippo Alberici, of Mantua, refers to an occasion upon which Henry personally presented degrees at Cambridge:[21]

You are first when you wage war, and you are the first to bestow the laurel wreaths upon learned men with your honored hand. Justly, therefore, may the emblems of a double triumph be allotted you. It is fitting that you be decorated both with the helmet and with the laurel.

Bernard André, the blind Poet Laureate of Toulouse, combined the duties of university teaching with the in-

[20] Public Record Office, MS E. 36–214, fol. 57 (May 1, 1506).
[21] MS Arundel 317, fol. 24. The poem is entitled "Ad Henricum Regem de honore per eum allato studiosis Cantabriæ F. Phil. Alb. carmen." The passage translated in the text reads:

Tu primus dum bella geris; tu laurea doctis
Primus honorata tradere serta manu.
Iure igitur duplici dentur tibi signa Triumpho:
Et galea, et lauro te decorare decet.

struction of princes. In 1486 the King granted "Bernard Andrew, poet-laureate," an annuity of ten marks "in consideration of the increase in virtue and learning coming to many persons at Oxford and elsewhere from his teaching."[22] André later undertook the education of the King's first son, Arthur.[23] He was occupied with this task for four years, from 1496 to 1500. The accomplishment of his princely pupil is amazing. André declares:[24]

I dare boldly affirm of my own knowledge that before he reached his sixteenth year [that is, by the time André ceased to be his teacher] he had either committed to memory or read with his own eyes and leafed with his own fingers, in grammar: Guarinus, Perottus, Pomponius, Sulpitius, Aulus Gellius, and Valla; in poetry: Homer, Vergil, Lucan, Ovid, Silius, Plautus, and Terence; in oratory: the *Offices*, *Letters*, and *Paradoxes* of Cicero, and Quintilian; in history: Thucidides, Livy, the *Commentaries* of Caesar, Suetonius, Cornelius Tacitus, Pliny, Valerius Maximus, Sallust, and Eusebius.

Didactic themes bulk large in a list of the works of Henry's scholars. Above all, the humanists were school teachers, imbued with a magnificent hope for the consequences of their labors. In that hope, the hope of a golden age of peace and virtue, they taught grammar and rhetoric, the wisdom of the ancients, morals and religion. The most important kind of instruction was, of course, the education of princes, the panacea of all political ills. Learning would fashion a wise and virtuous ruler, one who would govern wisely and virtuously. Renaissance princes did, in fact, become learned; whether they therefore became better governors is at least questionable. Faith in education as a cure-all

---

[22] *Materials for a History of the Reign of Henry VII*, in *Chronicles and Memorials*, LX (2), 62.

[23] André, *History of Henry VII*, edited by James Gairdner in *Chronicles and Memorials*, X, 6–7. André's predecessor as tutor to Arthur was one John Rede, of whom André thought highly (*ibid.*, p. 43). After André resigned the task in order to begin work on his *History*, Prince Arthur received instruction from an anonymous Scot (*Privy Purse Expenses of Elizabeth of York* (London, 1830), p. 28).

[24] *Op. cit.*, p. 43. The translation is mine.

has persisted until modern times, though with an important shift of emphasis—the dose, it is now thought, must be absorbed by the entire body politic, not by the head alone. The equations of learning to virtuous competence and of virtuous competence to political good remain tenets of every sanguine educator.

Accordingly, a considerable body of Renaissance literature concerns the education of rulers of states. Erasmus, More, Vives, Castiglione, Machiavelli, and Sir Thomas Elyot, to mention only the better-known writers, devoted themselves to teaching governors their trade. The court of the early Tudors had its share of such instruction. In requital of Prince Henry's support of his studies, Giovanni Boerio, probably Erasmus' pupil, whose father was physician to Henry VII, could find no better gift than a translation of Isocrates' oration, *De regno*.[25] Brother Stephen Baron, provincial of his order and lecturer at Cambridge, dedicated a *De regimine principum* to Henry VII.[26] He asked no compensation but that the King read the treatise frequently. Through the counsel of philosophers and theologians, he hoped, Henry's most glorious virtues might attain to absolute perfection.

A piece which in all probability was written by Bernard André, though it has not heretofore been attributed to him,[27] deals with the same subject. It is dedicated to Henry VIII and is entitled *Aristotelis ad magnum Alexandrum de vite*

[25] MS Additional 19, 553. The volume includes a dedication to the Prince, Latin translations of Isocrates and Lucian, and an epigram in praise of the Prince. The presentation must have occurred some time between the death of Prince Arthur (1502) and the death of Henry VII (1509), since the book is dedicated to Prince Henry, heir to the throne. See Allen, *Opus epistolarum Erasmi*, VIII, No. 2255.

[26] MS Royal 12 A xvi. The text of this was later printed by Wynken de Worde and also "in achademia parrhisiensi." It was evidently written near the end of the reign of Henry VII, for the printed editions are dedicated to Henry VIII. From another of Baron's books, *Sermones declamati coram alma universitate Cantabrigiense* (Wynken de Worde, n.d.), we learn that the author was an Observant Friar and confessor to Henry VIII. Baron is mentioned in the *Calendar of Patent Rolls (Henry VII)*, II, 568.

[27] See Appendix I, sec. 3.

institutione oratio.[28] The design of the work follows that of one of the most famous and popular books of the Middle Ages, *The Secret of Secrets* or *The Secret of Aristotle*. Like its prototype, it devotes itself to instructing the king in the proprieties of royal conduct and in the careful choice of counselors. It tacitly assumes that problems of state will be settled by the council, so that the king need not himself learn to cope with them. The *Oration* differs from the pseudo-Aristotelian work in its more "classical" Latinity, in its elimination of anachronisms, in its rejection of long digressions on medicine and physiognomy. It stresses particularly the importance of learning, manners, morals, and religion. In a prefatory section "Aristotle" advises his pupil to cherish the great example of his father, Philip of Macedon, who never departed from virtue, never lived in slothful idleness, who by the strength of his body and spirit overcame all perils, who loved money neither too much nor too little, enjoying present goods as a mortal, yet preserving and maintaining his wealth as though he should live forever. He was familiar with his friends and honored the studious before those linked to him by blood and nobility. Alexander can have no better model after which to pattern his life. Of course the author means that young Henry VIII will do well to imitate his royal father.

Grace entiere sur le fait du gouuernement dun prince, a French tract attributed to André, but quite possibly not his,[29] is also a treatise on government. The copy which remains appears in a most elegant folio volume which must have belonged to a noble family.[30] Apparently the treatise became quite popular, for there are two English translations of the prose body of the work.[31]

[28] MS Royal 12 B xiv, fol. 10.

[29] For a discussion of the attribution to André, see Warner, *Illuminated Manuscripts* (1903), plate 54.

[30] MS Royal 16 F ii.

[31] University College, Oxford, MS 85, fols. 136–179; Trinity College, Cambridge, MS O. 5. 6., fols., 65–69. Neither of these has heretofore been recognized

The date and occasion of the tract are given in the opening lines of the verse introduction:

En lan de septante & trente
Tenans quatorze cens de sente
Ung prince de royal noblesse
Qui en age de ieunesse
Est grant et excellent seigneur
Ordonne a estre greigneur
Par succession naturelle
Dit sagement parolle telle
Sur toutes chose ie desire
Que de la grace nostre sire
Ie puisse auoir entendement
De moy gouuerner sagement
Et de bien garder et tenir
Lestat ou dieu ma fait venir

Seventy and thirty and fourteen hundred make 1500. If the
book was written in England, as seems probable, the heir
to the throne so desirous of knowledge must have been
Arthur, Prince of Wales. The introduction explains that
certain members of the prince's council, observing the
laudable inclination of their charge, have decided to compile a treatise on government for him. The prose body of
Grace entiere is drawn, an English translator asserts,[32] from

thopynyons sentences and diffinicions of wyse philosophers and
other sage persoones Auncient and autentike // that is to sey in
the bible the wise Parables of Salamon in the booke of Ecclesiastes
Ecclesiasticus and diuers othir. The politiques and Ethiques of
the ffamous Philosophre Aristotle Thaduertisement of Vegecyus
in his trety made of the ffeete of Chiualrye and prudent counseyll
of Gyles in his Tretyse of Regiment and gouernaunce of Princes
and many othir writings of soufisaunt autorite wher ynne beth
shewyd parfyte Reules and notable conveyes by the whiche

as a translation of *Grace entiere*. The Trinity College copy is incomplete, containing
only the second and third divisions of the treatise. Although the two English
translations are related, they are not identical. On cursory examination, the University College text appears fuller and more elegant.

[32] University College, Oxford, MS 85, fol. 136.

kynges princes and othir lordys and estates may condue theire estates.

The prince is informed that he must govern in three respects: he must rule himself, his household, and his subjects. To rule himself properly, he must remember that he is a mortal and must therefore have humility. Government of the ménage depends upon the proper allotment of funds, part to the household, part to charity and remuneration of virtuous men, and part to a savings account. Finally, the prince must attend to his essential office, that of governing his subjects well. If he fails to fulfill it, he does not deserve the benefits of kingship. A good ruler is wise and provident, just and merciful. He knows how to select his counselors and how to bear himself in wartime. There follows a verse summary which ends the treatise.

The writers of the Renaissance not only advised princes to seek learning and virtue but also endeavored to provide them with textbooks which might ease the search. The school subjects perhaps most emphasized were grammar and rhetoric. This was natural for several reasons. First, grammar and rhetoric, which comprised the study of classical literature, were the special province of the humanists. Second, the ability to write and speak eloquently was of prime importance for princes who had to answer ambassadors and compose diplomatic letters. Finally, the study of grammar and rhetoric opened the entire wealth of classical knowledge to the comprehension of the noble pupil.

All of André's grammatical writings are lost, but a contemporary catalogue of his works[33] provides the titles. It is evident that he compiled books for a complete course in the humanist discipline. Many of the treatises were written expressly for Prince Arthur. They include a Latin vocabulary, several grammars, treatises on rhetoric and on elegant composition, an *Art of Letter Writing*, an *Orthography*,

[33] See Appendix I, sec. 1.

and an *Art of Memory*. In addition he prepared expositions and annotations for Cicero's *Letters*, Aulus Gellius, Pliny, Statius, Terence, the *Eclogues* and *Æneid* of Vergil, and Augustine's *City of God*.

André's outpouring of grammars, rhetorics, aids to composition, and annotations of the classics reflects the activity of the entire humanist group. Polydore Vergil, Erasmus, Colet, Linacre, William Lily, even Cardinal Wolsey contributed to the flood. The essence of the Renaissance which came to England in the late fifteenth century was a rebirth of Latin, with particular emphasis on oratorical and epistolary style. For the propagation of the new language, new textbooks were needed and needed quickly.

The learned of England compiled grammars for the presses of Caxton and Pynson and wrote commendations for textbooks written by their friends. A poem by André prefaces one of the earliest grammars printed in England.[34] Thomas More's first published work consists of commendatory poems to the elementary grammar, *Milk for Children*,[35] written by his friend, John Holt, usher of Magdalen. More praises the simplicity of Holt's method, warns the student that Latin cannot be learned in a day, and suggests more advanced grammars for further study, recommending particularly Phocas, Perottus, and, best of all, Sulpitius. Does this apparently professional advice mean that More taught grammar school?[36]

Pietro Carmeliano was intimately connected with the business of publishing textbooks for the study of grammar

[34] *Introductorium lingue Latine*, Wynken de Worde, 1495 (?), see Ames-Dibdin, II, 295–96; Duff, No. 231.

[35] Wynken de Worde, 1510?, Pynson, 1520? The grammar must have been written before 1500, since it is dedicated to John Morton who died in the course of that year.

[36] The suggestion that More taught grammar school has not previously been made, I believe. The fact that he was closely associated with Lily and with John and Nicholas Holt, all Latin masters, supports the conjecture. See below, p. 44.

and rhetoric. The colophon of Caxton's edition of the *Sex epistolæ* of Sixtus IV (after 1483), elegant models for school-boy themes, reads "Impresse per Willelmum Caxton / et diligenter emendate per Petrum Carmelianum Poetam Laureatum / in Westmonasterio." Carmeliano was linked to the Oxford printers, too, for his epigrams grace their edition of the *Letters of Phalaris* (1485). He supplies the names of the printers (Theodore Rood and Thomas Hunt), informs the reader of their nationality, and declares that their work excels that of the Venetians. A compendium of grammars for use in England, drawn from the works of Valla, Servius, and Perottus was published by Rood and Hunt, in 1483.[37] Again Carmeliano's commendatory poems function as do Caxton's prologues in less scholarly publications. Carmeliano names the author (unfortunately, by Christian name only, that is, "Joannes"), praises the book, and congratulates the patron at whose suggestion it has been compiled.

While the Renaissance schoolboy was receiving instruction in grammar, rhetoric, and literature, his manners, morals, and religion were not being neglected. Again a roster of the writers on these topics is a list of all the prominent humanists.

The previously mentioned catalogue of André's works includes two dialogues which obviously belong to the category of moral instruction. One of them, *Rationis et sensualitatis dyalogus* was probably a version of the work translated by Lydgate under the title *Reason and Sensuality*. The other, *De vera voluptate dyalogus*, suggests an attack on Valla's notorious elevation of the pleasures of sense to the position of the highest good.[38] Valla's *Elegantiæ* was

---

[37] *Compendium totius grammatice ex varijs autoribus . laurentio . seruio . perotto . diligenter collectum*, R. Pafroed, Deventer, 1489 (Duff, No. 30). Fragments of editions by Rood and Hunt (1483) also remain (Duff, Nos. 28, 29).

[38] See Appendix I (1) Nos. 7, 20. The suggested relationship between *Rationis et sensualitatis dyalogus* and *Reason and Sensuality* was pointed out to me by H. L. R. Edwards of Corpus Christi College, Cambridge.

praised by all England, but his ethical philosophy could find no welcome. *Rationis et sensualitatis dyalogus* was written for Prince Arthur and was declaimed before the King.

Among André's moral and religious writings there are several pieces which he dedicated to Henry VII's mother, Margaret, Countess of Richmond. She was a pious lady who, knowing no Latin herself, nevertheless gave liberal support to learned humanists who interested themselves in spiritual matters. Fisher, a friend of More, and like More a martyr, received her patronage. It was her munificence that established the professorship of divinity at Cambridge which Erasmus filled. At her request Caxton printed various edifying works. Giovanni Gigli gave her an exquisitely illuminated manuscript of *Liber precum*[39] and prefaced it with the double prayer that she surpass Nestor in years and be mindful of the donor of the book. To Margaret's influence must be attributed some part of the religious cast which colored the English Renaissance at its very inception.

The writings of Pico della Mirandola were particularly popular in England, probably because of their fortunate combination of sound Latin and sound morals. More's interest in Pico is attested by his English translations of *Three Epistles, An Interpretation of Psalm XV, Twelve Rules of Spiritual Battle*, and a life of Pico written by his nephew. French translations from Pico, including some of the pieces which More selected, were presented to Henry VII in two companion volumes,[40] apparently as New Year's gifts. *The Twelve Rules* also appears in a book of French translations of contemplative pieces by Pico and by Erasmus.[41] This last collection was given to the King by Gervase Amœnus, a pupil of Erasmus, and like Erasmus, a protégé

[39] MS Additional 33, 772.   [40] MSS Royal 16 E xxiv, xxv.
[41] MS Royal 16 E xiv.

of Lord Mountjoy. Amœnus explains in his dedication that the work was originally undertaken by his room-mate, Henry Hault, who, we learn from André's *Annals*,[42] was a scholar "utraque lingua peritus" and a pupil of André. After Hault's death in 1508, Amœnus completed and polished the book and carried out his friend's wishes by presenting it to the King.

HISTORY AND POETRY

Grammar, rhetoric, morals, and religion were of value not to the heads of states only, but to everyone; history, however, was the princely subject *par excellence*. Study of the deeds of his predecessors would provide a ruler with examples of good and of evil government—the good to be followed, the evil to be shunned. Claude de Seyssel, the French ambassador, could find no more appropriate gift for Henry VII than a French translation of Xenophon, royally inscribed on vellum.[43] In the dedication De Seyssel says that King Henry has a splendid library and enjoys both hearing and reading histories and other matters fit for a wise and noble prince. He is an experienced ruler, both in peace and in war, and will therefore recognize the value of the practical advice and warnings to be found in Xeno-phon's *Anabasis*, a work which, in the opinion of King Louis XII of France, should be divulged only to princes and to great personages.

The French ambassador's reference to Henry's fondness for listening to tales of the ancients was not merely diplo-matic flattery. In the catalogue of André's works I find *De Carthagine rapta dyalogus* and *Atheniensium ac Lacademoniorum*

---

[42] *Chronicles and Memorials*, X, 108.

[43] MS Royal 19 C vi. Jean Lascaris and De Seyssel collaborated on the book, Lascaris translating the Greek into Latin, and De Seyssel turning the Latin into French. They gave the work to Louis XII, who was much pleased. He wished to be the sole possessor of so rare a treasure, but Henry VII later proved so kind to De Seyssel that a second copy was made.

legatio, both of which are described as having been declaimed before the King.

Although all history was profitable to a prince, the history of his own land was of particular value. Not only did it provide examples directly applicable to his own affairs, but it also served to glorify the nation—to make its fame eternal. To Polydore Vergil, King Henry assigned the task of writing a polished history of England. Polydore produced a scholarly, reasoned, and well proportioned work which contributed enormously to the substance, style, and phraseology of almost every succeeding history.

About the time that Henry VII asked Polydore Vergil to write the deeds of his predecessors, he set Bernard André the duty of recording his own acts. While André was engaged in composing a connected tale of events from Henry's birth, he kept abreast of history in the making by writing yearly annals. He complains that each year the King insisted on examining the current chronicle, "which should never have been made public during his life."[44] Evidently Henry was well pleased with what André had written, for he rewarded him generously. The historian received forty shillings on New Year's Day in 1501 and one hundred shillings on the same holiday in 1506, in 1507, and in 1509.

When Henry VIII came to the throne, in 1509, André felt uncertain about the security of his position. The new king had younger and better scholars about him, and the old servant feared that he would be turned off. André begs for opportunity to finish and revise his history, to supply details omitted, and to retract doubtful and erroneous statements.[45] He realizes that the King receives eloquent eulogies daily.

Toutesfoys il ne repugne point a une si grande maieste & princificque haultesse dauoir beaucoup de hystoriographes Ainsi que de

[44] MS Royal 16 E xi, fol. 1: "ung chacum [sic] an il vouloit voir ce qui ne ce doit point monstrer durant la vie."
[45] *Ibid.*

la maieste diuine Et paternelle ymage nostre saulueur Jhesus crist ont este et sont quatre euangelistes grans hystoriens et iiii principaulx docteurs de leglise chrestienne de la louenge du quel nullz soit docte ou indocte est repulse en suppliant.

The appeal won; André was numbered among the new king's evangelists. He continued his chronicles and his court poetry; the King, for his part, continued the series of 100-shilling gifts each New Year's Day.

The functions of royal historian merged insensibly into those of royal poet. Both officers had as their duty the celebration in durable literature of the king's acts, and though the historian might restrict himself to prose, and the poet expand in verse, though the former might produce a consecutive narrative, and the latter devote himself to special occasions, they were nevertheless closely allied. So it was thought in Dryden's time, for that Poet Laureate, by the deed which gave him the office, was also named royal historiographer. Bernard André, officially historian to the king, was also the official "king's poet."[46]

How actively a king's poet performed his duties may be indicated by a list of the occasions poetically commemorated by Bernard André during the period 1485-89:[47]

1485: Henry's victory at Bosworth Field
1486: the coronation of the Queen
1486: the birth of Prince Arthur
1487: Henry's victory over Lambert Simnel
1487: the arrival of the papal legate (Giovanni Gigli)
1489: the assassination of the Earl of Northumberland
1489: the elevation of Arthur to the title of Prince of Wales
1489: the insolent poem of the French ambassador, Gaguin

The celebration of events during the reign of Henry VII was not restricted to the single voice of the king's poet. André tells an illuminating story concerning the visit of Robert Gaguin, the famous humanist, to the English

[46] He is called royal historiographer in MS Arsenal 418, fol. V, and king's poet in *Hymni Christiani Bernardi Andreæ* (Paris, 1517).

[47] *Chronicles and Memorials*, X, 35–36, 40, 41–42, 52–54, 54–55, 48–49, 44–46, 57.

court.[48] Gaguin had come as French ambassador to nego-
tiate a treaty of peace with England.[49] Although he made
a most eloquent speech, the ambassador achieved nothing,
and he vented his displeasure in a poetical attack leveled
at King Henry. Fortunately, England was strong not only
in arms but in eloquence as well:[50]

Giovanni Gigli of happy memory, a man most learned in things
human and divine, made a witty satire and replied in the king's
name to the orator . . . Then Pietro Carmeliano of Brescia,
famous poet and orator and most worthy king's secretary, in a
witty poem (which I cannot reproduce owing to his absence at
this time) poured scorn to perfection on the sour French jester;
to say nothing of the biting epigram of that most eloquent
orator Cornelio Vitelli . . . We ourselves also, being sealed of
the poets' tribe, raved upon the fellow, not (as they) in a few
lines, but in almost two hundred: truly there is nothing bolder
than a bad poet! . . . Thus, hooted and hissed out by these and
many like compositions, he departed in a great rage.

The more elaborate occasional poems often assumed a
character approaching historical narrative. Of this type is
Carmeliano's *Suasoria læticiæ pro sublatis bellis ciuilibus et
Arthuro principe nato / epistola.*[51] The poem begins, epic
fashion, in the middle. Richard III is reigning. God, looking down upon England, most beautiful of the countries of
the earth, is shocked by the intestine war and its attendant

[48] *Ibid.*, pp. 55–57.
[49] Gaguin's first trip to England began August 17, 1489, and ended before
September 24. A second embassy, during which the poetic affray must have occurred, began October 24, 1489, and ended before February 25, 1490 (*La Faculté
de décret de l'Université de Paris au xvᵉ siècle*, M. Fournier and L. Dorez [Paris, 1913],
III, 242, 246–47, 263).
[50] Translated from André's *History* by H. L. R. Edwards, in "Robert Gaguin
and the English Poets," *Modern Language Review*, XXXII (1937), 430–34. I have
taken the liberty of omitting the title "lord," applied to Carmeliano and Gigli by
Mr. Edwards. *Dominus*, which is the title André uses, is a term applied to holders
of the degree of Bachelor of Arts and to other clerks and clerics.
    Edwards prints the poems written by Gaguin, Carmeliano, and Gigli from
Trinity College, Cambridge, MS O. 2. 53. Comparison with the versions in MS
Additional 33, 534, fol. 3 and in *Notes and Queries*, Series ii, VIII, 411–12 would
have produced a somewhat better text.
[51] MS Additional 33, 736.

horrors. He asks the council of saints to propose a means of terminating the struggle. They suggest that the spirit of Henry VI be called on for advice. Henry appears, and although he understands that God knows everything, relates to Him nevertheless the course of events in England from the time he lost his throne to the nadir of the fortunes of young Henry Richmond, now helpless in a Breton prison. He begs that God release the hero. The request is granted, Bosworth is fought, the tyrant and murderer Richard dies, Elizabeth of York becomes queen, and finally, Arthur is born, or rather reborn after centuries of burial. Rejoice, oh England!

Also verging on straightforward history are the eulogies of Johannes Opiciis.[52] The first piece in the beautiful little volume of Latin poems which he presented to Henry VII,[53] concerns the King's expedition into France, in 1492. Opiciis must have found it rather difficult to fashion a heroic poem from the poor materials of history. There had been an ineffective siege of Boulogne and a peace treaty which repaid to the King the costs of the war, costs for which his subjects had been especially taxed. Yet, heroic the tale appears in Opiciis' resounding narrative. The soldiers move about with the tread of the warlike ancients; the siege of Boulogne echoes the grandeur of the siege of Troy.

The second poem in Opiciis' book is an eclogue, "De eiusdem serenissimi ac inuictissimi regis laudibus . . / sub pretextu inclitæ rosæ purpureæ per dialogum." Melibœus can scarcely recognize Mopsus since when last he saw him Mopsus was pale, unhappy, and ill cared for, but now he

[52] His name is usually given as Opicius. Although Tanner thought him an Englishman (*Bibl. Brit.-Hib.*, p. 562), it is probable that he was related to one Peter de Opiciis, merchant of Montserrat (or possibly Montferrat), who appears in the King's account book in 1507 (Public Record Office, MS E. 36-214, fol. 180). Examples of his poetry will be found in *Chronicles and Memorials*, X, lx–lxii, and in W. F. Schirmer, *Der englische Frühhumanismus* (Leipzig, 1931), pp. 150–51.

[53] MS Cotton Vespasian B. IV.

appears spruce and cheerful. Mopsus explains the glad transformation allegorically. There is a garden surrounded on all sides by walls and by streams, which is beautiful with the various fragrance of sweet blossoms. In the garden is a red rose, a bloom of most beautiful color, which has been gracious enough to fasten itself to a snow-white flower. Under the figure of the red rose Melibœus is told the history of the great king who is bringing the golden age back to the earth. Grateful for the story, he bestows a wreath of laurel on Mopsus.

André, too, wrote a topical pastoral poem: "De Carolo Francie in Italiam egloge due."[54] This is lost, but André's allegorical celebration of Henry's reign, *Les Douze Triomphes de Henry VII*, does remain.[55] It is a comparison of the deeds of Hercules with those of the King of England. Interpreted properly, Hercules' exploits represent his conquest of Envy, personified by Juno. King Henry's career also consists of a campaign against Envy, realized in the person of Margaret, Duchess of Burgundy. This remarkable coincidence invites the author to examine further the correspondence between his hero and the son of Jupiter. The terrible boar is obviously Richard III, who used the boar as a cognizance. The Amazon queen must be understood as another appearance of the envious Margaret. The dragon who guards the golden apple is Maximilian, Emperor of the Romans, and the apple itself is the guerdon of peace and alliance with the King of France. The allegory fails only when the Greek hero weakly succumbs to Envy and dies ignominiously. Envy shall never conquer King Henry, a greater than Hercules.

It is unnecessary to pursue further the catalogue of humanist writings in England. Henry VII and his sons were instructed in grammar, morals, and history. They

[54] See Appendix I (1), No. 18.

[55] Edited by Gairdner in *Chronicles and Memorials*, X, 133–53. Gairdner's English translation is found *ibid.*, pp. 307–27.

were hymned beyond measure. Every royal act was the occasion for an outpouring of poetical praise; every royal virtue was set down for the wonder of posterity. The new fashion of the courts of Italy had come to England.

But it was the new Italian fashion with a difference. There was little lightheartedness among the writings of Henry's orators, little literature for the sake of enjoyment. All was morality and religion and solid learning. The court of England was a sober court, and its leaders appreciated such praise as that which Giovanni Gigli heaped upon John Morton, then bishop of Ely, later cardinal and chancellor, in the dedication of a treatise on the canonization of saints:[56]

Your Lordship . . . . is most highly characterized by piety, wisdom, prudence, humanity, practical knowledge, and experience, and is furthermore excellently learned in those good disciplines which are particular necessities both for the conduct of the public affairs of any kingdom whatever, and for the discovery of truth— I say of truth, of solid and pure truth, truth divorced from all sophisticated levity and dialectical vanity.

This emphasis on piety and usefulness in learning is precisely the emphasis of Colet and the later English humanists. The wantonness and frivolity of the Italian revival and the vain logic chopping of the schools of Paris are equally to be shunned. Eloquence must be devoted to the service of God and country.

ALIEN ORATORS IN ENGLAND

Of the orators and poets employed by Henry VII, remarkably few were English. William Celling, Gunthorpe, Colet, and John Skelton almost exhaust the list. Celling died in 1494, and Gunthorpe in 1498. Colet's service was restricted to the last few years of the reign.

In contrast to the paucity of Englishmen, the crowd of foreigners in the royal service during the reign of Henry

[56] MS Arundel 366, fols. 1-2. The translation is mine.

VII takes on the character of mass invasion. All of the Latin secretaries, all of the French secretaries, most of the ambassadors to Italy, and many of the King's chaplains were aliens. Only one explanation is possible. A nation imports the commodities it lacks. During the reign of Henry VII, England exported wool and tin; it imported fine cloth, wines, and scholars of rhetoric. Poets and orators were needed, and there was not enough native talent for the purpose. It was therefore necessary to have recourse to foreign mercenaries. Even the University of Cambridge was forced to hire an Italian, one Caius Auberinus, to compose such of its letters as demanded elegance.[57] For epistles directed to the Queen Mother, Margaret, the Vicar of Trumpington sufficed.

Of the foreigners who came to England in the early Tudor period, many seem to have immigrated because they hoped to find a market for their literary talents. But aliens who had been living in England for other reasons remained to influence English scholarship. Numbers of Italian merchants appear in the records as residents of England. Had they formed a quiet colony in Fenchurch Street, the present study could ignore them. But they came with the advantage of an Italian education and helped to infect English society with the fever of the new learning. They took an active part in the business of the nation, became controllers of the Change at Calais, and collectors of the Customs at Bristol. They entered the court and played cards and dice with the king—unfortunately for the king, it seems.[58] The family of

---

[57] "[His] fee was at the rate of twenty pence for an epistle. The same person was employed to explain Terence in the public schools." (Cooper, *Annals of Cambridge* (Cambridge, 1842), I, 240).

[58] For example:

> . . . . Domyngo Lomelyn,
> That was wont to wyn
> Moche money of the kynge
> At the cardys and haserdynge

(Skelton, *Why Come Ye Not to Court*, ll. 1187-90).

Bonvisi traded in wool; Antonio Bonvisi was an intimate
friend of More. Numerous commercial Spinelli are found in
the time of Henry VII; Thomas Spinelli was one of the
busiest ambassadors of the next reign. An Italian physician
was employed at court; his sons went back to Italy to study
under the tutelage of Erasmus, and one of them dedicated
a book of translations from Lucian and Isocrates to the
King's son, Prince Henry.[59] Perhaps the most important
source of scholarly Italians in England was the papal service. Adrian of Castello, Giovanni Gigli, Polydore Vergil,
and Andrea Ammonio, each of whom found a place in the
English diplomatic corps, had originally come to England
as emissaries of the pope.

Italians were not the only learned foreigners at the
court of Henry VII. Bernard André, of Toulouse, wrote
histories and occasional poems. The royal library was cared
for by a Frenchman, Quentin Poulet. Giles Duwes taught
French to the princes and succeeded Poulet as librarian.
Henry Hault translated into French a group of devotional
writings; Jacques Hault gave books to King Henry and
prepared disguises and pageants for the entertainment of
the court.[60] Spaniards came to England in the train of
Katherine, bride of Prince Arthur and later of Prince
Henry. A Scot tutored the elder prince.[61] Erasmus, the
Dutchman, sought to enter royal service, or at least to
partake of royal patronage.

MORE AND HIS FRIENDS

The More-Erasmus-Linacre-Ammonio-Colet circle apparently represented the "outs" during the reign of Henry

[59] The physician was Giambattista Boerio. See Allen, *Opus epistolarum Erasmi*,
I, No. 267, and VIII, No. 2255.
[60] The King gave him forty shillings for each of two books, once on January 1,
1506 (Public Record Office, MS E. 36–214, p. 25), and again on January 2, 1508 (*ibid.*,
p. 230). He received numerous payments for disguisings and pageants between
1498 and 1500 (P. R. O., MS E. 101–414–16, December 3–5, 1497; February 1,
1498; November 11–16, 1498; March 3–5, 1499; MS E. 101–415–3, February 14, 1500).
[61] See above, p. 15, n.

VII. More's political career was cut short by an eloquent speech he made before Commons, in which he opposed the King's demands for new taxation. Linacre begged for a chance to succeed André as tutor to Prince Arthur, but he got neither that position nor the post of physician to the King, though both are often attributed to him.[62] Ammonio, despite the patronage of Lord Mountjoy, Erasmus' pupil, was unable to find an entry into the King's service.[63] Erasmus himself made two visits to England and was greatly disappointed by the failure of material advantage. Colet was more successful than any of the group; he became dean of St. Paul's, and during the last three years of the reign he preached sermons before the King.[64] Thus, in contrast to the excellent nourishment received by André, Carmeliano, the Gigli, and Polydore Vergil, the More circle profited little from the patronage of Henry VII. Various explanations are possible. For one thing, More and his friends arrived too late. Giovanni Gigli, André, and Carmeliano had all been active at the very beginning of the reign; Adrian of Castello came to England four years later. Silvestro Gigli was his uncle Giovanni's natural successor; Polydore Vergil was a nephew of Adrian. Consequently, when More's friends came to court, they found the best places taken by scholars old in the service. A second reason for the coolness of the welcome accorded the friends of Thomas More may have been their disturbing freshness and originality. Henry VII, a solid individual by all accounts, surely was troubled by the bright humor of More and Erasmus, by their gay and irresponsible gamboling in the new academic pastures. Set beside the sober scholars in his employ, the young men must have appeared contaminated with the vicious frivolity of Italy, where learned

---

[62] See Allen, *Opus epistolarum*, I, 274.

[63] *Ibid.*, I, 455.

[64] Public Record Office, MS E. 36–214, pp. 136, 146, 245, 255, 326, 342. He received twenty shillings for each sermon.

men wrote love lyrics and elevated pleasure to the position of the highest good.

The death of the old king opened new opportunities to the More circle. More gave Henry VIII a volume of poems in his honor, beautifully inscribed on vellum, ornamented with roses red and white entwined with the pomegranates of Queen Katherine.[65] Ammonio poured forth a poetic libation.[66] Erasmus hurried all the way to England from Italy. Although the proceeds of these efforts probably failed to live up to the expectations which prompted them, they at least represented an improvement over the yield of the previous reign. Ammonio supplanted Carmeliano as Latin secretary.[67] Linacre became king's physician. Erasmus remained in England for a five year sojourn and returned frequently thereafter. More did not immediately find the new reign profitable, but eventually he attained the highest position ambition could aspire to, that of chancellor of the realm.

But the fact that Henry VII dealt less generously with the More circle than did his son does not mean that he failed to patronize humanist scholars. Since most of our information about the Renaissance in England has been derived from Erasmus' letters, we are in danger of mistaking the fortunes of the More coterie for those of the entire humanist group. That Henry VII did employ scholars and that he rewarded them richly is sufficiently proved by his beneficence to such "orators" and "poets" as Carmeliano, André, and the Gigli.

With rich rewards at stake, it is not out of nature that scholars should have quarreled among themselves—should have praised and taken favors from their luckier brethren,

[65] MS Cotton Titus D IV. The pieces in the volume were printed at the head of More's *Epigrams*.

[66] See Allen, *op. cit.*, I, No. 218.

[67] The change occurred in 1513. Carmeliano became royal luter. See *Letters and Papers*, I (1920), Nos. 1970 (ii), 2053 (2.), 1956.

while they belittled them behind their backs. Competition for patronage by the older and younger groups of scholars set the stage for a great deal of "backbiting." With André and Carmeliano, the More circle maintained an appearance of friendship. André loaned Erasmus twenty nobles and tried to introduce him to a possible patron, Richard Bere, Abbot of Glastonbury.[68] Erasmus wrote commendatory poems for the blind poet's publications.[69] But his real opinion of André appears in his irritable references to André's dunning for the twenty nobles, and in his intense relief when Lord Mountjoy paid the debt.[70] In a letter to Richard Bere he characterizes André as a man of insignificant talent.[71] He accuses him of having kept Linacre from the royal service and asserts that he does not know for what merit Henry VII favored him.[72]

[68] Allen, *op. cit.*, V, No. 1490.

[69] They deserve reprinting because they do not appear in the collected works of Erasmus (1703-6) nor in the recent careful *Erasmi opuscula* (edited by W. K. Ferguson, The Hague, 1933). One of the epigrams is appended to André's *Hymni Christiani* (Paris, 1517), fol. 2.

> *In hymnos Bernardi Andreæ Tolosatis poetæ regii Erasmi Roterodami*
> *Hexasthicon*
>
> Mæonius vates ac Thracius Orpheus olim
> Hymnidicis cecinit numina vana modis:
> Bernardina chelys veros canit ordine diuos
> Gaudens omniiugis diuariare metris.
> Hæc lege cui pietas cui sunt cœlestia cordi:
> Illa iuuant aures: hæc refouent animum.

The other is attached to André's *Commentary on St. Augustine* (MS Arsenal 418, fol. V):

> *Erasmi Roterodani theologi in commentarios / D. B. Andree tholo-*
> *zani Poete Regii / Super opus / Aurelij Augustinj / de ciuitate dei /.*
>
> Doctor Augustine sacre celebris author pagine
> Tua graui scalebat [Qy. *scatebat*?] antehac ciuitas caligine
> Et parum liquebat oculis impericioribus
> Ecce Bernardus labore plurimarum noctium
> Luculentis sic retexit cuncta commentariis
> Vt queant vel lusciosis perspici dilucide
>
> τέλος

[70] Allen, *Opus epistolarum Erasmi*, I, Nos. 248, 254.   [71] *Ibid.*, V, No. 1490.

[72] John Noble Johnson, *The Life of Thomas Linacre* (London, 1835), p. 172. Johnson suggests that Erasmus' epigram "In cæcum tragœdiarum castigatorem" is an attack on André.

This kind of thing is to be expected from Erasmus, but it is a little shocking to find Thomas More following the same trace. André's *Hymni Christiani*, which Erasmus commended, was written with More's advice and help, and André was grateful.[73] Like Erasmus, More graced André's book with a commendatory epigram. At least, it appears to be a commendation. In the *Hymni Christiani* it is entitled "In Hymnos Bernardi Andreæ Tolosatis poetæ regii, Thomæ mori Hexadecastichon." But suspicions are aroused when the poem reappears among More's collected epigrams with the title, "In quendam qui scripserat Hymnos de divis, parum doctè, testatus in Præfatione, se ex tempore scripsisse, nec servasse leges carminum, & argumentum non recipere eloquentiam."[74] On re-examination, More's "eulogy" savors strongly of double meanings:[75]

[73] After replying to one of his commendators, Giovanni Boerio, André addresses More (*op. cit.*, fol. 83):
> "Ad Morum de eodem carmen trimetrum Trochaicum, acatalecticum.
> Nunc iambeis trochaicum metiar
> Damno chori parumper obsequere
> More sub tua tamen lima recinens
> Finies paucis quod optarunt proceres."

And again:
> "Ad eundem trochaicum tetrametrum Acatalecticum.
> More quod iubes trochæo lusitauimus probe
> Quo Boerio Ioanni gratias rependimus:
> Hymnulos qui non disertos laudat & probat meos
> Quicquid autem laudis ille buccinat velut Maro
> Ecce soli Christe tibi reddimus perenniter."

I can make little of the first line of the first of these two epigrams. Perhaps André refers to More's suggestion that he write his answer to Boerio in trochaics. Nor do I understand "damno chori."

[74] More, *Thomæ Mori opera omnia* (Frankfurt, 1689), p. 245.

[75] "Hic sacer Andreæ cunctos ex ordine fastos
> Perstringit mira cum breuitate liber.
> Ipsos quos cecinit superos dum scriberet omnes
> Credibile est vati consuluisse suo.
> Nam subito scripsit, sed sic vt scribere posset
> Quantumuis longo tempore non melius.
> Et pia materia est: priscisque intactus ab ipsis
> Seruatus fato est huic operi iste stylus . ."

Opera (1689) reads "Non" instead of "Nam" in the fifth line, which is clearly wrong. The edition of 1566 (Louvain, p. 26) confirms the reading in *Hymni Christiani*.

With marvelous brevity, this holy book by André embraces the whole almanac in order. It is likely that the very saints whom he sang all gave counsel to their poet while he wrote. For he wrote extempore, but in such manner that he could not have written better had he taken much longer. And the subject matter is pious. For this work, his style has by fate been preserved intact from the ancient models themselves.

The last sentence betrays the spirit of the epigram. No humanist could have written it without tongue in cheek. It was rather a good joke to have André print the piece in front of his book.

Carmeliano, too, was treated shabbily by More and his friends. He gave Erasmus a splendid gift and was repaid with an ode in which he was named high priest of elegance and prince of literature.[76] But when Carmeliano wrote a false quantity into a mock epitaph[77] on the King of Scots (killed at Flodden, in 1513), Erasmus and his correspondent Ammonio, giggled gleefully.[78] This was not the only time Carmeliano slipped. In a poem written to celebrate the betrothal of the Princess Mary to Charles of Castile (1508), he called Prince Henry "princeps cui nemo secundus."[79] More pounced on the expression. I translate freely:[80]

[76] *Erasmi opera omnia* (1703-6), I, 1221.

[77] Carmeliano's epitaph is found in a manuscript copy (MS Additional 29, 506) of a book on Flodden which was printed by Pynson. The false quantity referred to does not appear in the manuscript, which is to be expected, since Ammonio says that he pointed it out to the author before publication.

[78] Allen, *Opus epistolarum*, Nos. 280, 282.

[79] *Solemnes cerimonie & triumphi nuper habiti* (Pynson, n. d.). The Grenville copy is on vellum. The line to which More refers reads "Henricus frater / princeps cui nemo secundus."

[80] The subject of the epigram has not previously been identified, I believe. The Latin follows (More, *Opera* [1689], p. 245):

In Stultum Poetam.

Scripserat Æneam nulli pietate secundum,
    Vates secundus nemini.
Quidam igitur Regem dum vult laudare, Maronem
    Pulchrè æmulatus scilicet,
Hic, hic est, inquit, Princeps cui nemo secundus.
    Hac laude Rex indignus est,

On a Foolish Poet
"To none is Æneas in piety second,"
Wrote the poet who's second to none.
A mimic of Vergil, of wit not too fecund,
An elaborate eulogy spun.
Quoth he, "Here's a prince to whom nobody's second!"
(This title the prince hadn't won.)
If to each the accounting in justice be reckoned,
This is the way it should run:
"Here is a bard to whom nobody's second;
A prince who is second to none!'

Despite false quantities and grammatical errors André and Carmeliano represent the effective beginning of humanist scholarship in England. There had been students of classical literature before them, of course.[81] Free, Grey, Tiptoft, and Gunthorpe had studied in Italy. At Christ Church a long tradition of humanist learning, beginning with visits by Manuel Paleologus in 1400 and by Manuel Chrysoloras in 1406, was crowned with the labors of William Celling, the prior of the monastery, who was a friend of Politian, a collector of Greek manuscripts, and an ambassador of Henry VII.[82] But it was primarily André, Carmeliano, and their mates who taught England that the study of the classics was a profitable discipline, one which led to favor at court.

Of course, More, Colet, and Erasmus were not mere rhetoricians like the petty poets and orators employed by

---

Ipse sed est Vates dignissimus: ergo age demus
Utrique laudem debitam.
Hic, hic est igitur Vates, cui nemo secundus,
Rex qui secundus nemini.''

[81] There is an excellent discussion of fifteenth-century humanism in England in *Der englische Frühhumanismus*, by W. F. Schirmer (Leipzig, 1931), which may be supplemented by E. C. Wright, "Continuity in XV Century English Humanism," *PMLA*, LI, 370–76. Schirmer does not treat of the foreign scholars in the employ of Henry VII, however. Opiciis (Schirmer calls him "Opicius") receives some discussion (pp. 150–52) because Schirmer, on Tanner's authority, believes he may have been an Englishman. But see above, p. 27.

[82] Schirmer, *op. cit.*, pp. 154–62.

Henry VII. More's lightness of touch and his sweet reason-
ableness, Colet's hatred of timeserving and his breadth of
religious outlook, and the cutting intelligence of Erasmus
set them far above the rout of King Henry's scholars. The
difference between the two groups is symbolized by the
difference in their use of Latin. More and Erasmus use it
fluently as a native idiom; Carmeliano, the Gigli, and
André strain hard after effect, desperately parading their
erudition. But however much Colet, More, and Erasmus
transcend the tradition of Henry's secretaries, ambassadors,
and historians, they are not apart from that tradition.
They, too, seek royal patronage or, at any rate, accept it
unsought. They too think of learning as pre-eminently an
invaluable tool to be employed in the service of the State
for the increase of virtue and prosperity. They too instruct
princes, write grammars and rhetorics, expound morals
and religion, compile histories, and celebrate royalty in
extravagant poems. True, they do these things more skill-
fully than did their predecessors, they do them with more
freedom and imagination, and they have a wider range of
interests. But if Henry VII had not realized the value of
humanistic learning to the business of the State, if he had
not found it desirable to imitate the new foreign fashion
of the Mæcenas king, More and Colet and Erasmus would
have had no tradition of English humanism to transcend.

It is in this tradition that I propose to set John Skelton.
As I will try to show in the following chapter, his training,
his occupations, his literary matter, and his style all
identify him as one with André and the other orators of
the Tudor court. A deal of sound scholarship has been ex-
pended in an effort to prove that Skelton was no scholar.
It has been asserted that his reading was not exceptionally
wide, that his Latin was not exceptionally good, that his
knowledge of Greek was nil, that his views on education,
politics, and religion differed from those of More and

Erasmus.[83] With these specific contentions there is no quarrel. Certainly More and Erasmus were more learned in the humanities than was Skelton. Their political, educational, and religious philosophies were more "modern" than his. But More and Erasmus cannot be taken as the criteria of humanism. They are not the representatives of the movement, but its outstanding products. Skelton is not typical of Renaissance learning, either. Nevertheless, the type is to be found both in More and in Skelton. For they share what is perhaps the basic tenet of the Renaissance of learning, that by means of eloquence, the world may be made virtuous and the orator prosperous.

[83] R. L. Dunbabin, "Skelton's Relation to Humanism," *Modern Language Review*, XII (1917), 129-37.

John Skelton, Humanist

THE DEGREE of Poet Laureate was conferred upon Skelton by the three universities of Oxford, Louvain, and Cambridge. Skelton's possession of the laurel crown and the pride with which he wore it constitute the most direct proof of his membership in the circle of humanists.

This is true despite the fact that the precise significance of the laureateship for Englishmen of the Renaissance is difficult to discover. It is clear, at least, that it did not designate a poet pensioned for the specific task of celebrating king and country. John Dryden was the first to bear the name in that modern acceptation.[1] Earlier Laureates were, not state officers, but holders of a title of honor, a title which several writers might possess at the same time. Skelton wore the laurel wreath during the reign of Henry VII; so, too, did Pietro Carmeliano, Bernard André, and John Kay.[2]

The most famous of Renaissance laureations is the ceremony in honor of Petrarch which took place at the Capitol, in Rome, in 1341. The official patent by which the title was granted[3] declares that ancient Rome had made a practice of honoring the triumphs of Cæsars and poets with crowns of laurel, that the custom had been in disuse for thirteen hundred years,[4] that Francis Petrarch, poet and

[1] E. K. Broadus, *The Laureateship* (Oxford, 1921), p. 59.

[2] Carmeliano signs himself "Petri Carmeliani Brixiensis Poetæ Laureati . . . Carmen" in MS Royal 12 A xxix. André is described as Poet Laureate in a royal patent already cited (see above, p. 15). John Kay, Poet Laureate, translated into English *The Siege of Rhodes* (c. 1483, Duff, No. 75). He may be the Johannes Caius who, in company with Bernard André, wrote a commendatory poem for *Introductorium lingue Latine* (Wynken de Worde, 1495). John Key, a Carmelite of Cambridge, was ordained deacon of Ely in 1487 (Venn).

[3] *Petrarchæ opera* (Basle, 1581), III, 6–7.

[4] Despite the assertion of Petrarch's patent, the custom of granting laurel

historian, desired to be granted the wreath, not for vain-glory, but in order to stimulate the souls of the studious with a similar ambition and thus to revive the neglected disciplines of poetry and history. To prove his worth, the document asserts, Petrarch submitted himself to the examination of King Robert of Sicily, who, after having read some of the poet's works, judged him deserving of the honor. The patent proceeds to relate that Ursus, Count of Anguillaria, as the King's deputy, accordingly crowned the poet and historian with his own hands, and, by the authority vested in him by the said King and by the Senate and the people of Rome, conferred upon him the privilege of composing new books and poems, and of reading, dis-puting, and interpreting, in Rome and elsewhere, such writings of the ancients as concern the arts of poetry and history. Petrarch's laurel, in short, was the equivalent of a *ius ubique docendi*.

Later laureations seem to have been cut after the Petrarchan pattern. The grant of the wreath remained a royal prerogative, which was exercised in favor of scholars versed in the literature, oratory, and history of the ancients. Writers so decorated were given the equivalent of an academic degree, that is, they were privileged to teach their discipline in the schools. A particularly interesting in-stance is represented by the founding of the College of Poetry and Rhetoric at the University of Vienna, by Maximilian I, in 1501. The King of the Romans declared his decision to establish, throughout his towns and peoples, schools of Latin literature modeled after the fashion of ancient Rome, whence would come leaders skilled in the science of government. These leaders, having been made prudent by the study of the ancients, would further the

---

wreaths to poets had not been unknown for thirteen hundred years. See Du Resnel, in *Memoires de litterature, tirez des registres de l'Academie Royale des inscriptions*, X, 508 ff.

good and holy life by their writings.[5] For this purpose, he chose Conrad Celtes, who had been laureated by the King's father, Frederick III, to give ordinary lectures in poetry and oratory at Vienna. To Celtes and to Celtes' successors he granted the right to create new Poets Laureate of those who were found worthy after diligent examination. Maximilian, nevertheless, did not by this grant of power impede his own privilege of crowning with laurel.[6]

Oxford, Cambridge, and Louvain granted Skelton the degree of Poet Laureate. An item of information as to the course in poetry at the University of Louvain is available. In 1478, many years before Maximilian's foundation at Vienna, the Duke and Duchess of Brabant, in the hope that the science of poetry would prove of value to the State, established a course of lectures in the University to be delivered by one Lodewic Bruyn, who is described as a Poet Laureate.[7]

Laureation of "poets" was not very common either at Oxford or at Cambridge.[8] The statutes of neither institu-

[5] The deed is quoted in John Selden's *Titles of Honor* (London, 1631), pp. 406-8. Selden goes into the matter because he wishes to explain to his friend Ben Jonson the history of the honor Jonson had gained.

[6] In Germany the practice of laureation persisted into the seventeenth century. Selden (*op. cit.*, pp. 402-5) lists the right to laureate among the prerogatives of the counts Palatine, who derived it by patent from the emperor. He describes a laureation ceremony which took place at Strasbourg in 1616. Professor Jefferson Butler Fletcher has pointed out to me a late and remarkable instance of a laureation at Rome. The affair is recorded in a handsomely printed volume entitled *Atti della solenne coronazione fatta in Campidoglio della insigne poetessa D.na Maria Maddalena Morelli Fernandez* (Parma, 1779). Corilla, as the estimable lady was known by the members of the Arcadian Academy, had achieved great reputation as a poet, particularly because of her ability at improvisation. In 1776, after examinations on sacred history, revealed religion, moral philosophy, physics, metaphysics, heroic poetry, law, eloquence, mythology, harmony, fine arts, and pastoral poetry, she was granted the laurel wreath at an elaborate ceremony before a numerous and distinguished audience. She was also given a diploma confirming the grant by the authority of the Senate and the Roman people.

[7] *L'Ancienne Faculté de théologie de Louvain* (Louvain, 1911), pp. 73-74. Skelton's teacher at Louvain was probably, not Bruyn, but Franciscus de Crementis, also Poet Laureate and later a friend of Erasmus, who began to read in 1492 (see below, p. 63).

[8] Laureation of "poets" must not be confused with baccalaureation. At Cam-

tion provided for the ceremony. Skelton was the only Laureate ever created at Cambridge, and he was admitted to the title merely on the basis of his studies at Oxford and Louvain.[9] Since no further details are given, it is impossible to know what requirements Cambridge set for the honor. The meaning of the ceremony at Oxford is almost equally obscure. Skelton's laureation at that institution (*c.* 1488) falls within a period for which the university registers are missing. However, I find two later grants of the laurel at Oxford. One was bestowed on John Bulman, a scholar of the art of rhetoric, in 1511.[10] He was permitted to lecture on any book concerning that art and, furthermore, was granted the laurel, on condition that he read publicly and gratis the first book of Cicero's *Offices* and the first book of the same author's *Letters*. The second wreath went to Robert Whittinton, the famous Tudor grammarian, in 1513.[11] Because he had studied rhetoric for fourteen years and had taught children for twelve, he was presented with the laurel on condition that he compose one hundred verses (*C carmina*). A little later Whittinton received a dispensation permitting him to wear a silken hood, and on the following day *insignitus est laurea*.

Several other Oxford students received permission to teach grammar and rhetoric under very similar stipulations at about the same time but were not granted the laurel. In 1511 Maurice Byrchynshaw, like Whittinton a student of rhetoric for fourteen years, was granted the right to teach in the faculty of rhetoric if he composed a hundred verses

---

bridge a laureation ceremony accompanied the granting of the bachelor's degree (Caius, *Historiæ Cantabrigiensis academiæ* [London, 1574], p. 122), a custom to which Alberici refers (see above, p. 14). But a Poet Laureate is not the same thing as a baccalaureate.

[9] *Grace Book B (I)*, edited by Mary Bateson (Cambridge, 1903), p. 54 (1493): "Conceditur Johanni Skelton poete in partibus transmarinis atque oxonie laurea ornato ut aput nos eadem decoraretur."

[10] *Statuta antiqua universitatis Oxoniensis*, edited by Strickland Gibson (Oxford, 1931), p. lxxxviii.

[11] C. W. Boase, *Register of the University of Oxford* (Oxford, 1885), I, 299.

"de nobilitate Universitatis."[12] A few months afterward Byrchynshaw, now described as *baccalarius grammatices*, was allowed to lecture on any book on the art of poetry except Ovid *De arte amandi* and Pamphilus *De amore*. In the course of the following year Richard Smyth, for sixteen years a student of rhetoric, was asked to write a hundred verses in praise of the university and a comedy on the same subject.[13] In 1513 Thomas More, a student and teacher of grammar for fourteen years, was required to compose an epigram to be attached to the doors of the Church of St. Mary the Virgin.[14] But as far as the registers indicate, none of these graduate grammarians and rhetoricians was laureated, except Bulman and Whittinton. The *usual* insignia given to such scholars were the rod and the birch, emblems of the schoolteacher's trade. At Cambridge there were also degrees in grammar, but the examination poem, the rod and birch, and the laurel do not appear.

It is difficult to understand the relation between the honor of laureation and the degree in grammar and rhetoric. That there was a connection, the cases of Bulman and Whittinton demonstrate. Yet the inconsistencies are striking. Why should some grammar students receive the laurel and others not? Furthermore, both at Oxford and at Cambridge degrees in grammar were clearly minor honors. At both institutions the statutory requirements were less strict than were those for other degrees, and at Cambridge, the fees for grammarians' commons were lower than those collected from inceptors in arts. Nevertheless, Skelton and Whittinton strut in their laurel wreaths as though they had attained unique dignities.

---

[12] *Ibid.*, p. 298.   [13] *Ibid.*, p. 299.

[14] *Ibid.* I know of no reason why this Thomas More may not be identified with the author of *Utopia*. If he was teaching grammar before 1500, as his commendatory poems to Holt's *Milk for Children* suggest (see above, p. 20), the fourteen years of instruction are accounted for. The fact that Thomas More of the Oxford register was required to write an epigram lends further support to the identification, for in 1513 the humanist was engaged in making a collection of epigrams.

Perhaps there was confusion in the universities themselves. Grammar had long represented the lowest rung in
the educational scale. Old statutes provided for the training of teachers of that essential but elementary subject, and
for the conference of the degrees of Bachelor and Master
of Grammar. But suddenly, in a complete reversal of academic values, the students of humane letters, of grammar
and rhetoric, claimed the honor of being the academic
élite. The claim could not be ignored, for it had the powerful support of kings and princes. On the continent the
innovators left the old institutions and entered new academies which were established for them, usually under royal
grant. The College of Poetry and Rhetoric at Vienna has
already been mentioned. At Louvain the College of Three
Languages arose. Francis I created the College of France.
Spanish humanism was planted at Alcala. In England,
however, no such radical changes occurred. The universities of Oxford and of Cambridge tried to fit the new learning into the framework of the old curriculum. The only
place for it within that framework was the faculty of
grammar and rhetoric. It is evident that attempts were
made to refurbish the mean dignities of the elementary
faculty in order to bring them into closer correspondence
with their recently acquired importance at court. At Cambridge, for instance, the ancient office of master of Glom-
mery (said to be a perversion of *Grammary*) was metamorphosed into the post of public orator, the incumbents
of which were granted a regular salary and a rank higher
than that of any Master of Arts.[15] But the statutes record
no parallel change in the degrees assigned to adepts of the
new literary discipline. Pressure for such a change there
must have been, however. Those who had drunk of
"Helicon's well," who were trained to fill important
places in the affairs of state, could scarcely have been

[15] Caius, *Historiæ Cantabrigiensis academiæ*, p. 129; *Documents relating to the University and Colleges of Cambridge* (London, 1852), I, 431–34.

satisfied with the minor degrees of Bachelor and Master of Grammar. It seems likely that laureation of "poets" at Oxford and at Cambridge was a tentative expedient devised to accommodate the demand. The ceremony, sanctified by Petrarch's example, was both convenient and appropriate. But for some reason it did not take hold, and it disappeared from the universities without leaving a trace on the statute books.

What Skelton says of his own laureation supports the conclusion that it was an unusual honor granted to him by the favor of both the university and the king:[16]

> A kyng to me myn habyte gaue:
> At Oxforth, the vniversyte,
> Auaunsid I was to that degre;
> By hole consent of theyr senate,
> I was made poete lawreate.

The laurel, then, was conferred upon Skelton not by the usual Congregation of Regents, but by unanimous vote of the "senate," that is, the Great Congregation of Regents and Non-Regents. It is not clear whether the king's "habit" and the laurel wreath were bestowed on separate occasions, or whether they were both symbols of a ceremony in which the king and the university concurred. At any rate, it is certain that the "habit," too, represented attainment in the humane discipline. Its academic nature is disclosed by the fact that Henry's grant of the gown was later confirmed by the University of Cambridge.[17] It was probably the same gown which moved someone to ask Skelton the question, "Why wear ye *Calliope* embroidered with letters of gold?"[18] To which Skelton, Laureate, made this answer:

> Calliope,
> As ye may se,
> Regent is she

---

[16] "Poems against Garnesche," Skelton, *Works*, I, 128.
[17] See below, p. 102.   [18] Skelton, *Works*, I, 197-98.

Of poetes al,
Whiche gaue to me
The high degre
Laureat to be
Of fame royall

Skelton's garland of laurel, therefore, was a stamp of excellence in an academic discipline, a discipline technically pertaining to the minor faculty of grammar. But students of humane letters had become so valuable to the nation that the king himself took part in honoring them. Between Skelton's wreath and that allotted to Petrarch there is no great difference. In both cases the laurel was granted to scholars who by their constant study of ancient literature had rendered themselves capable of teaching poetry and oratory to others and of using their pens in the service of the State.

The humanists believed that by means of the persuasive power of eloquence, peace and virtue could be brought to the earth. It was that belief which gave meaning and value to the study of the classics, which justified the place of the new learning in the courts of princes. John Skelton, translating from Diodorus Siculus, expands his original in eloquent exposition of this high concept of eloquence. The italicized words are pure Skelton:[19]

. . first there reigned among theym [the Atlantians] a kyng whos name was celum [Uranus] which *through his faconde eloquence and crafty dispositive of lusty utteraunce* so used to persuade the people en commen which agrest were and of wilde conuersation tofore ledyng theire lives bestially in the busshye wildrenes here and there disparsed to arrect theire coraiges theym self to assemble in compaignyes to gedre and cittees to bilde for theire habitations and thus *through the sugyrd and swete electuaries of his persuasives*

[19] Corpus Christi College, Cambridge, MS 357, fol. 184. The corresponding passage in the Latin of Poggio, which Skelton translated, reads: "Scribunt autem primum regnasse apud eos Cœlum hominesque antea per agros dispersos ad coetum condedasque urbes exhortatum a fera eos agrestique vita ad mitiorem cultum traduxisse" (Jehan Petit, Paris, n.d., fol. LXVIII). The parallel Greek version may be found in the Loeb edition of Diodorus, II, 262–63.

ornately ennewed with wordes of pleasure he brought theym of theire
rude and wilde conuersation unto a more quyete and ordynate
enstitution of honest demeanour and sadde guydyng acqueynted
theym by all usuall experience theym self to enure with tilthe
of lande and sowyng of sedes with many other thynges metely
and right expedient for the necessarye behofe of mannes bodily
sustynaunce

Not only did Skelton have a humanist training and a
humanist faith, but he also pursued occupations that
paralleled perfectly those followed by the other scholars
of Henry VII. It is possible that the title of *regius orator*
which was granted to him by Henry VIII implied service
as an ambassador or secretary.[20] But for the present purpose
it is sufficient that during the reign of Henry VII he was
employed as tutor to the King's son and as court poet. As
I will try to show in the following discussion, his career
under the first Tudor fits so neatly the pattern established
by his brother Laureates, Bernard André and Pietro Carmeliano, that it is necessary to conclude that his position
at court was similar to theirs.

André was tutor to Arthur, Prince of Wales; Skelton
taught Henry, the King's second son. Both schoolmasters
gave their charges sound humanist educations. Prince
Arthur's classical learning has already been described.
Skelton boasts a similar accomplishment on the part of his
pupil:[21]

> I yaue hym drynke of the sugryd welle
> Of Eliconys waters crystallyne,
> Aqueintyng hym with the Musys nyne

Skelton's grammars, like André's, have all disappeared.
An invaluable catalogue of his works which appears in his
Garland of Laurel provides the titles, however. "New
grammar in English compiled" (l. 1182) was of course a
Latin grammar written in English, like Holt's *Milk for*

---

[20] See below, pp. 131–33.
[21] "Poems against Garnesche," Skelton, *Works*, I, 129.

Children. The item "Of Tully's *Familiars* the translation" (l. 1185) is illuminated with the side note: *concedat laurea lingua*, which emphasizes the rhetorical purpose. "His comedy *Achademios*," (l. 1184), was less obviously a school-book. But it is to be remembered that the school drama flourished as a technique for teaching good Latin and that several candidates for Oxford degrees in grammar were required to write comedies, one of which was explicitly restricted in topic to "praise of the University."[22] Perhaps Skelton's *Achademios* was composed to satisfy the requirements for the degree of Poet Laureate at Oxford. At any rate, it was probably not written for purposes of entertainment exclusively. "The book to speak well or be still" (l. 1175) probably derived from the *Tractatus de doctrina dicendi et tacendi*, a popular rhetoric written by Albertano of Brescia.

Skelton also wrote several tracts on the subject of government. The list in the *Garland of Laurel* includes "the Book of Honorous Estate" (l. 1172), "Royal Demeanance worship to win" (l. 1174), and "Sovereignty, a noble pamphlet" (l. 1191). These are all lost, unfortunately. But two of his treatises on the subject are extant, the morality play *Magnificence* and *Speculum principis*. The circumstances under which the latter was composed are recorded in the *Garland* (ll. 1226-32):

> The Duke of Yorkis creauncer whan Skelton was,
>   Now Henry the viij. Kyng of Englonde,
> A tratyse he deuysid and browght it to pas,
>   Callid *Speculum Principis*, to bere in his honde,
>   Therein to rede, and to vnderstande
> All the demenour of princely astate,
> To be our Kyng, of God preordinate

Like the other humanists, Skelton busied himself with moral and religious instruction. Among the lost works

[22] See above, p. 44.

listed in his catalogue are "the Book how men should flee sin" (1. 1173), "to learn you to die when ye will" (1. 1176), "Of Vertu . . the sovereign interlude" (1. 1177), "The False Faith that now goeth" (1. 1179), "Good Advisement, that brainless doth blame" (1. 1186), and a translation of the great French moral allegory, *La Pèlerinage de la vie humaine* (ll. 1219–22). Another item of the *Garland* list,

> . . a deuoute Prayer to Moyses hornis,
> Metrifyde merely, medelyd with scornis (ll. 1381–82)

scarcely sounds like a moral tract. That it was, nevertheless, is proved by a passage which occurs in *La Pèlerinage*. Moses asks Reason:[23]

> Wherof sholde myn hornys serve?
> Thys staff ek, with the sharpë poynt,
> Telleth me fro poynt to poynt,
> Be they nat maad, by good resoun,
> For punysshynge and Correccioun;
> Myn hornys, for to takë wrak
> On shrewës, & to putte abak?

Reason answers:

> Thogh thyn hornys & pyk also
> Be yovë to the, bothë two,
> ffor Punysshyng & for chastysyng
> Off folkys Rebel in werchyng;
> Yet fyrst thow sholdest hem dyrecte,
> And with fayrnesse hem correcte

But one need not rely on titles of books no longer extant for evidence that Skelton was a teacher of morals. The stated purpose of his satires is the destruction of vice. Even though *Elinor Rumming*, a poem which describes a group of country wives at a tavern, seems nothing but a revel in vulgarity, it surely has an underlying moral purpose. Here is Skelton's picture of the gluttonous Elinor (ll. 12–41):

[23] The translation is Lydgate's, *The Pilgrimage of the Life of Man* ("Early English Text Society [Publications]," E. S., Nos. 77, 83, 92), ll. 1580–86, 1599–1604.

Her lothely lere
Is nothynge clere,
But vgly of chere,
Droupy and drowsy,
Scuruy and lowsy;
Her face all bowsy,
Comely crynklyd,
Woundersly wrynkled,
Lyke a rost pygges eare,
Brystled wyth here.
　　Her lewde lyppes twayne,
They slauer, men sayne,
Lyke a ropy rayne,
A gummy glayre:
She is vgly fayre;
Her nose somdele hoked,
And camously croked,
Neuer stoppynge,
But euer droppynge;
Her skynne lose and slacke,
Grained lyke a sacke;
With a croked backe.
　　Her eyen gowndy
Are full vnsoundy,
For they are blered;
And she gray hered;
Jawed lyke a jetty;
A man would haue pytty
To se how she is gumbed
Fyngered and thumbed

Unpleasant enough, to be sure. But compare Saint Thomas
More, preaching soberly in *The Four Last Things*:[24]

If God would never punish gluttony, yet bringeth it punishment
enough with itself: it disfigureth the face, discoloureth the skin,
and disfashioneth the body; it maketh the skin tawny, the body
fat and fobby, the face drowsy, the nose dripping, the mouth
spitting, the eyes bleared, the teeth rotten, the breath stinking,
the hands trembling, the head hanging, and the feet tottering . . .

[24] *The English Works of Sir Thomas More* (London, 1931), I, 496.

More and Skelton are drawing on the same tradition and using it for the same moral purpose. Skelton's crime is not that he portrayed Elinor, but that he did it too vividly.

Skelton's contribution to the literature of ancient history was his translation of the *Historical Library* of Diodorus Siculus from the Latin version of Poggio. Skelton's selection of this very popular work is not surprising. It was a solid historical treatise, from which noble men might draw examples, and it was a classic and therefore endowed both with elegance and with authenticity. Of course, the *Historical Library* is full of tall tales, and Diodorus himself is decently skeptical of some of them. But Skelton generally overlooks the doubt and holds for the reliability of his stories. Apparently not everyone was equally gullible, for, late in the work Skelton bursts into a tirade against incredulous readers:[25]

. . . we now adayes passe ferre the tapetes of good maner & forme of humanyte / in that that many of theyr wylful affectionat mynde depraue auncyent wryters that touche many thynges that seme to theym incredyble for cause that theyr moche endulled witte can not atteyne ne suffiseth not to come ne atteyne to the parfyght notyce & knowlege of so hygh a processe / But syth it ne is possible for us to moeue yow unto credence but yf ye lyste / yet shal ye not discorage us to put in remembraunce as wonderful thynges as any as we haue recounted yet in this byhalue / accordyng as we fynde wreton in precedentys of formar recorde

If the accuracy of Diodorus satisfied Skelton, his rhetoric did not. The beginning of Skelton's translation is literal enough to please a Latin master who cares nothing for idiomatic English. But as the work proceeds, new adjectives creep in, together with linking sentences, explanatory digressions, and other embellishments, until, toward the end it becomes a problem of some difficulty to find the kernels of Diodorus in the mass of Skelton. If the relation-

[25] Corpus Christi College, Cambridge, MS 357, fol. 249. No justification for this passage can be found either in Diodorus or in the Latin of Poggio.

ship of the length of Skelton's Book I to the corresponding
Latin of Poggio[26] be taken as unity, then the ratio of
Skelton's Book II to Poggio's Book II equals 1.3, of
Skelton's Book III to Poggio's Book III, 1.9, of Book IV,
2.4, and of the fragment of Book V, 3.3. One hesitates to
extrapolate the proportions of the lost Book VI. A single
instance of Skelton's technique of translation will serve.
Diodorus had said, "After this, Hera sent two serpents to
destroy the babe [Hercules] but the boy gripped the neck
of a serpent in each hand and strangled them both."[27]
Here is Skelton's version:[28]

She [Juno] thenne enpoysond with the uenymous serpentis of
Saturnyne malyce enfestryd in her herte / fretyng and gnawyng
upon the passionat agonye of enuyous bytternesse compassed in
hir restles mynde / how she myght be reuengid upon this innocent babys / wherfore in releuement & moche easyng of her
angry stomack / by her magyke & deuynacioun she sente two
dragons to the chylde / where as he laye in his cradel / of purpose that they sholde stynge hym mortally unto his fynal deth /
This infaunte so pratyly lyeng & lufsomly laughyng in his
swadelyng bondes / nothyng abasshyd of the gastly & horryble
sight of these ij dredeful serpentis / but as it had ben of deuyne
instynction he forcybly brake & lcsed the bondis to haue out his
praty lytil armys and wonderly anymated with boldenes of
courage he toke in eche hande one of theym harde by the necke /
and thurgh deuyne vehemencye of enstrengthyd compression /
he so enstraytted their golettis & throtis / that inmediately
he strangled theym bothe to the deth /

In the field of occasional poetry Skelton's works closely
parallel those of Bernard André. If one may judge by titles,

The Tratyse of Triumphis of the Rede Rose,
Wherein many storis ar breuely contayned
That vnremembred longe tyme remayned[29]

[26] Poggio (and Skelton) divide the first book of Diodorus into two. Skelton's
Book III is therefore Book II of the Greek, and so on.

[27] *Diodorus*, Loeb, II, 370–71. Poggio's Latin reads: "Iuno deinceps duos dra-
cones ad perdendum misit puerum. quos ille utraque manu faucibus apprehensos
strangulauit" (*op. cit.*, fol. LXXVIII).

[28] *Loc. cit.*, fol. 234.   [29] *Garland of Laurel*, ll. 1223–25.

must have been like André's *Les Douze Triomphes*.[30] A gloss
on this passage from the *Garland of Laurel* reads, "Notat
bellum Cornubiense, quod in campestribus et in patentiori-
bus vastisque solitudinibus prope Grenewiche gestum est,"
which is a reference to a battle with Cornish rebels at
Blackheath, one of the stories "briefly contained" in
André's allegory. During the year 1489 three events of
national importance occurred. The King's first son, Arthur,
was entitled Prince of Wales in an elaborate ceremony.
André celebrated the occasion with the ode *De Arturi
Principis Creatione*.[31] Skelton's contribution to the festivities
was "Prince Arthur's Creation."[32] In April, 1489, the Earl
of Northumberland was assassinated while he was engaged
in collecting the king's taxes. André mourned in a poem
entitled *De Nortumbrorum comitis nece*.[33] Skelton wrote an
elegy "Upon the Dolorous Death and Much Lamentable
Chance of the Most Honorable Earl of Northumberland."[34]
Late in the year the French ambassador, Gaguin, insulted
the King of England. André, Carmeliano, Giovanni Gigli,
and Cornelio Vitelli responded to the attack.[35] Skelton,
too, joined the chorus: "The Recule against Gaguin of the
French Nation."[36]

It is, therefore, in terms of the humanist tradition established at the court of Henry VII that John Skelton must
be interpreted. His training, his belief in the power of
eloquence, his occupations, his literary matter, and his
style all identify him as a colleague of André, Carmeliano,
and the other scholars of the King.

One great difference there is. Whereas Carmeliano
wrote for King Henry in Latin, and André in Latin and
French, Skelton restricted himself almost entirely to his
native tongue. There are a few Latin pieces from his pen:
the *Speculum principis* and a scattering of epigrams. The lost

[30] See above, p. 28.   [31] *Chronicles and Memorials*, X, 44–46.
[32] *Garland of Laurel*, l. 1178.   [33] *Chronicles and Memorials*, X, 48–49.
[34] Skelton, *Works*, I, 6–14.   [35] See above, p. 26.   [36] *Garland of Laurel*, l. 1187.

comedy *Achademios* was probably written in Latin, since it seems that Skelton knew no Greek. But aside from *Speculum principis* and *Achademios*, every one of the works which Skelton found worthy of mention in the *Garland of Laurel* catalogue has an English title, and, if we may judge by those which remain extant, every composition with an English title was written in English. While André lamented the death of the Earl of Northumberland in Latin, Skelton grieved in English. There is no reason to doubt that the "Recule against Gaguin" and "Prince Arthur's Creation" were also written in the vernacular. His grammar and his rhetoric were English; he made English versions of Tully's *Familiars* and of Diodorus' *Library*. In sum, Skelton, the academically trained student of the classics, devoted himself busily to translating into his native idiom the learning, the substance, and the form of humanist literature.

He is entirely conscious of the importance of what he is doing, of the fact that he is opening to the populace at large the rich glories of the science of rhetoric, formerly hoarded in the academies. At the close of the *Garland of Laurel*, in which Skelton sets forth his claim to renown, he addresses his book, not with the traditionally timorous "unlearned though I be, my will is good," but in the full pride of Renaissance learning (ll. 1521–28):

> Ite, Britannorum lux O radiosa, Britannum
> Carmina nostra pium vestrum celebrate Catullum!
> Dicite, Skeltonis vester Adonis erat;
> Dicite, Skeltonis vester Homerus erat.
> Barbara cum Latio pariter jam currite versu;
> Et licet est verbo pars maxima texta Britanno,
> Non magis incompta nostra Thalia patet,
> Est magis inculta nec mea Calliope.

"Though most of the writing is in English, not more rude does my Thalia appear, not more unlearned my Calliope." And in a parallel English "envoy" (ll. 1533–52):

Go, litill quaire,
Demene you faire;
Take no dispare,
Though I you wrate
After this rate
In Englysshe letter;
So moche the better
Welcome shall ye
To sum men be:
For Latin warkis
Be good for clerkis;
Yet now and then
Sum Latin men
May happely loke
Vpon your boke,
And so procede
In you to rede,
That so indede
Your fame may sprede
In length and brede.

The allegory of the *Garland* provides another indication of Skelton's conception of his place in English literature. In the course of the vision, his three great predecessors, Gower, Chaucer, and Lydgate, lead him first to the pavilion of the learned Pallas (ll. 442–48), and thence to the temple of the Queen of Fame. This means, clearly, that it was the inspiration of these poets that persuaded Skelton to the study of literature by means of which he achieved celebrity. But Skelton is careful to distinguish himself from Gower, Chaucer, and Lydgate. They were great poets, he agrees, but they lacked the symbol of learning in the humanities, the laurel crown (ll. 393–97):

Togeder in armes, as brethern, enbrasid;
  There apparell farre passynge beyonde that I can tell;
With diamauntis and rubis there tabers were trasid,
  None so ryche stones in Turkey to sell;
  Thei wantid nothynge but the laurell

Skelton is not guilty of an exaggerated boast. He was in-

deed the first humanist to devote himself to the writing of
English poetry. And so Erasmus must have been informed:[37]

> O Skelton, worthy of eternal fame,
> Why should thy fount of speech pour on my name
> The meed of praise, for I have never sought
> Pierian grottos, nor drunk water brought
> From the Aonian fountain, liquor which
> The lips of poets ever doth enrich.
> But unto thee Apollo gave his lyre,
> Thou playest the strings taught by the Muses' choir;
> Persuasion lies like honey on thy tongue
> Given by Calliope, and thou hast sung
> A song more sweet than dying swan's by far,
> And Orpheus self yields thee his own guitar,
> And when thou strik'st it savage beasts grow mild,
> Thou leadest oaks and stayest torrents wild,
> And with thy soul-enchanting melodies
> Thou meltest rocks. *The debt that ancient Greece*
> *To Homer owed, to Vergil Mantua,*
> *That debt to Skelton owes Britannia,*
> *For he from Latium all the muses led*
> *And taught them to speak English words instead*
> *Of Latin;*[38] *and with Skelton England tries*
> *With Roman poets to contend the prize.*

There is another important difference between Skelton
and rhetoricians such as André and Carmeliano. Like More,

[37] Translated by Preserved Smith in *Erasmus* (New York, 1923), p. 62, from MS
Egerton 1651, fol. 6. The italics are mine. The Latin has been reprinted in Appendix
III of Smith's *Erasmus;* in *Erasmi opuscula*, edited by W. K. Ferguson (The Hague,
1933), p. 29; and by Ian A. Gordon, in *London Times Literary Supplement*, Sept. 20,
1934, p. 636. It also appears, with minor variants, in the American edition of Dyce's
Poetical Works of John Skelton (Boston, 1871), I, lxvii, "transcribed from a MS. (in
the collection of the late Mr. B. H. Bright), consisting of *Hymni*, &c., by Picus
Mirandula." Despite the attribution to Pico, Erasmus' authorship is certain, for
the Egerton MS is a copy of the volume which Erasmus presented to Prince
Henry. See below, pp. 71–73.

[38] Smith's translation is not altogether justified by the Latin:

> Primus in hanc Latio deduxit ab orbe Camenas,
>> Primus hic edocuit
> Exculte pureque loqui . . . .

Nevertheless, though Erasmus does not explicitly say that Skelton taught the
muses to speak English, his comparison of Skelton to Homer and Vergil clearly
shows that he considers Skelton to be the father of English literature.

Colet, and Erasmus, Skelton transcends the tradition from which he springs. Like them he is endowed with a quality of his own which makes it impossible to ticket him neatly as a member of any school. But Skelton's spirit takes him a very different path from that followed by the friends of More, a path which leads to the works of "beastly" Skelton who "fabricates a kind of literary mud"[39] "pleasing only to the popular ear," or, if one prefers, of Skelton the brilliant and courageous satirist, the unique example of an English poet of individual genius in the century and a half between Chaucer and Wyatt.

[39] H. A. Taine, *History of English Literature*, translated by Van Laun (1872), I, 139.

Tutor to the Prince

THE FIRST clear notice of the existence of John Skelton appears in the dedication of Caxton's *Eneydos*, in 1489. Of Skelton's career before that time little is known and nothing is certain. Where the poet came from, of what family, when he was born, when he attended the university, how he found his place at court are questions to which none but the most tentative of answers can be given. Until 1489 there is nothing but doubtful scraps and more doubtful conjecture.

"DISPARAGE YE MINE ANCESTRY?"

Skelton's enemy, Sir Christopher Garnesche, apparently did disparage the poet's ancestry.[1] Skelton's only answer was, "you are disposed for to lie." And despite much scholarly labor there is nothing more positive to be said on the subject. The most careful student of the genealogic problem concludes:[2]

The Skelton family, quite distinct from the Norfolk Sheltons, originated in the North, in Cumberland and Yorkshire. By the fifteenth century members were scattered over the whole island, and ranged from sheriffs and gentlemen, vicars and maltmen to university bigwigs, cooks, whores, and pirates. Regarding Skelton himself, facts are non-existent and tradition is almost useless, depending as it does upon accident, whim, or actual error.

Unfortunately, even the statement that Skeltons and Sheltons were unrelated may be questioned, for I find a John Skelton (not the poet) appointed to the rectory of Shelton, Norfolk, in 1518, a living normally in the gift of

[1] Skelton, *Works*, I, 128.
[2] H. L. R. Edwards, "John Skelton: a Genealogical Study," *The Review of English Studies*, XI (1935), 418.

Sir John Shelton.[3] Under the circumstances, there can be no point in guessing.

The date of the poet's birth is almost equally uncertain. Only two solid items of information have any bearing on the problem: Skelton was Poet Laureate in 1489, and he died in 1529. Presumably, he was not less than twenty years old when the university honored him, and it is doubtful that he lived to be over one hundred. It is relatively safe to conclude, therefore, that he was born between 1430 and 1470. If the Skelton who became Bachelor of Arts at Cambridge in 1480 was the poet,[4] and if he was the usual sixteen or seventeen years of age when he received the degree, then Skelton, Laureate, was born in 1463 or 1464. But if it is assumed that one of the requirements for the Oxford degree of Poet Laureate was fourteen years of grammar school teaching (Whittinton and the others who received degrees in grammar claimed such service[5]), then Skelton's acquisition of the degree in 1488 or 1489 proves that he must have been born by 1455 at the latest. His birth year is usually given as "1460?" and if the question mark be kept in mind, there is no harm in retaining the date. It has the advantage of giving him a decent seventy years of life.

"ALMA PARENS O CANTABRIGENSIS"

Somewhat more secure ground is reached in the matter of Skelton's university. The poet himself settles part of the question:[6] "Cantabrigia Skeltonidi laureato primam mammam eruditionis pientissime [*sic*] propinavit." But the Cambridge records are not very helpful. A number of Skeltons are recorded in this period,[7] but none who can with cer-

---

[3] Norwich Diocese Institution Book XVI, fol. 45. This John Skelton cannot be Skelton, Laureate, for he died before April 2, 1523 (Institution Book XIV, fol. 179).

[4] See below, p. 61.   [5] See above, pp. 43–44.   [6] Skelton, *Works*, I, 207.

[7] For example, Master Skelton in 1456–57 (*Cambridge Grace Book A*, p. 11), Skelton, inceptor in Arts in 1462 (*ibid.*, p. 32), Master Skelton of Michaelhouse

tainty be identified as our poet. The most likely of the lot is Dominus Skelton, *questionist* (about to become Bachelor of Arts) on March 18, 1480. But it is also possible that the *questionist* was one William Skelton, of Peterhouse.[8] There is no evidence that the poet took the degree of Bachelor or Master of Arts at Cambridge, and if he did not, his name would not appear in the records.

It is possible that Skelton met influential friends at Cambridge. He may have known John Blythe, later bishop of Salisbury, John Syclyng, later master of Godshouse, and John Fisher, adviser to the Lady Margaret.[9] At the end of Skelton's elegy on the Earl of Northumberland is a respectful quatrain addressed to William Ruckshaw, Doctor of Sacred Theology. Ruckshaw,[10] a Peterhouse man, became Master of Arts in 1460–61 and received his degree in theology in 1480. He must have been considerably Skelton's senior, therefore, and perhaps he was his tutor. In 1480 Ruckshaw entered the service of the Earl of Northumberland and was installed succentor of York. His connection with Peterhouse continued, however, for in 1492 he gave the college a silver-enameled spice plate weighing thirty-one ounces.

"I WAS MADE POET LAUREATE"

Skelton surely attended Cambridge; quite as surely he graced the sister university. Caxton refers to him as Laureate of Oxford.[11] So, too, do the records of the University of Cambridge,[12] which, in 1493, conceded to "John

---

in 1466 (*ibid.*, pp. 59, 64), Dominus Skelton, *questionist*, March 18, 1480 (*ibid.*, p. 134).

[8] T. A. Walker, *A Biographical Register of Peterhouse Men* (Cambridge, 1927), I, 101.

[9] See below, pp. 70–71.

[10] Biographical information concerning Ruckshaw is to be found in *Testamenta Eboracensia IV* ("Surtees Society [Publications]" No. 53), pp. 231–33, and in *A Biographical Register of Peterhouse Men*, I, 56–57.

[11] See above, p. 4.

[12] *Grace Book B (I)*, p. 54. See above, p. 43 n.

Skelton, poet, laureated at Oxford and abroad," the privilege of a similar decoration. Tradition, indeed, associates the poet more closely with Oxford than with Cambridge. *The Merry Tales of Skelton*, a contemporary collection of anecdotes concerning the poet,[13] begins: "Skelton was an Englysheman borne as Skogyn was, and hee was educated and broughte vp in Oxfoorde: and there was he made a poete lauriat." In another tale[14] a dinner companion asks Skelton, "Be you of Oxforde or of Cambridge a scoler?" Skelton said, "I am of Oxford." But it is probable that this tradition depends upon the fact that it was Oxford which first granted Skelton the title Laureate. The poet himself, while he calls Cambridge *alma parens*, refers to Oxford rather impersonally, as though he were not a member of that university, but a stranger honored by it:[15]

> At Oxforth, the vnyversyte,
> Auaunsid I was to that degre;
> By hole consent of theyr senate,[16]
> I was made poete lawreate.

Aside from Caxton's "late created Poet Laureate in the University of Oxford," written in 1489, and Skelton's assumption of the title in a poem composed during the same year,[17] there is no evidence bearing directly on the date of the poet's first garlanding. A curious calendar which Skelton uses in some of his later writings seems to take its origin from an event which occurred in October or November, 1488,[18] and the happening so celebrated may well be the Oxford laureation, of which Skelton was inordinately proud.

The Cambridge ratification of the Oxford degree of Poet Laureate mentions a similar honor granted by a continental

---

[13] Reprinted in Skelton, *Works*, I, lvii–lxxiii.   [14] Tale iii.

[15] Skelton, *Works*, I, 128.

[16] "Senate" is properly used of the governing body of Cambridge, not of Oxford.

[17] The elegy on Northumberland.   [18] See below, pp. 173–74.

university. That this foreign university was Louvain is
indicated by the title of a eulogy of Skelton addressed to
him by the grammarian, Robert Whittinton:[19] "In claris-
simi Scheltonis *Louaniensis* poetæ laudes epigramma."
Louvain probably granted the degree after Oxford, for it is
the Oxford degree to which Skelton and his contemporaries
continually refer. The date of the Louvain ceremony must
therefore fall between 1488, when it is presumed that
Skelton was laureated at Oxford, and 1493, when the
foreign degree was mentioned in the Cambridge register.[20]

COURT POET

In 1489 Caxton announced not only that Skelton had
just been created Poet Laureate at the University of Oxford, but also that he was a learned scholar, capable of
mending any fault in Caxton's translation of *Eneydos*, and
that he had englished both the *Historical Library* of Diodorus and Cicero's *Familiar Letters*. During the year in
which Caxton's eulogy was printed, Skelton composed
three court poems, all on subjects also treated by the king's
poet, Bernard André.

Unquestionably Skelton was at this time desirous of
receiving royal patronage. In his translation of Diodorus
he admonished rulers to favor the learned and warned them
that neglect of that duty would entail serious consequences.
Diodorus had accounted for the names of each of the Muses
by reference to an appropriate quality from which the name
was derived: "Erato [the *lovely* one], because she makes

---

[19] *Opusculum Roberti Whittintoni* (Wynken de Worde, 1519); Skelton, *Works*, I,
xvi–xix.

[20] It is therefore probable that Skelton's teacher at Louvain was Francisco de
Crema, Poet Laureate, who began to lecture in 1492. De Crema's predecessor in
the chair of poetry established by the Duke and Duchess of Brabant was Lodewyc
Bruyne, Poet Laureate, who apparently ceased to read in 1482 (H. De Jongh,
L'Ancienne Faculté de théologie de Louvain [Louvain, 1911], pp. 73–74). If Skelton
studied under De Crema, he was taught by a man "most learned in literature"
who was host to Erasmus in 1498 (Allen, *Epistolæ*, I, No. 76).

those who are instructed by her men who are desired and worthy to be *loved*."[21] The pun was lost in passage through Poggio's Latin translation (which Skelton used), and the English scholar, without knowledge of the meaning of the original Greek, seized the occasion to exalt his trade and to plead for patronage:[22]

The sixte [Muse] is named dame Erato / whiche thurgh her bounteuous promocioun hir scolers and discyples bryngeth unto so noble auaunsement / that whan she hath enryched theym with the gloryous tresour of connyng & wysedom / they shal stande in faueur of ryal pryncis / and so atteyne unto the spirytual rowme of prelacye or other temporal promocioun / but yf folye by his fantasie disguysed with his gylded habillementis of worldly vanyte Induce noble astates to daunce the comyn trace of abusion / wherupon sone after ensueth extreme confusion of fallyble fortune ful of deceyte

The facts that Skelton had achieved the honor of the laurel, that Caxton's eulogy was included in a dedication to Prince Arthur, and that the poet was engaged in paralleling André's Latin poems on court events with English ones suggest that by 1489 he had already achieved entrance into the service of Henry VII.

It has recently been proposed that Skelton's position was that of tutor to Prince Arthur.[23] The strongest argument for the hypothesis is the appearance of Caxton's praise of Skelton in a foreword addressed to the three-year-old prince. It is also pointed out that although Skelton claims to have written the little instruction book *Speculum principis* (1501) expressly for Prince Henry, the pamphlet addresses "princes," not "the prince," and the conclusion is drawn that Skelton tutored Arthur as well as Henry. But the use of the plural is probably only a literary formality, designed to secure for the tract the appearance of universal

[21] *Diodorus*, Loeb edition (Harvard University Press, 1935), II, 364–65. The italics are mine.

[22] Corpus Christi College, Cambridge, MS 357, fol. 231.

[23] F. M. Salter, "Skelton's 'Speculum principis,'" *Speculum*, IX (1934), 30–33.

applicability. Although Skelton may have been teaching a single pupil, his precepts were of value to all of the ruling class.[24] Since Bernard André clearly asserts that he taught Arthur from 1496 to 1500 and mentions as a predecessor only John Rede,[25] there seems to be little room for Skelton. It is possible, however, that he did give Arthur instruction in the elements. The precise nature of the poet's employment in 1489 remains in the unhappy realm of "perhaps" and "it is possible that." But it is certain that he had sought royal service, and it is probable that he had already achieved it.

THE FIRST POEM

Skelton's earliest extant poem, the elegy "Upon the Dolorous Death and Lamentable Chance of the Most Honorable Earl of Northumberland,"[26] exhibits the mature poet in little. Like André, Skelton mourned the noble Earl and extolled his virtues. But unlike André's complaint, Skelton's is not altogether a stiff rhetorical exercise. The poet was already the master of the sharp phrases that became the usual weapons of his later works; he knew how to saber an enemy from a galloping verse. And the germ of the moral philosophy that animates *Magnificence* and the satires on Wolsey is to be found in this early poem. The nature of Skelton's ethical system appears in the reproof which he addresses to the murderers of Northumberland, the riotous commons:

> I say, ye comoners, why wer ye so stark mad?
> What frantyk frensy fyll in your brayne?

[24] If the form of address of *Speculum principis* is to be understood literally, it must be concluded that Skelton had no idea as to who would read his book: "Quisquis es — genus nullum, ordinem nullum, condicionem nullam, sexum nullum excipio, princeps licet magnificentissimus . . ." (*ibid.*, p. 35).

[25] See above, p. 15 n.

[26] It is possible that "Of the Death of the Noble Prince, King Edward the Fourth" antedates "Northumberland," but there is good reason to doubt the attribution to Skelton (Brie, "Skelton-Studien," *Englische Studien*, XXXVII [1907], 27).

Where was your wit and reson ye should haue had?
  What wilful foly made yow to ryse agayne
  Your naturall lord? alas, I can not fayne:
  Ye armyd you with will, and left your wit behynd;
  Well may you be called comones most vnkynd.
                                        (ll. 50–56)

Skelton conceived that the essence of morality, both personal and political, was to be found in the relationship ob-
taining between will (freedom of action) and wit (reason).
Will, or liberty, as Skelton explains in *Magnificence* (ll. 74–
80), is the desire of every man:

  I say, there is no welthe where as lyberte is subdude;
  I trowe ye can not say nay moche to this;
  To lyue vnder lawe, it is captyuyte;
  Where drede ledyth the daunce, there is no ioy nor blysse;
  Or howe can you proue that there is felycyte,
  And you haue not your owne fre lyberte
  To sporte at your pleasure, to ryn and to ryde?

But, the poet insists, human desires need restraint. Unless
will is ruled by wit, there follow wild excess, riot, and the
ruin of worldly felicity (ll. 132–37):

Lyberte   What, lyberte to measure then wolde ye bynde?
Measure   What ellys? for otherwyse it were agaynst kynde:
         If lyberte sholde lepe and renne where he lyst,
         It were no vertue, it were a thynge vnblyst;
         It were a myschefe, yf lyberte lacked a reyne,
         Where with to rule hym with the wrythyng of a rest

Thus the commons slew Northumberland because their
will was unbridled. The concept runs through every one of
Skelton's political poems. Years later, the poet asserts that
it is the willfullness of the world that is bringing ruin
upon it:[27]

         For wyll dothe rule all thynge,
         Wyll, wyll, wyll, wyll, wyll,
         He ruleth alway styll.
         Good reason and good skyll,

[27] *Why Come Ye Not to Court*, ll. 102–9.

> They may garlycke pyll,
> Cary sackes to the myll,
> Or pescoddes they may shyll,
> Or elles go rost a stone

"Will" did not remain an abstract concept for Skelton. When the foregoing lines were written (1522), will had become identified with the solid, powerful reality of Cardinal Wolsey, unbridled ruler of England.

The rashness of Skelton's assault upon Cardinal Wolsey was itself adumbrated in the early poem on Northumberland. Even in 1489 he betrayed his inability to modulate his voice to the gentle tones required of a court poet. The elegy is dedicated to the son and heir of the dead Percy, "Ad libitum cujus ipse paratus ero." But if the young Earl gave Skelton employment or patronage in response to this request, it must have been over the protests of his whole army of retainers. For Skelton was not satisfied to attack the murderous commons:

> Barones, knyghtes, squiers, one and all,
>   Together with seruauntes of his famuly,
> Turned their backis, and let their master fal,
>   Of whos [life] they counted not a flye;
>   Take vp whose wold, for ther they let him ly.
> Alas, his gold, his fee, his annual rent
> Upon suche a sort was ille bestowed and spent!
>
>   (ll. 92–98)

Thus, even in the first of his extant poems Skelton found it impossible to "flatter, glose, and paint." If there was an evil to be attacked, if unfettered will ruled in high places, Skelton could not contain himself. As poet and scholar he seems to have considered himself the apostle of reason and of moderation and to have conceived it his duty to whip erring humanity into line. But it was a violent, intemperate man that professed this philosophy of the golden mean. It was a quixotic, indignant spirit that clothed itself in the garments of that most subservient of creatures, the court poet.

When Skelton was introduced by Caxton, in 1489, therefore, he appeared complete. He was possessed of a degree testifying to his accomplishment in humane letters. He was the author of occasional poems and of solid works, useful to kings and princes. He was already a disciple of the philosophy that guided the thought of his later years. And he was an outspoken, irascible fellow, unable to curb his tongue to his own advantage.

TOWN AND GOWN

In 1495 the relations of the University of Cambridge with the townspeople were seriously disturbed.

The controversy was not a passing incident but was based upon a deep-rooted difference concerning questions of privilege, jurisdiction, control of markets, fairs and trading generally. The university on the one hand, the town on the other, had obtained respectively from successive sovereigns concessions whose bearing upon prior concessions to the other party was not duly weighed, and the resultant duality of authority had divided town and gown since the middle of the thirteenth century.[28]

The particular occasion of the trouble of 1495 is not known. But if one may judge by the number of trips to London made by the representatives of the university, it was serious enough. The senior proctor, the vice-chancellor, and Master Syclyng, Master of Godshouse (later Christ's College) carried the burden of the business, which kept them away from the university for long periods. Commencement time forced the vice-chancellor to return to Cambridge, and Syclyng was left alone in London to urge the university's cause. His expense account contains some interesting items. On a Wednesday after Pentecost he took breakfast and dinner with Master Skelton "who was with

[28] A. H. Lloyd, *The Early History of Christ's College Cambridge* (1934), pp. 230–31.

the bishop of Salisbury.''[29] On the following Saturday he again had breakfast with Master Skelton, this time at Symson's, in Fleet Street.[30] Several years later, in 1501, a new contention arose between town and gown. Syclyng was made senior proctor in 1500-1501, possibly because of his experience in matters of controversy. He spent almost the whole year in London and Westminster, leaving a deputy to perform his duties at Cambridge. On a Wednesday during Hilary term he had dinner with Master Skelton, and on the following Tuesday and Wednesday the two dined together again. On Thursday Skelton sat in Syclyng's room, and they talked over a penny drink before a penny fire.[31]

It seems likely that this Master Skelton, warmed, fed, and wined by the University of Cambridge, was Skelton the poet. The appearance of these items in the expense account indicates that university business was involved in his entertainment. For the furthering of its cause Cambridge required the assistance of lawyers, men in royal favor, orators, and letter writers. The doctors of the Court of the Arches dined frequently at the University's cost. Letter writers reaped a harvest. Sir Reginald Bray, a favorite of the King, received payments for preparing rolls and documents. When Syclyng made his second expedition, in 1501, Skelton the poet was certainly employed as tutor to Prince Henry. As he was both a courtier and a rhetorician, he was doubly qualified to assist the university which he had attended in his youth. I know of no other Master Skelton busy at court during this period. And if the Skelton of the 1501 account was the poet, surely the Skelton of the 1495 record must have been.

It becomes interesting, therefore, to consider the people

[29] *Grace Book B* (I), p. 92.
[30] *Ibid.* Symson's in Fleet Street is not the same as the modern Simpson's in the Strand, which was established in 1828 (Lloyd, *op. cit.*, p. 232).
[31] *Grace Book B* (I), pp. 148–49.

with whom the Skelton of the Cambridge expense accounts was associated. Syclyng,[32] like Skelton, was a student of grammar, in which faculty he incepted in 1481. In 1490–91 he became master of Godshouse, a position which he continued to hold through the metamorphosis of Godshouse into Christ's College, until his death in 1506. It was during his administration that the Lady Margaret refounded the institution and provided it with its new name and with a set of statutes which reflect, some historians assert, the influence of Erasmus. But even before Margaret's beneficence, the College had been a center for the study of grammar and the training of grammar-school teachers. Syclyng, who had taken a degree in the faculty of grammar and was employed in the capacity of university orator, was well fitted to head Godshouse and to entertain John Skelton, Poet Laureate.

John Blythe, the bishop of Salisbury in whose company Skelton was found in 1495, was another "orator." He had taken the degree of Master of Arts at Cambridge, in 1482, and, after receiving a number of ecclesiastical preferments, he was raised to the episcopate, in 1495. In 1492 he was made master of Rolls, and from 1493 to 1495 he served as chancellor of the University of Cambridge. In the latter capacity he delivered a speech of welcome to King Henry VII, the Queen Mother, and Prince Arthur on the occasion of their visit to the university.[33]

Syclyng became Master of Grammar in 1481, Blythe, Master of Arts in 1482. One recalls the Skelton, *questionist*, of 1480.[34] Perhaps—it is only a guess, of course—Syclyng's visit to London in 1495 reunited three school friends who had sat together at Cambridge lectures. Perhaps it was the

[32] An excellent biography of Syclyng is to be found in Lloyd, *op. cit.*, chap. xiv and xv.

[33] There is an elegant manuscript copy of his oration in the Bodleian Library, an abstract of which is printed in *Chronicles and Memorials*, XXIV (1), 422–23.

[34] See above, p. 61.

influence of John Blythe, the chancellor, that procured for Skelton the only degree of Poet Laureate that Cambridge seems ever to have conferred. Perhaps it was through Syclyng's friend John Fisher that Skelton received appointment as schoolmaster to Prince Henry. For Fisher, another Master of Grammar at Cambridge (1480), was the spiritual adviser of Lady Margaret, and Margaret was charged with the education of the King's younger son.[35]

"THE HONOR OF ENGLAND I LEARNED TO SPELL"

After 1494 Skelton's biographer does not reach certainty again until 1498 and 1499. In March, April, and June, 1498, John Skelton, *poeta laureatus*, was ordained successively subdeacon, deacon, and priest by the bishop of London.[36] His rapid advancement through the clerical orders does not itself betray the pressure of royal favor, for such procedure seems to have been common. But in November, 1498, a few months after Skelton became priest, Henry VII made an offering of twenty shillings at "Master Skelton's mass."[37] There can be little doubt that this Master Skelton was the poet, and the fact that he said mass before the King places him definitely among those in favor at court.

The marvellous collection of Erasmus' letters illuminates every corner of Renaissance Europe. In 1499 the great humanist came to England, and the bright light which enveloped his movements fell for a moment on John Skelton. Erasmus tells[38] how Thomas More, visiting him at the country house of Lord Mountjoy, suggested that they walk together to the nearby town of Eltham, where all the King's children, with the exception of Arthur, were

[35] C. A. Halsted, *Life of Margaret Beaufort* (London, 1839), pp. 196–97.

[36] Register "Hill" (1485–1506). The precise dates are March 31, April 14, and June 9.

[37] Public Record Office, MS E.101–414–16 (November 11–16, 1498): "Item for offring at master Skeltons masse   xx s."

[38] Allen, *Opus epistolarum Erasmi*, I, No. 1 (p. 6).

receiving their schooling. Erasmus was rather annoyed to find that More had brought along a manuscript to give to Prince Henry, while he, caught unawares, had nothing to present. His chagrin was further deepened, for while they sat at dinner he received a note from the young Prince asking for a poetical gift. Erasmus could not answer extempore. He spent the next three days working feverishly and managed to put together a little book of poems, consisting chiefly of scraps which he found in his trunk.[39] To these old pieces he added a leaven of new material: a prose dedication, an ode entitled "A Description of Britain, King Henry VII, and the King's Children," and the eulogy of Skelton, a translation of which is quoted on page 57 above. In the first two, as well as in the last, Skelton is honorably mentioned. The dedication assures Prince Henry, "There is in your household that light and glory of English letters, Skelton, who is capable not only of stimulating your appetite for learning, but of satisfying your hunger as well."[40] And again, in the ode to the King and his children, Erasmus says,[41] "Now the boy Henry, happy in the name of his father, is introduced to the sacred fountains of the Muses by the poet Skelton."

Like certain other pieces in the volume which Erasmus presented to Prince Henry, the poem which he devoted to the praise of Skelton does not appear in the editions of his collected works. It has been supposed that it was intentionally omitted because Skelton failed to make an appropriate answer. What justification there is for this guess I do not know. The first lines of Erasmus' poem certainly

[39] MS Egerton 1651. See *Erasmi opuscula*, ed. by W. K. Ferguson (The Hague, 1933), p. 26.

[40] Allen, *op. cit.*, I, No. 104: "et domi haberes Skeltonum, vnum Britannicarum litterarum lumen ac decus, qui tua studia possit non solum accendere sed etiam consummare."

[41] *Opuscula*, p. 27:

"Iam puer Henricus genitoris nomine lætus
Monstrante fonteis vate Skeltono sacros."

indicate that Skelton, not Erasmus, had made the first move in the contest of mutual congratulation:

> Why should thy fount of speech pour on my name
> The meed of praise . . .

Of course, Erasmus' eulogy of Skelton cannot be taken as evidence of genuine respect born of close acquaintance with the poet's works. It is for his English writings that Erasmus praised Prince Henry's tutor, and Erasmus knew no English. Perhaps More was his informant. But whether or not Erasmus knew of Skelton's literary attainments, he understood that Skelton professed to be a poet and rhetorician and that he was in favor at court and therefore in position to do a good turn for a needy fellow scholar.

That Skelton was Prince Henry's first schoolmaster is implied by the lines:[42]

> It plesyth that noble prince roialle
> Me as hys master for to calle
> In hys lernyng primordialle.

In Tudor times, noble children often began their studies at the age of four. It is possible, therefore, that Skelton assumed the task of instructing Prince Henry as early as 1494 or 1495. The hypothesis is somewhat strengthened by the fact that when Skelton dedicated the *Speculum principis* to the newly crowned Henry, about the year 1510, he included in the manuscript volume an epigram entitled "Ad tanti principis maiestatem in sua puericia, quando erat insignitus Dux Eboraci."[43] The last clause may be understood to mean that the epigram was written either "when he was created Duke of York," that is, in 1494, or "during the period when he was called Duke of York," that is, any time between 1494 and 1502, when Henry was made Prince of Wales. In a recent discussion of the *Speculum principis* manuscript,[44] the latter interpretation is proposed

---

[42] Skelton, *Works*, I, 129.   [43] Salter, *Speculum*, IX (1934), 36–37.
[44] *Ibid.*, p. 29.

and accepted. It is argued that the description of Henry in the epigram as *clarus alumnus* is not appropriate to a three-year-old, and that the phrasing of the epigram suggests that it was not written for a special occasion. But *alumnus* means "nurseling" as well as "student," and in my opinion, the praise given to Henry seems at least as applicable to an infant as to a lad of twelve. The epigram states that the new rose is worthy of the tree from which it comes; Henry is of noble blood on his mother's side as well as on his father's; child though he be, nobility flourishes in him; neither Narcissus nor Hyperion excels him in beauty. Final proof that the occasion of the poem was the ceremony at which Henry was created Duke of York is offered, I think, by the line "En nouus Ebra[u]cus merito redimitus honore." The modern editor prints "Ebrancus," which means nothing. It should be "Ebraucus," the mythical founder of York, and the date 1494 is therefore certainly correct. But the fact that Skelton addressed the Prince in that year cannot be taken as proof that he was already a member of his household.

Skelton probably remained schoolmaster to the Prince until 1502. *Speculum principis*, the treatise which he wrote for his pupil, is dated at Eltham, August 28, 1501. Eight months later, on April 29, 1502, the Duke of York's schoolmaster received a gift of forty shillings from the King.[45] I am inclined to think that this payment was an addition to Skelton's regular salary and that it marked the end of his service as tutor to the Prince. Since no other disbursement to Skelton as tutor appears in the King's account books, it is probable that his regular income was received from some other source, perhaps from the Lady Margaret, who supervised the young Henry's education. The forty shillings, therefore, seems to have constituted

[45] Public Record Office, MS E. 101-415-3: "Item to the duc of yorks scolemaster   xl s."

an exceptional gift. Such bonuses were often bestowed on faithful retainers at the close of their service. In July, 1502, for example, Prince Arthur's schoolmaster, a nameless Scot, received twenty shillings from Queen Elizabeth "at his departing."[46] The occasion for the Scot's departure was the death of his pupil, heir to the throne of England, in April, 1502. It may have been the same misfortune that terminated Skelton's connection with the household of the younger prince. A great change had taken place in the status of the young Duke of York, a change which undoubtedly entailed a reorganization of his ménage. The future king does not live at the same rate as the brother of the future king. In any case, Skelton was no longer Henry's schoolmaster in 1504, for in that year he was resident in his rectory of Diss, in Norfolk.[47] In 1504–5 the Prince had a new teacher, one William Hoone.[48] Skelton's service as tutor ended, therefore, between 1501, when *Speculum principis* was written, and 1504. The probability is that the death of Prince Arthur occasioned his dismissal, which was sweetened by the King's gift of forty shillings in April, 1502.

Concerning the substance of Skelton's instruction of Prince Henry, there is information to be found in *Speculum principis*. The treatise begins with a series of examples drawn from classical history proving that virtue is more important to a ruler than wealth or nobility of blood. The point is reinforced by appropriate quotations from reliable authorities: Cato, Scipio, Horace, the pseudo-Aristotle. Those princes, therefore, that wish to excel in majesty must be virtuous and learned. Skelton has another reason for urging virtue and learning on his pupil, a reason which depends on a striking departure from the precepts of the traditional instruction books. He does not devote a long

---

[46] *Privy Purse Expenses of Elizabeth of York*, p. 28. The tutor also received four pounds from the king on June 25, 1502 (P. R. O., MS E.101-415-3).
[47] See below, p. 81.   [48] Cambridge *Grace Book* Γ, p. 37.

section to explaining how the prince should choose his council. Instead, he warns him that advisers are a poor staff, that those who claim knowledge are untrustworthy, those who are doubtful are useless. The prince himself must learn to govern his State; he cannot rely on his servants. The pamphlet proceeds to list the horrible examples of vicious rulers: Ezechiel, Pilate, Manasses, and Saul, each one of whom came to a bad end. From their disasters, princes may learn bitter lessons. Skelton fears that what he must now say will be unpleasant to hear. Nevertheless, like Juvenal and Lucilius, he must physic his auditor, and he will be unfaithful to his task if he omits it. However sure your state may seem, says Skelton, it is not impossible that catastrophe may overtake you, miserable exile, such as your ancestors suffered. You may expect wounds and wretched disaster, times of evil omen, incalculable secret hatreds hidden behind courteous language, horrible war, rare sweetness and endless tribulation, frail spirits apparently sure today but worth nothing tomorrow, unsuspected perils, unavoidable crises. Having frightened his little pupil into docility, Skelton closes his *Speculum* with a torrent of precepts. The prince is told to beware of gluttony, drunkenness, lasciviousness, ingratitude, flattery, miserliness, and thriftlessness. One of the "sentences" which Henry probably memorized reads, "Choose a wife for yourself; prize her always and uniquely."[49] The flow of precepts ends with the injunction that the prince read chronicles and histories, and he is advised to pattern himself after various classical examples of kindliness and justice.

COMMITTED TO THE KING'S PRISON

Master Skelton of the Cambridge accounts is not the only Skelton whose identification is rendered difficult by the existence of a numerous throng of namesakes. "John

[49] "Coniugem tibi delige quam unice semper dilige."

Skelton" occurs twice in the Act Book of the Court of Requests,[50] a court composed of the members of the King's
Council. On May 14, 1501, the court ordered that the case
of Peter Ottey *versus* John Skelton be postponed until nine
o'clock of the following day in hope of concord between
the disputants, and Skelton was required on pain of a
penalty of forty pounds to appear before Richard, Bishop
of Ely, and the others of the Council unless an agreement
had been reached in the meantime. There is no further
record of the case, nor does the court record provide any
information as to the cause of the quarrel. I find nothing
more about Peter Ottey, unless he is Peter Otley, a chaplain
presented by the King to the parish church of Wanstede
in 1504.[51]

On June 10, 1502, John Skelton appeared before the
same court by virtue of an obligation in which the Prior
of St. Bartholomew's and others were held by Sir Reginald
Bray, second husband of Lady Margaret, and by others.
The court ordered that Skelton be committed to the keeper
of the king's prison. This imprisonment does not, of course,
represent punishment for a crime. Skelton seems to have
been a surety for a loan, or a party to it, and he was probably released when the obligation was settled.

Whether this John Skelton (or these John Skeltons)
can be identified with the poet, I cannot say. It seems
likely, on the whole. The suit between the Prior of St.
Bartholomew's and Bray involved both church and court,
a combination nicely suited to Skelton, priest and court
scholar. If Ottey is the same as Otley, Skelton was engaged
in a dispute with an appropriate enemy, a cleric in royal
favor. However, even if the discoveries concern Skelton,
Laureate, they are not particularly illuminating; Skelton's
appearance as a surety and the threatened penalty of forty

[50] See Appendix II.
[51] *Calendar of Patent Rolls* (*Henry VII*), II, 374 (August 20, 1504).

pounds indicate the possession of considerable wealth, and the presumption of Skelton's culpability in his disagreement with Ottey suggests that the poet was as contentious in life as in literature.

THE BOWGE OF COURT

There remains a further source of information concerning Skelton's life at the court of Henry VII. It is the poem called *Bowge of Court* which Skelton must have written before 1501, since it was printed while Wynken de Worde was still at Westminster.[52] The word *bowge* is derived from the Old French *bouge*, meaning "kitchen," and "bowge of court" was the official designation of the diet of meat and drink furnished to the king's servitors at the court.[53] The topic of the poem, the treachery and ill manners of courtiers competing for place, is typical Renaissance; the dream form is typical Middle Age; but the poem is nevertheless true Skelton and one of the best of his works.

The poet, after providing a conventional astronomic date and after making the conventional apologies, settles down to sleep, not in the conventional arbor, but at Harwich port in my host's house called Power's Key. He dreams of the "Bowge of Court," a ship which carries that royal merchandise Favor. The dreamer, named Dread, is given the jewel of Bon Aventure, and with a crowd of other adventurers, sues to Fortune: "And we asked Favor, and Favor she us gave." So ends the prologue. Fortune at the helm, Favor aboard, the ship sets sail. It would be a pleasant voyage, were it not for Dread's fellow passengers: Favel (flattery), Suspicion, Harvy Hafter (trickster, or wrangler), Disdain, Riot, Dissimulation, Deceit, and

[52] Helen Stearns Sale, in "The Date of Skelton's 'Bowge of Court,' " *Modern Language Notes*, LII (1937), 572–74, assigns the date 1499.

[53] In Rymer, *Fœdera*, XIII, 374 (1513) is a grant to Marcellus de la More, principal surgeon of the court: "Habendum . . . dictum Officium dicto Servienti nostro, durante Vitâ suâ, cum Feodis & Vadiis . . . simul cum omnibus Allocationibus tàm *le Bouge the Courte*."

Subtlety. In his vivid painting of these individuals, Skelton
shows that he is able to write spirited conversation in
poetry, to hit off character in a line or in half a line, to
suggest action, atmosphere, and interplay of personalities
through the medium of dialogue, talents which make one
wonder why *Magnificence* is not a better play than it is.
Dread, looking at Harvy, the trickster, says (l. 238):

> my purse was halfe aferde

Says Riot (ll. 386–88):

> Pluck vp thyne herte vpon a mery pyne,
>   And lete vs laugh a placke or tweyne at nale:
> What the deuyll, man, myrthe was neuer one!

Deceit confidentially whispers (ll. 512–18):

> . . by that Lorde that is one, two, and thre,
>   I haue an errande to rounde in your ere:
> He tolde me so, by God, ye maye truste me,
>   Parte remembre whan ye were there,
>   There I wynked on you,—wote ye not where?
> In A *loco*, I mene *juxta* B:
> Woo is hym that is blynde and maye not see!

The intrigue, the falseness, the indecency of courtiers are
too much for Dread. He decides to leap overboard,

> and euen with that woke,
> Caughte penne and ynke, and wrote thys lytyll boke.
>   (ll. 531–32)

How much of the *Bowge of Court* is autobiographical is a
question which Skelton challenges the reader to answer
(ll. 537–39):

> I wyll not saye it is mater in dede,
>   But yet oftyme suche dremes be founde trewe:
> Now constrewe ye what is the resydewe.

And indeed the individual reader must himself decide
whether or not the vivid characterization of the passengers
of the *Bowge of Court* can be taken as evidence of their substantial existence. But from certain passages in the poem

the biographer may corroborate what he has already assumed—that Skelton found favor at court because of his learning. Says Favel to Dread, welcoming him to the ship of the lady, Royal Favor (ll. 150–57):

> Deynte to haue with vs suche one in store,
>   So vertuously that hath his dayes spente;
>   Fortune to you gyftes of grace hath lente:
> Loo, what it is a man to haue connynge!
> All erthly tresoure it is surmountynge.
>
> Ye be an apte man, as ony can be founde,
>   To dwell with vs, and serue my ladyes grace;
> Ye be to her yea worth a thousande pounde

It is this "cunning" which Skelton had so "virtuously" acquired that provides the unifying element which binds together the scattered scraps of information as to his life at the court of Henry VII. His outburst of court poetry in 1489 followed immediately upon his laureation at Oxford. It was as court scholar that the University of Cambridge called upon him in its need. His learning in the rhetorical discipline made him a fit tutor for the son of a king. Perhaps Skelton also wrote songs and plays and prepared pageants and "devices" for the delectation of the court. He surely provided Henry VIII with such entertainment, and a discussion of these activities has therefore been left to a later chapter, in which Skelton's career at the court of his former pupil will be considered.

The fact that Henry VII appreciated Skelton's talents as a poet is indicated by his gift of a gown on which the word "Calliope" was embroidered in letters of silk and gold.[54] But it is Favel, or flattery, who values Skelton's services at a thousand pounds. Henry VII did not. Presumably Skelton, as Prince Henry's tutor, received a regular salary, ten marks (£6. 13s. 4d.) yearly, if the wage allotted Palsgrave for teaching Henry VIII's daughter, the Princess Mary, be taken as standard.[55] In reward for Skelton's

[54] See above, pp. 46–47.   [55] *Letters and Papers*, II (2), 1459 (1513).

labors the King's account book records only twenty shillings for the mass celebrated in 1498 and forty shillings given to the Duke of York's schoolmaster in 1502. To these emoluments must be added the rectory of Diss, a living which was in the King's gift because of his confiscation of the possessions of the Fitzwater family, the usual patron. King Henry had presented it in 1498 to his already well beneficed chaplain, Peter Greves.[56] There is no patent recording either Greves' resignation or Skelton's institution, nor does the transfer appear in the bishop's register at Norwich. The date of the poet's appointment is therefore uncertain. It must precede April 10, 1504, on which day, Skelton, as rector of Diss, witnessed the will of his parishioner Margery Cowper.[57] Perhaps Greves resigned the living shortly after he was granted Portpull prebend in St. Paul's, on December 15, 1501.[58] In that case, it may be that the gift bestowed on Skelton as the Duke of York's schoolmaster, in April, 1502, included not only forty shillings but a rectory as well.

Although Skelton's share of the "Bowge of Court" was small compared to the largesse bestowed upon André and Carmeliano, he was certainly not turned off without a penny. Nor is there any indication that the poet was dismissed because he fell into the King's displeasure. Perhaps, like Dread, he left of his own will because he could no longer stomach the servility and intrigue demanded of a courtier. Yet, it is true, he was eager enough to return when Henry VIII ascended the throne, in 1509. Until more information is found, one must rest content with the statement that Skelton, having served Henry VII, received his reward and departed.

[56] *Calendar of Patent Rolls (Henry VII)*, II, 136 (July 19, 1498); Norwich Institution Book XII, fol. 203 (August 16, 1498).

[57] Norwich Consistory Court, Register "Rix" (1504–1507), fol. 112: "Theise beyng witnesse *Master* John Skelton laureat *parson* of disse and *Sir* John Clarke sowle preest of the same towne"

[58] *Calendar of Patent Rolls (Henry VII)*, II, 266.

The Origin of Skeltonic Rhyme

IN MANY respects Skelton left the court of Henry VII fully formed. When he undertook his duties as parish priest of Diss, he was already both a scholar learned in the humanities and a man who had known the court and had conversed with peers and princes. The *Bowge of Court* (*c.* 1499) exhibits a mature poet, possessed of a vivid, individual style, and a genius for satirical portraiture. Skelton had already assumed his philosophy of temperance, and he had already betrayed his inability to practice it. But Skelton had not yet found his most brilliant role, that of the astute pamphleteer who dared to attack whatever of evil he saw in the world regardless of the personal danger involved. And he had not yet invented the remarkable verse pattern which rendered such attacks devastatingly effective; he had not discovered how to

> wrest vp my harpe
> With sharpe twynkyng trebelles,
> Agaynst all suche rebelles[1]

Skeltonic verse and Skelton are inseparable. The association is, I dare say, closer than that between the Spenserian stanza and Spenser, between euphuistic prose and Lyly. The wholly individual character of Skeltonics was clearly recognized by the sixteenth century. In the plays concerning Robert, Earl of Huntington (1601), Skelton is brought upon the stage as master of ceremonies. Whenever he appears blank verse changes to the explosive rattle typical of *Colin Clout* and *Elinor Rumming*. Jonson, similarly, puts Skelton into a masque (*The Fortunate Isles*) and has him speak after his own unique fashion. Imitators

[1] *Colin Clout*, ll. 492–94.

of the style often refer to Skelton directly; one finds[2]
A Merry-Mad Letter in Skelton's Rime, a *Skeltoniad*, and two
Skeltonical Salutations. Several of these were written a full
century after Skelton's death.

The form, then, was identified with its creator, and
never lost its name, never merged with the general stock of
English verse patterns, even though it enjoyed a period of
considerable popularity. And this, one might conjecture,
was due to the fact that there existed in English no body of
poetry sufficiently like it by which it might be assimilated.
Skelton's rhyme stands out unmistakably from the rest of
English verse forms.

But even an atypical individual has his parents, and it is
well to know the parents before designating him a "sport."
Before considering the antecedents of the Skeltonic pattern
which have been suggested by students of the problem and
before proposing my own theory, it is necessary to set the
discussion on the basis of a definition of the form.

It is not easy to describe Skeltonics in the terms usual to
prosody. One might almost say that the outstanding
characteristic of the form is its formlessness. If, for instance, we wish to establish verse length, we are brought
up short by such a passage as the following, from the
morality play, *Magnificence*. It begins:

> Lo, this is
> My fansy, I wys:
> Nowe Cryst it blysse!

And the passage ends:

> I blunder, I bluster, I blowe, and I blother;
> I make on the one day, and I marre on the other;
> Bysy, bysy, and euer bysy,
> I daunce vp and downe tyll I am dyssy;
> I can fynde fantasyes where none is;
> I wyll not haue it so, I wyll haue it this.

(ll. 984–1054)

2 See Skelton, *Works*, I, cxxvi–cxxix.

The first line has three syllables, the last eleven. It is true
that Skeltonics run generally to short verses, but there are
enough lines of four, five, and six beats to forbid elevating
the characteristic of brevity into an invariable term of the
definition. Rhythmical looseness, however, is invariable.
It is an unusual passage in which one finds a dozen lines of
uniform beat.

Skelton's unashamed laxity of verse form cannot be
explained in terms of the upsetting language change often
invoked to account for the irregularities which are found in
fifteenth and early sixteenth-century poetry, for the same
freedom characterizes Skelton's Latin doggerel as well:[3]

> In malitia vir insignis,
> Duplex corde et bilinguis;
> Senio confectus,
> Omnibus suspectus,
> Nemini dilectus

Since no one could have had any trouble achieving perfect
regularity in Latin accentual verse, it is evident that Skelton did not wish to be regular. He makes perfectly clear
that he is conscious of his own unorthodoxy. Says Counter-
feit Countenance in the play of *Magnificence*:[4]

> But nowe wyll I, that they be gone,
> In bastarde ryme, after the dogrell gyse,
> Tell you where of my name dothe ryse.

Colin Clout protests (ll. 53–58):

> For though my ryme be ragged,
> Tattered and iagged,
> Rudely rayne beaten,
> Rusty and moughte eaten,
> If ye take well therwith,
> It hath in it some pyth.

And in *Why Come Ye Not to Court* occurs this passage, mocking the formalists:[5]

[3] Skelton, *Works*, I, 168.   [4] Lines 412–14.   [5] Skelton, *Works*, II, 66.

> Hoc genus dictaminis
> Non eget examinis
> In centiloquio
> Nec centimetro
> Honorati
> Grammatici
> Mauri.

The grammarian referred to is not Terentianus Maurus, as Dyce has it,[6] but Maurus Servius Honoratus, the Vergilian commentator, whose *Centimetrum* was a popular textbook throughout the Middle Ages and the Renaissance. Servius wrote no *Centiloquium*, as far as I can discover. Of course Skelton's appeal to his authority is itself written in a meter not to be found among the grammarian's "hundred."

Skeltonical rhyme is as formless as Skeltonical rhythm. One rule is firm: Skeltonics are never cross-rhymed. But there are no other rules. Rhymes occur *ad lib.*, in groups of two, three, eight, ten; even longer runs are found. I select a well-worn illustration, the opening lines of *Colin Clout*:

> What can it auayle
> To dryue forth a snayle,
> Or to make a sayle
> Of an herynges tayle;
> To ryme or to rayle,
> To wryte or to indyte,
> Eyther for delyte
> Or elles for despyte;
> Or bokes to compyle
> Of dyuers maner style,
> Vyce to reuyle
> And synne to exyle;
> To teche or to preche,
> As reason wyll reche?

For this is what people say of the honest satirist:

> His hed is so fat,
> He wotteth neuer what

[6] Skelton, *Works*, II, 375.

Nor wherof he speketh;
He cryeth and he creketh,
He pryeth and he peketh,
He chydes and he chatters,
He prates and he patters,
He clytters and he clatters,
He medles and he smatters,
He gloses and he flatters;
Or yf he speake playne,
Than he lacketh brayne,
He is but a fole;
Let hym go to scole,
On a thre foted stole
That he may downe syt,
For he lacketh wyt;
And yf that he hyt
The nayle on the hede,
It standeth in no stede;
The deuyll, they say, is dede,
The deuell is dede.

This single passage contains rhyme groups of two, three, four, and five lines. The only generalization that one can draw is that Skelton tends to rhyme as long as he can—and he is an amazingly fecund rhymester. His facility in rhyming is, in fact, the most striking aspect of his manner. And so it appeared to his imitators, one of whom found forty-five words to rhyme with "nations."[7]

Concomitant with the fondness for strings of rhyme is a passion for parallel structure. Nothing is said once. If an adjective is used, a dozen others irresistibly follow on its tail. Phrase begets phrase, and clause, clause, each in its kind. If he "chides," then he "chatters"; he "prates" and he "patters"; he "clitters" and he "clatters"; he "meddles" and he "smatters." If Henry's "nobility" is eulogized,[8] we shall inevitably hear of his "magnanimity," his "animosity," his "frugality," his "liberality," his

---

[7] *The Image of Ipocrysy*, in Skelton, *Works*, II, 427.
[8] *Duke of Albany*, Skelton, *Works*, II, 81.

"affability," his "humanity," his "stability," his "humility," his "benignity," his "royal dignity," and we should hear of more, too, only, as Skelton puts it,

> My lernyng is to small
> For to recount them all.

It is striking that no such marked insistence on parallelism is to be found in Skelton's poems which are written in the traditional rhyme royal. It is a trait which belongs to the Skeltonic form.

Skeltonics are, then, at the opposite pole from formal stanzaic poetry. Verse length and meter are irregular; rhymes are not ordered. Positively one can speak only of an inordinate fondness for rhyme, a similar addiction to catalogues in parallel structure, and a tendency toward short verses.[9]

Unfortunately, it has been the last characteristic, brevity of line, that has been seized upon by most of the investigators of the problem as the essential element of the Skeltonic pattern and therefore as the one for which a

[9] It is clearly incorrect to define the form as "riming trimeter lines forming a verse paragraph closed by one diameter [sic] line" (J. M. Berdan, *Early Tudor Poetry* [New York, 1920], p. 167). In fact, the passage used to illustrate this definition (the introduction to *Colin Clout* quoted above) contains few verses which are clearly of three beats and consists chiefly of verses of two accents. Even if lines like "He cryeth and he creketh" be scanned as three-footed, with an awkward accent on *and*, no Procrustes can stretch
> Vyce to reuyle
> And synne to exyle
In an earlier treatment of the same subject (*Romanic Review*, VI [1915], 365) Berdan observes of the identical quotation: "Its form consists in the use of short irregular lines, tied together by rhyme. The rhyme is usually in couplets, although, as in the passage cited, it may continue into triplets or more, a feature that gives a breathless, undignified effect." With this description I have no quarrel.
I prefer Brie's definition, however, since it emphasizes the paramount importance of rhyme: "Es besteht aus kurzzeilen von ein bis vier, meistens drei hebungen, die in gruppen von zwei bis acht, ja gelegentlich von noch mehr durch reim miteinander verbunden sind, so jedoch, dass die reime sich niemals kreuzen. Dem reime fällt hierbei die wichtigste rolle zu. Er wird die eigentliche seele des metrums, der zuliebe die verse gebaut werden" ("Skelton-Studien," *Englische Studien*, XXXVII [1907], 78). See also F. Pyle in *Notes & Queries*, CLXXI, 362.

source must be sought. But if short lines are sufficient to
define the form, then

> Fashioned so slenderly,
> Young and so fair

are Skeltonical verses. Most of the songs of the court of
Henry VIII are written in "linekins," as Saintsbury calls
them. This is one of Wyatt's:[10]

> With serving still
> This I have won,
> For my good will
> To be undone.
>
> And for redress
> Of all my pain,
> Disdainfulness
> I have again

Here are short lines in combination with a regular beat,
regular rhyme, and cross rhyme. This is not our form.

There are numerous varieties of short verse forms in
medieval literature. In consequence, each scholar has found
Skeltonic analogues to his own taste. Guest[11] decides on a
split Old English alliterative line (he also suggests the
lais and *virelais* of the fifteenth century); Saintsbury[12] cites
his favorite *Nut Brown Maid;* Sir Sidney Lee,[13] of course,
produces French parallels.[14]

---

[10] *The Poetry of Sir Thomas Wyatt,* ed. E. M. W. Tillyard (London, 1929), p. 109.

[11] *A History of English Rhythms* (London, 1882), pp. 396–97.

[12] *A History of English Prosody* (London, 1906), I, 242–43.

[13] *The French Renaissance in England* (Oxford, 1910), pp. 103–7.

[14] Berdan adds to shortness of line as the defining characteristic the quality of
abruptness and incoherence which is displayed by Skelton in many of his poems
(*Romanic Review,* VI [1915], 364 ff.). Such abruptness and incoherence Berdan also
finds in the French *fatrasie* and in the Italian *frottola.* He does not, however, believe
that Skelton borrowed from the French or from the Italian. Rather, he would
explain all three appearances by reference to a common origin: rhymed accentual
Latin verse.

But Skelton is more incoherent in the rhyme royal *Speak, Parrot* than in any
of the poems which he wrote in the Skeltonic form. I have been unable to find
examples of the *fatrasie* or the *frottola* which resemble Skeltonics. Surely many

The essential characteristics of the Skeltonic form, loose rhythms and torrents of rhyme, are not easy to find in medieval poetry. There is a restricted group of medieval Latin poems which resemble Skeltonics in point of rhyme. Classical Latin poets studiously avoided rhyme. With the development of accentual verse in the early Middle Ages, however, rhyme came to be employed sporadically on the same plane as alliteration, punning, and the other verbal tricks listed in the *Arts of Poetry*. It grew so exceedingly popular that it became a necessity rather than a gaud. During this period poems were written in which every line was rhymed, but the rhyme followed no set plan. The effect was, in fact, very much like Skeltonics in point of rhyme. To this form the name "tirade rhyme" has been given.[15] It was short-lived. As early as the eleventh century a regularizing tendency had set in. Poems came to be rhymed in regular groups; in couplets throughout, in threes throughout, in sixes throughout. Cross rhyme appeared and stanzaic structure.

If we are to believe that these early tirade rhymes supplied Skelton with the cue for his technique, then we must imagine a poet basing his style on the slender survivals of a fashion dead four hundred years. Moreover, the hypothesis fails entirely to explain why Skelton's freedom in rhyme is accompanied by freedom in rhythm. The Latin tirade rhymes beat with perfect regularity.

---

verse forms were used by the medieval Latin poets. There may be analogues to Skeltonics among them, though I have found few which satisfy the requirements both of rhythm and of rhyme. Of the two examples Berdan presents, one is a "componista," rhymed in couplets, which the author of *Epistolæ obscurorum virorum* ascribes to Peter Nigellinus. The other is a verse description of Wales from Ranulph Higden's *Polychronicon*, containing some rhyme runs, it is true, but exhibiting perfectly regular rhythm. Neither seems an adequate parent for the Skeltonic offspring.

[15] W. Meyer, *Gesammelte Abhandlungen zur mittellateinischen Rythmik* (Berlin, 1905), II, 123: "Gruppen von beliebiger Grösse haben denselben Reim. Diese Reimart, der Tiradenreim, ist demnach die älteste Form des lateinischen Reimes; sie findet sich bis in das 11. Jahrhundert."

Indeed, the attempt to ascertain Skelton's original by means of analogues alone can never arrive at more than plausibility, even if the proposed prototype should satisfy all the formal requirements. For such an approach cannot prove that Skelton knew the analogous pattern, knew it well enough, had been struck by it so that he wished to copy it, had transformed it into the Skeltonics we know.

The recent publication of Skelton's *Speculum principis*,[16] the Latin treatise written for the instruction of Prince Henry, provides a better ground. It includes passages closely resembling Skeltonics, yet belonging to a firm and well established tradition:[17]

Habes consiliarios, scios aut nescios, illos incertos, istos inualidos. Solus sapis: O saxum! O lapis! Scias prodesse, in munero esse. Componis diuicias, fallaces delicias quibus adicias interitus primicias. Quas te gloriabundum et martis alumnum. Non ferias gladio indocto labio. . .

Iram cohibeas. Neminem irrideas. Fidem serua. Scurras increpa. Sussoros obiurga. Constanciam ama. Cogita de fama. Sit bona non vana. Diu delibera. Loquere pauca.

The passages quoted are typical of large sections of the *Speculum principis*. That this prose is brother to the verse of *Colin Clout* is beyond question. The heaps of rhyme, the free rhythms, the alliteration, the strings of parallels mark it unmistakably. Although no such proof is needed, Salter, the editor of the *Speculum principis*, points to the style of these sections for indisputable evidence of Skelton's authorship of the pamphlet.[18] But the treatise is not written in Skeltonic verse at all. The form is that of Latin rhymed prose.

It is unnecessary to discuss at length the origins and development of this curious kind of writing. There is an exhaustive treatment containing thousands of illustrations in

[16] Ed. by F. M. Salter, in *Speculum*, IX (1934), 33–36.
[17] *Ibid.*, pp. 34–36.   [18] *Ibid.*, p. 34n.

Polheim's *Die lateinische Reimprosa*.[19] For the present purpose, the barest outline will suffice. It is difficult for moderns to associate rhyme with anything but poetry. We are
willing to accept poetry without rhyme, but not rhyme
without poetry. This has not always been true. Classical
authors, in fact, often used rhyme in prose, although they
avoided it in poetry. Rhymed prose was considered a
proper rhetorical figure. The Greeks called it ὁμοιοτέλευτον;
the Latins, *similiter desinens*. All the text books described it
and prescribed it. The trick of prose rhyme was to be used
with classical moderation, however. Thus the author of
the *Rhetoric to Herennius* cites the following passage as an
example of the figure: "Turpiter audes facere, nequiter
studes dicere, vivis invidiose, delinquis studiose, loqueris
odiose," but he adds a strong warning against excess.[20]

During the Middle Ages, however, rhymed prose, like
rhymed poetry, became fashionable, and the fashion grew
beyond bounds. From the eleventh century to the four-
teenth century it enjoyed a tropical growth. Complete
prose works in which every pause is marked by rhyme are
quite common. In fact, papal edicts were issued against
preachers whose chief interest was, not exhortation, but
rhyme. Eventually the fad cracked of its own weight, and
ὁμοιοτέλευτον, except for infrequent if robust revivals, returned to its classical function of occasional ornament. The
passages quoted from *Speculum principis* are evidence that
such revivals continued to occur. They are entirely typical
of the style in its highest fever. A few examples of the form
will suffice to show that the *Speculum* is of the tradition.
One such passage is cited as a side note to Barclay's translation of the *Ship of Fools*:[21]

. . . Aliis adulantes, aliis detrahentes, aliis inuidentes, mordaces
vt canes, dolosi vt vulpes, superbi vt leones, exteriùs vt oues,

[19] Berlin, 1925.   [20] *Op. cit.*, IV, 20, 28; IV, 22 f., 32.
[21] London, 1570, fol. 257.

interiùs vt lupi rapaces, sine authoritate iudices, sine visu testes, sine processu doctores, postremò falsi accusatores, et omni virtute carentes.

A late fifteenth-century collection of sermons describes lawyers:[22]

Advocati sunt Sicut canes litigantes Sicut rane garrulantes Sicut libre ponderantes Sicut protheon se mutantes Sicut Lacus se celantes Sicut lingue egrotantes

And the following occurs in an eleventh-century *Life of Abbot Gerard:*[23]

Salubri sarcinæ gaudent succedere, gaudent contingere, gaudent convehere, gaudent deosculari, gaudent munerari, gaudent venerari. . .

One offshoot of the medieval rhymed-prose tradition led to the development of a Latin hymn form so closely resembling Skeltonics that one student of the subject, Friedrich Brie, has concluded (erroneously, I believe) that it constituted Skelton's original.[24] This variety of the hymn, known as the "sequence," began as unrhythmical prose.[25] Here is an example of the early, or Notkerian type of sequence:

Alleluia

qui regis sceptra
forti dextra
solus cuncta,

tu plebi tuam
ostende magnam
excitando potentiam

[22] Paulus Wann, *Sermones de septem vitiis* (1514), quoted by Polheim, *op. cit.*, p. 457.
[23] *Vita Gerardi abbatis Broniensis*, in *Monumenta Germaniæ historica, Scriptorum tomi XV pars II* (Hanover, 1888), p. 662.
[24] *Englische Studien*, XXXVII (1907), 78–83.
[25] F. J. E. Raby, *A History of Christian Latin Poetry* (Oxford, 1927), p. 213: "The original Sequences . . were texts or proses fixed to an existing melody. This melody was divided into parts, which . . were repeated by alternate choirs usually of men and boys. So the structure of the text was bound to follow the structure of the melody, and the text was, in fact, a piece of unrhythmical prose."

præsta dona illi salutaria.

quem prædixerunt prophetica
vaticinia
a clara poli regia
in nostra,
Iesu, veni, domine arva.[26]

The prose is without regular rhythm, but it is clearly
marked by rhyme. Sometimes a two-syllable rhyme is employed in the early sequences:

Flos pudicitiæ,
Aula mundiciæ,
Mater misericordiæ,
Salve, virgo serena,
Vitæ vena,
Lux amœna,
Rore plena,
Septiformis spiritus
Virtutibus
Ornantibus
Ac moribus
Vernantibus.[27]

This is one of the sequences quoted by Brie as analogues to
Skeltonics. There is certainly a close resemblance between
the forms. But I believe that the resemblance is due to the
fact that both forms rise from the rhymed-prose tradition.

It is evident that these sequences, the passages quoted
from Barclay and from the *Speculum principis*, and indeed
almost every example of rhymed prose have, in addition to
their rhyme, a loosely rhythmical effect. This is a direct
consequence of the fact that a very important use of the
rhyme ornament, perhaps its most important use, was to
emphasize the parallelism of parallel structures. Similarly-
organized expressions are almost inevitably of similar
length and similar beat. Parallel structure, both grammatical and thematic, was much stressed by the rhetoric

[26] *Ibid.*, p. 214.   [27] Brie, *Englische Studien*, XXXVII, 81.

textbooks of medieval and Renaissance times. Indeed, the
body of instruction in rhetoric was directed at the ex-
pansion of simple statements by lists of similes, lists of
examples, lists of antitheses. And when the structures set
in parallel are brief, the end of each starred by a rhyme, a
staccato rhythm is the necessary result. The effect is like
that of falling down a long flight of stairs, bumping soundly
at every step.

When, in the mid-sixteenth century, rhetorics for
English composition came to be written, they included
ὁμοιοτέλευτον in the list of stylistic ornaments. It was regarded as a perfectly respectable device; Gorgias had used
it in Greek, and Cicero in Latin. Thomas Wilson, in his
Art of Rhetoric (1560),[28] translates the term as "like ending,"
and gives the following as an example: "The rebels of
Northfolke . . . through slaverie, shewe nobilitie: in deede
miserably, in fashion cruelly, in cause devillishly." Like
the author of the *Rhetoric to Herennius*, however, he is
very emphatic in counseling moderation:[29]

Diuers in this our time delite much in this kinde of writing,
which beeing measurably vsed, deliteth much the hearers, otherwise it offendeth . . . I speake thus much of these ii. figures
[*like ending*, and a related rhyme color, *like failing*], not that I
thinke folie to vse them (for they are pleasant and praise worthy)
but my talke is to this ende, that they should neither onely nor
chiefly be vsed, as I know some in this our time, do ouermuch
vse them in their writings. And ouermuch (as all men knowe)
was neuer good yet.

Thus, in moderation, it was used by Roger Ascham,
and with somewhat less moderation, by Lyly and the other
elegants of Elizabeth's time. Perhaps Thomas More over-
steps Wilson's bounds:[30]

thou seest, I say, thyself, if thou die no worse death, yet at the
leastwise lying in thy bed, thy head shooting, thy back aching,

[28] Edited by G. H. Mair (Oxford, 1909), p. 202.   [29] *Ibid.*, p. 203.
[30] *The English Works of Sir Thomas More* (London, 1931), I, 468.

thy veins beating, thine heart panting, thy throat rattling, thy flesh trembling, thy mouth gaping, thy nose sharping, thy legs cooling, thy fingers fumbling, thy breath shortening, all thy strength fainting, thy life vanishing, and thy death drawing on.

But there were some for whom rhymed prose had become an obsession. Thus Wilson writes,[31] "Some end their sentences all alike, making their talke rather to appeare rimed Meeter, then to seeme plaine speeche, the which as it much deliteth being measurably vsed, so it much offendeth when no meane is regarded." His horrible example is a preacher:

I heard a preacher deliting much in this kind of composition, who vsed so often to ende his sentences with wordes like vnto that which went before, that in my judgement there was not a dosen sentences in his whole sermon, but they ended all in Rime for the most parte. Some not best disposed, wished the Preacher a Lute, that with his rimed sermon he might vse some pleasant melody, and so the people might take pleasure diuers waies, and dance if they list. Certes there is a meane, and no reason to vse any one thing at al time, seing nothing deliteth (be it neuer so good) that is alwaies vsed.

A story about just such a riming preacher is told in Rastell's *A Hundred Merry Tales:*[32]

A certayne frere there was whiche, vpon Our Lady day the Annuncyacion, made a sermon in the Whyte Freres in London, and began his antetexte thys wyse. Aue Maria gracia plena dominus tecum &c. These wordes, quod the frere, were spoken by the aungell Gabryell to Oure Ladye, whan she conceyued Christe; which is as moche to saye in our mother tonge as: all hayle, Mary, well thou be; the sonne of God is with the. And furthermore the aungell sayde: thou shall conceyue and bere a sonne, and thou shalt call his name Jesum; and Elysabeth thy swete cosyn, she shall conceyue .he swete Saynt John. And so he proceded styll in his sermon in suche fonde ryme, that dyuers and many gentylmen of the court that were there began to smyle and laughe.

[31] *Op. cit.*, p. 168.   [32] Tale liii.

Literary examples of the exaggerated use of "like ending" are comparatively rare in English. Nevertheless, they occur. The following passage was written by Andrew Boorde:[33]

better it is not to set up a howseholde or hospytalyte. then to set up howseholde lackynge the performacion of it, as nowe to ronne for maler, and by & by, for salte, nowe to sende for breade, and by and by to sende for a shepes hed, & nowe to sende for this, and nowe to sende for that, and by & by he doth sende, he can not tel for what / suche thynges is noo prouysion, but it is a great abusyon. Thus a man shall lose his thryfte. And be put to a shyft, his gooddes shall neuer increase, and he shall not be in rest nor peace, but euer in carke & care. For his purse wyll euer be bare. Wherfore I do counceyll euery man. to prouyde for hym selfe, as soone as he can. For yf of implementes he be destytuted, men wyl call hym lyght wytted. To set up a howse, & is not able to kepe man nor mowse. Wherfore let euery man loke or he lepe. For many cornes maketh a great hepe.

It is true that neither this passage nor the sermon quoted by Rastell is very much like Skeltonics. One difference resides in the fact that the rhymed "cola" of the cited passages are longer than they usually are in Skelton's poems. Nevertheless, the examples serve to show that an exaggerated form of English rhymed prose did exist in the sixteenth century.

There is, however, an instance of English rhymed prose which reveals an astonishing degree of similarity to Skeltonics. The resemblance is so close that the kinship of the two forms is unmistakable. In fact, the prose book has been erroneously described as an imitation of the Skeltonic verse pattern.[34] That it is prose, not verse printed as prose, is made evident by the circumstance that the rhymed passages are found in unrhymed surroundings. The book is a warning addressed to the nobles of England, enjoining

[33] *The boke for to lerne a man to be wyse in buyldyng of his howse* (Robert Wyer, n. d.), Sig. B4.
[34] Skelton, *Works*, I, cxvii–cxviii.

them to beware of Spanish domination.[35] The author, John Bradforth, declares that some Spaniards can cleverly hide their evil nature:

Whose mischeuouse maners a man shal neuer knowe, till he come vnder their subiection. But then shall ye perceiue perfectly their puffed pride, with many mischeffes beside, their prowling, and poling, their bribinge and shauinge, their most deceitfull dealing, their braging and bosting, their flatteringe and faininge, their abominable whore huntynge with most rufull ruling, their doings vniust, with insaciate lust, their stout stubbernes, croked crabbednes and vnmeasurable madnes in enui, pride and lecherie, which thei saie, god loueth hartelie, vaine glorie, and hipocrisie with al other vilanie, of what kind soeuer it be: supersticion, desolacion, extorcion, adulacion, dissimulacion, exaltacion, suppression, inuocacion, and all abominacion: with innumerable moe mischeues, whiche I coude plainlie declare

He lists the commodities which the Spaniards tax:

wine white and reade, with all other wines beside, salt white and graye, al thinges must pay, small nuttes and wall nuttes, cheries, and chest nuttes, plumbes, damassens, philbeardes and al both gret & smal whatsoeuer thei maye se to fede the pore commenalte, Salmon and hearing, this is a shamefull thing, tench ele or conger, this shall kepe vs vnder, and make vs die for hunger, flounders, floucke, plaice or carpe, here is a miserable warke

That Skelton, like Bradforth, was passionately addicted to the prose figure of "like ending" in Latin is clear from the rhyming passages of *Speculum principis*. Nor are examples of his use of the form in Latin restricted to the *Speculum*. His Latin prose is almost invariably rhymed. Thus in "Against Venemous Tongues":[36] "Novarum rerum cupidissimi, captatores, delatores, adulatores, invigilatores, deliratores, &c," and "Inauspicatum, male ominatum, infortunatum se fateatur habuisse horoscopum."

[35] *The Copye of a letter, sent by John Bradforth to the right honorable lordes the Erles of Arundel, Darbie, Shrewsburye, and Penbroke, declaring the nature of Spaniardes* (no printer, c. 1555).

[36] Skelton, *Works*, I, 135.

It is evident that Skelton employed the same trick in his English prose. His translation of Diodorus Siculus, though one of his earliest works, exhibits a few rhymed passages, of which the following is an example:[37]

alle of hole assente endronkynd with drowsy deuocioun prayen god bachus that hath bathed theym in his blysse / that eche to other may goulp vp his galon / halyng the hanope / catchyng the collocke / & kyssyng the cuppe With drynkehayl to gydre

But the tricks of prose ornament are most apparent in Skelton's *Replication against Certain Young Scholars* (1528). The Introduction to the pamphlet is strongly marked by rhythm, alliteration, and rhyme:[38]

. . these demy diuines, and Stoicall studiantes, and friscaioly yonkerkyns, moche better bayned than brayned, basked and baththed in their wylde burblyng and boyling blode, feruently reboyled with the infatuate flames of their rechelesse youthe and wytlesse wontonnesse, enbrased and enterlased with a moche fantasticall frenesy of their insensate sensualyte, surmysed vnsurely in their perihermeniall principles, to prate and to preche proudly and leudly, and loudly to lye

Other sections of this very Introduction provide evidence which renders almost certain the proposed derivation of Skeltonics from the tradition of Latin rhymed prose. Skelton has very considerately quoted in the margins beside the text of the Preface portions of his Latin prose version of it. It is possible to observe, as though in the moment of transition, the metamorphosis of Latin rhymed prose into English Skeltonics. In the Latin occurs:[39]

Rhetoricari incomposite, logicari meticulose, philosophari perfunctorie, theologisari phrenetice, arguit in concionatore, nedum lucidum intervallum, sed continuam pertinacemque mentis alienationem, fæculentam, amurcatam, temulentam, &c.

This, like the rest of the Latin version, is typical rhymed prose. The parallel English version, as has already been

---

[37] Corpus Christi College, Cambridge, MS 357, fol. 226.
[38] Skelton, *Works*, I, 209.   [39] *Ibid.*, I, 208.

seen, is also ornamented with rhyme. But one portion of
the English, that which corresponds with the Latin prose
just quoted, is not only rhymed but also divided into
verses:

> A lytell ragge of rethorike,
> A lesse lumpe of logyke,
> A pece or a patche of philosophy,
> Than forthwith by and by
> They tumble so in theology,
> Drowned in dregges of diuinite,
> That they iuge them selfe able to be
> Doctours of the chayre in the Uyntre
> At the Thre Cranes, . .

Skelton thus clearly announces that his "ragged rhyme" is
the English equivalent of Latin rhymed prose.

In brief, then, this is the argument. Aside from the
religious hymnal sequence, no poetical analogue to Skeltonics exists. Excessive use of the prose figure, "like
ending," in short parallel clauses (technically called
clausulæ) creates a form very much like Skeltonics. That
rhymed prose was familiar to Skelton's contemporaries, we
know. We know, too, that Skelton practiced such prose,
both in Latin and in English. And finally, Skelton manifestly equated Latin rhymed prose and English Skeltonics.

It is difficult, of course, to comprehend the transition of
prose into poetry. Perhaps, like the audience of Wilson's
preacher, Skelton suddenly recognized the dancing quality
of his own rhymed prose. The illuminating Preface to the
Replication shows exactly how the transformation might
have occurred. The passage of Skeltonics beginning "A
lytell ragge of rethorike" does not constitute a complete
sentence. It is, in fact, the end of a prose sentence. The
words immediately preceding it are:

. . whan they [the scholars] haue delectably lycked a lytell of
the lycorous electuary of lusty lernyng, in the moche studious
scolehous of scrupulous Philology, countyng them selfe clerkes

exellently enformed and transcendingly sped in moche high
connyng, and whan they haue ones superciliusly caught

Here the prose breaks off, and the poetry—at least it is
printed as poetry—begins. And, after a brief Skeltonic
passage, the Preface reverts to a highly ornamented and
rhymed prose. Clearly, there is no great difference between
Skelton's poetry and Skelton's prose, nor did the poet
himself erect a high wall between them.[40]

Naturally, the mere arrangement of rhyming *clausulæ*
in separate lines entails certain changes. In transforming a
prose pattern into a poetic one, Skelton was bound to
regularize somewhat. In a prose passage rhymed *clausulæ*,
strung out across a page, may be long or short without
offense, but the visible appearance of a column of verses
requires an approach to regularity. Line length becomes
more even; rhythm becomes smoother. Wilson's preacher
rhymed almost every pause; *Colin Clout* is rhymed throughout. Furthermore, once the form had become a verse form,
it was laid open to the influence of traditional verse patterns. Skeltonics occasionally echo the Latin rhyming
hexameter, the English alliterative line, and the lyrical
measures common to all medieval languages. Yet despite
the inevitable smoothing and normalizing tendency, the
transformation did not go far enough to eliminate the
essential irregularity of rhymed prose. The uneven verse
lengths, the loose, staccato rhythms, and the floods of
rhyme which characterize Skeltonics testify to the primary
origin of the form.

[40] It is particularly interesting, in view of the present theory, that the Skeltonic
meter should strike the ear of a modern poet as a close approximation to the
rhythms of ordinary speech. Mr. W. H. Auden acutely observes (*The Great Tudors*,
ed. by K. Garvin [London, 1935], pp. 62–63): "The skeltonic is such a simple
metre that it is surprising that fewer poets have used it. The natural unit of
speech rhythm seems to be one of four accents, dividing into two half verses of
two accents. If one tries to write ordinary conversation in verse, it will fall more
naturally into this scheme than into any other . . . Skelton is said to have spoken
as he wrote, and his skeltonics have the natural ease of speech rhythm."

What Skelton calls his "bastard rhyme" represents, therefore, an exaggerated development of the classical prose figure "like ending." Its classical origin does not make it respectable, of course, nor did Skelton think it so. Surely he knew the injunction against the excessive use of rhyme in the *Rhetoric to Herennius*. Moreover, by the time Skelton wrote, rhymed prose had had its medieval fling, and the exaggerated employment of it had become a thoroughly discredited fashion. His use of the form in *Speculum principis* and in the English Skeltonics must have constituted a deliberate refusal to obey the rules he had learned in school. He found in it an effect which he wished to produce and which he could achieve in no other way. The style he invented had the liberty of prose and the sharpness of poetry. It invited him to display his fecundity of phrase and epithet. It gave him room for the flow of his imagination and the torrent of his anger. He could produce with it either the gentle patter of *Philip Sparrow* or the repeated hammer blows of *Colin Clout*. In short, it gave him liberty to speak.

Skelton at Diss

IN THE ungainly church of the unprepossessing market
town of Diss, Skelton the court scholar evolved into a
writer of independent originality. Not only did he
learn to "wrest up his harp with sharp twinking trebles,"
but he found new uses for his pen, personal uses, divorced
from the requirements of courtly composition. Skelton did
not lose his learning or forget his pride in it. He continued
to express his faith in the power of rhetoric to confer eternal
praise and blame, to force the vicious from their evil ways.
During his residence at Diss he seems to have maintained
an association with Cambridge, which was but a day's
journey away. In 1504–5, not long after he had undertaken
his parish duties, he was granted by the University the
right to wear the habit which had been conferred upon
him by Henry VII.[1] If the costume had no academic impli-
cation, it is difficult to understand why Skelton thought it
necessary to ask Cambridge to ratify the royal grant. The
fact that he secured the privilege suggests that he planned
to visit the University occasionally. The gown would have
had little meaning at Diss, but it would have been most
useful at the University, where scholars were jealous of
their academic insignia. And it is probable that Skelton
did return to Cambridge in 1507, for two poems which
he wrote in that year were copied out by the Vicar of
Trumpington,[2] who was regularly employed as university
scribe. Skelton the court scholar remained a scholar—but

---

[1] *Grace Book* Γ (Cambridge, 1908), p. 37: "Item conceditur Johanni Skelton poete
laureato quod possit stare eodem gradu hic quo stetit Oxoniis et quod possit vti
habitu sibi concesso a principe."

[2] Skelton, *Works*, I, 173. For information concerning the Vicar, see the Cambridge *Grace Books*.

he was no longer at court. In his Norfolk home he addressed hymns of praise, not to royalty, but to a young
lady being educated at a convent near Norwich; he attacked neither false courtiers nor insolent ambassadors,
but his personal enemies, obnoxious neighbors of Diss. For
a few years Skelton's pen was in no service but his own.

TWO KNAVES SOMETIME OF DISS

If we may judge by what remains of his writings,
Skelton's life in Diss was scarcely a peaceful rustication.
Perhaps he was not greeted with the deference which a
scholar and courtier expects as his due. Perhaps boredom
made him irascible. At any rate he made enemies, graceless
characters, indeed, if his report may be trusted. One was
John Clerk, a wealthy reprobate who is accused of raging
"like a camel" against Christ and, I suppose, against His
representative in Diss.[3] Clerk's will, which was probated
on April 14, 1506, proves that he really existed.[4] It shows
nothing of the alleged depravity, of course, but contains
the usual pious sentiments and charitable bequests. Another of Skelton's enemies was Adam Uddersall, Bailiff of
Diss.[5] According to the poet, he was a rapacious fellow
who extorted money from the townspeople, hated the
clergy, and oppressed the Church. His will has not been
found, so that it is impossible to grant him even the slight
mitigation of a charitable end.

Skelton did not attack Clerk and Uddersall until after
they died. His poems "Of two knaves somtime of Diss" are
mock epitaphs. There is a "trental" for Clerk:

[3] Skelton, *Works*, I, 168–71.

[4] Norwich Consistory Court, Register "Rix" 1504–1507, fols. 460–61. The
testator was not Sir John Clerk, soul priest of Diss, as H. L. R. Edwards suggests
(*London Times Literary Supplement*, May 22, 1937) but "old John Clarke," perhaps
Sir John's father. Sir John, the priest, was named as the executor of John's will,
and appeared before the probate registry.

[5] Skelton, *Works*, I, 171–73. Adam is also described in the *Garland of Laurel*,
ll. 1247–53.

Jam jacet hic starke deed,
Neuer a toth in his heed.
Adieu, Jayberd, adue,
I faith, dikkon thou crue!
Fratres, orate
For this knauate,
By the holy rode,
Did neuer man good
(ll. 41–48)

Uddersall receives an equally devout tribute:

Belsabub his soule saue,
Qui jacet hic, like a knaue!
Jam scio mortuus est,
Et jacet hic, like a best.
Anima ejus
De malo in pejus. Amen.
(ll. 25–30)

Speaking ill of a man after his death was not considered so unmannerly during the Renaissance as it is today. Carmeliano wrote a jubilant epitaph on King James IV of Scotland, killed in battle at Flodden.[6] Ammonio, it is true, thought Carmeliano's invective "womanish." But Ammonio's friend, More, composed an epitaph on James little more kindly than that written by Carmeliano.[7] Skelton, it must be admitted, was particularly fond of the device of evening scores after the death of his opponents, for there are other instances of the practice to be found among his works.[8]

WARE THE HAWK!

A third quarrel is recorded in *Ware the Hawk!*[9] This time Skelton does not reveal the name of his opponent.[10] He

[6] MS Additional 29, 506, fol. 14.   [7] More, *Opera* (1689), p. 247.

[8] E.g., *In Bedel* (Skelton, *Works*, I, 175) and the attack on Meautis, the King's French secretary (*Why Come Ye Not to Court*, ll. 781–817).

[9] Skelton, *Works*, I, 155–67.

[10] Possibly his name was Smith. The suggestion would give point to the following lines placed conspicuously at the very end of the poem:

Masyd, wytles, smery smyth,

was a "parson beneficed," the poet says, who found no
better place to train his hawk than inside the church of
Diss (ll. 46–59):

> Streyght to the sacrament
> He made his hawke to fly,
> With hogeous showte and cry.
> The hye auter he strypt naked;
> There on he stode, and craked;
> He shoke downe all the clothis,
> And sware horrible othes
> Before the face of God,
> By Moyses and Arons rod,
> Or that he thens yede,
> His hawke shoulde pray and fede
> Vpon a pigeons maw.
> The bloude ran downe raw
> Vpon the auter stone

Meanwhile, Skelton must have remained outside the
church, impotently furious, for the falconer, fearing his
sport would be disturbed, had barred the doors. At length,
however, Skelton managed to enter.[11] He found no shame-
faced submission. Instead of apologizing meekly, the
brazen sporting parson

Hampar with your hammer vpon thy styth,
And make hereof a syckyll or a saw,
For thoughe ye lyue a c. yere, ye shall dy a daw.
There was a John Smyth of Diss whose will was proved in 1529 (Norfolk Arch-
deaconry Register 1524–31, fol. 177).

[11]. . wyth a prety gyn
I fortuned to come in
(ll. 93–94)

How does one get into a church when the doors are bolted? A possible explanation
of Skelton's pretty ingenuity is to be found in the unusual structure of the Diss
church. The western tower stands apart from the rest of the edifice, and is connected with it only by a hollow arch. From the space beneath this arch, one door
leads into the church, and another into the tower. In Skelton's day, if the church
door were bolted, one might have entered and climbed the tower, passed through
the arch, and descended by a small door (now blocked up) into the nave of the
church. Perhaps it was by means of this devious route that the irate Skelton con-
fronted the falconer.

> sayde that he woulde,
> Agaynst my mynde and wyll,
> In my churche hawke styll.
>   (ll. 97–99)

Skelton took the matter up with the ecclesiastical court, but

> the Scrybe was feed,
> And the Pharasay
> Than durst nothing say,
> But let the matter slyp,
> And made truth to trip;
> And of the spiritual law
> They made but a gewgaw,
> And toke it out in drynke[12]
>   (ll. 151–58)

Some slight satisfaction Skelton had, nevertheless. He presented the hawking priest with "a tabull playne" and challenged him to make sense of it (after l. 238):

> Sicculo lutueris est colo būraarā
> Nixphedras uisarum caniuter tuntantes
> Raterplas Natābrian umsudus itnugenus.
> 18. 10. 2. 11. 19. 4. 13. 3. [4]. 1. tēualet.

If Skelton's victim failed to unravel the mystery, he must have gone through life wondering what horrible curse had been inflicted on him. But if, like Henry Bradley, he labored long and finally arrived at the solution, he discovered only that Skelton proclaimed himself the phœnix of Britain:

> Sic, velut est Arabum phenix avis unica tantum
> Terra Britanna suum genuit Skeltonida vatem.[13]

[12] Although Skelton declares the affair was registered in the "official's books," a search of such of the court records as remain at Norwich produced no information.

[13] The *Academy*, August 1, 1896. The first three lines (and the word *temualet* of the fourth) are coded by inversion of syllabic order and introduction of useless letters. As for the numbers: "Skelton denotes the consonants by the numbers marking their places in the alphabet, and the vowels by the numbers 1, 2, 3, 4, 5. The three figures 2, 3, 4, have thus a twofold value: they may either mean B, C, D, or E, I, O respectively." Skelton uses the number code again in an attack on one Rogerus Stathum (*Garland of Laurel*, after l. 751).

PHILIP SPARROW

Norwich diocese was not all unpleasantness, however. In contrast to the epitaphs on John Clerk and Adam Uddersall, *Philip Sparrow* is as delightful a dirge[14] as has ever been written. Jane Scroupe, a pretty young lady staying at Carrow Nunnery, close to Norwich, had lost her pet bird, Philip, to the unsentimental hunger of Gib, the cat. Jane mourns and reminisces, damns the assassin, and begs that heaven receive her sparrow's soul. Alas, she cannot write a proper epitaph, for her learning is but small. She has read hundreds of romantic stories (she tells some of them to prove it), but the weighty classics are too "diffuse" for her.[15] And rude English is scarcely an appropriate medium for so enduring a composition as an epitaph. Very timidly, therefore, she writes a few lines of simple Latin to set on her sparrow's tomb.

Appended to the poem is Skelton's charming "commendation" of Jane, a eulogy which suggests that she was not quite such a child as might be supposed from the naïveté of her complaint, and that Skelton, despite his priestly office, was capable of thinking about her a little indecorously. He protests there is no harm in thinking however (ll. 1199–1203):

> No man can let me thynke,
> For thought hath lyberte,
> Thought is franke and fre;
> To thynke a mery thought
> It cost me lytell nor nought.

[14] For the relation of Skelton's poem to church ritual for the dead, see I. A. Gordon, " 'Philip Sparrow' and the Roman Service Book," *Modern Language Review*, XXIX (1934), 389–96.

[15] It is Jane, not Skelton, who prefers Chaucer's "pleasant, easy, and plain" language to Lydgate's higher sententiousness (ll. 788–812). In the *Garland of Laurel*, Skelton, like the rest of his contemporaries, puts the two English classics on the same plane.

THE MERRY TALES OF SKELTON, LAUREATE

Tradition has it that Skelton's wantonness was not of the imagination exclusively. It is said that despite the thunderings of his bishop, Richard Nikke, he kept a mistress at Diss. To appease the episcopal wrath, Skelton brought his superior a present of two capons. The reception was most ungracious. But Skelton was not easily cowed:

Skelton sayde, My lord, my capons haue proper names; the one is named Alpha, the other is named Omega: my lorde, sayd Skelton, this capon is named Alpha, thys is the fyrst capon that I dyd euer geue to you; and this capon is named Omega, and this is the last capon that euer I wil giue you: & so fare you well, sayd Skelton.[16]

On the following Sunday, Skelton revenged himself on his tattling parishioners. He preached on the text, "Vos estis."

Thou wyfe, sayde Skelton, that hast my childe, be not afraid; bring me hither my childe to me: the whyche was doone. And he, shewynge his childe naked to all the parishe, sayde, How saye you, neibours all? is not this child as fayre as is the beste of all yours? It hathe nose, eyes, handes, and feete, as well as any of your: it is not lyke a pygge, nor a calfe, nor like no foule nor no monstruous beast. If I had, sayde Skelton, broughte forthe thys chylde without armes or legges, or that it wer deformed, being a monstruous thyng, I woulde neuer haue blamed you to haue complayned to the bishop of me; but to complain without a cause, I say, as I said before in my antethem, *vos estis*, you be, and haue be, & wyll and shall be knaues, to complayne of me wythout a cause resonable.[17]

These stories are told in the *Merry Tales of Skelton* (published in 1567), a book of anecdotes about the poet which Skelton's editor, Dyce, characterizes as a "tissue of extravagant figments which was put together for the amusement of the vulgar."[18] Despite the late date of publication and the apparently popular character of the pamphlet, however, it is not altogether worthless as a

[16] *Merry Tales of Skelton*, in Skelton, *Works*, I, lvii–lxxiii, Tale vi.
[17] *Ibid.*, Tale vii.   [18] Skelton, *Works*, I, xxx.

source of biographical information. For it is probable that the *Merry Tales*, though published almost forty years after Skelton's death, is part of a tradition which had grown up either during the poet's lifetime or within a few years after he died. First, it should be noticed that among the papers that came into the possession of Thomas Cromwell between 1530 and 1532 is a piece entitled *The Jests of Skelton*.[19] The pamphlet is no longer extant, but, to judge by the title it must have been either a collection similar to the *Merry Tales* or an early edition of that jestbook itself. Second, the text of the *Merry Tales* suggests that its author was a contemporary of Skelton. One of the stories[20] tells of an epitaph that Skelton wrote for a knave of Oxford called Swanborn.[21] The author of the jestbook declares: "I knewe him when that he was a boye in Oxforde; hee was a littell olde fellowe, and woulde lye as fast as a horse woulde trotte." In another tale[22] the writer betrays a close acquaintance with the Oxford of Skelton's day: "[Skelton] did com late home to Oxforde, and he did lye in an ine named the Tabere whyche is now the Angell." There really was a Tabard on High Street, and its name was changed to the Angel not long before 1523.[23] Third, one of the merry tales, that which concerns Skelton's gift of Alpha and Omega to the Bishop of Norwich, was current while the poet was alive, for it appears in Rastell's *A Hundred Merry Tales*[24] which was published about 1525.

The fact that the jestbook tradition of Skelton had begun even during his lifetime makes it likely that there is truth to be found in the stories. Some of them are obviously figments. The tricky miller who steals Skelton's sheets while the poet lies abed[25] is too much of a stock character

---

[19] *Letters and Papers*, VII, No. 923 (vii).   [20] Tale v.

[21] The epitaph quoted consists of lines taken from the poems on John Clerk and Adam Uddersall.   [22] Tale i.

[23] *A Cartulary of the Hospital of St. John the Baptist*, ed. by H. E. Salter, Oxford Historical Society (1914), I, 184.

[24] *A C Mery Talys*, Rastell, n.d. (see *Short Title Catalogue*). The tale in question is reprinted in Skelton, *Works*, I, lxxiv–lxxv.   [25] Tale xiii.

to be real. There are other stereotypes. But quite as obviously the *Merry Tales* contains a modicum of history.
Skelton is represented as an Oxford Laureate and as rector
of Diss. It is stated that he was imprisoned at Westminster
at the commandment of Cardinal Wolsey, that he sued for
peace and gained it. He is described as a witty poet and a
writer both of mock epitaphs and of serious ones. So much
is certainly true. It is probable, therefore, that some of the
residue is also true.

Anecdotes, whether of the sixteenth century or of the
twentieth, are scarcely reliable biographical information.
Good stories are always in search of well-known protagonists. Better than, "A man said," is "A gentleman of Kent
said," and better than either is "Erasmus of Rotterdam"
or "Patch, the king's fool." And since the fame of a popular
wit dies, while a good joke is immortal, the same story is
often found attributed to characters separated by centuries
in time and by oceans in distance. On the other hand,
orphaned anecdotes usually choose appropriate parents.
Conscious witticisms cannot be assigned to dolts, nor un-
conscious drolleries to the clever. A jest concerning a long
nose must be told about a man who is reputed to have one.
Although the stories about Skelton may be of doubtful
authenticity, it is likely that the portrait of the poet
which emerges from them is founded on fact.

Mistress Skelton is by no means an improbability. The
jestbook tradition of her existence is supported by the
earliest extant biography of the poet, that compiled by
Edward Braynewode, an industrious antiquary whose collections concerning English poets of the early Tudor period
gave Bale much information for his *Scriptorum illustrium
maioris Brytanniæ catalogus* (1559 [?]).[26] Braynewode seems
to have been one of Skelton's contemporaries, and his

---

[26] Braynewode's biography of Skelton is found copied out in Bale's notebook,
which has been printed under the title *Index Britanniæ scriptorum* (ed. by R. L.
Poole and Mary Bateson, Oxford, 1902), p. 253.

biography was probably written about 1549,[27] but twenty years after the poet died. Of Skelton's mistress, Braynewode says:[28]

Under Richard, the pseudo-Bishop of Norwich, Skelton kept a woman whom he had secretly married. He called her a concubine in order to avoid the reproach of Anti-Christ. On his death bed, however, he confessed that he had always considered her his lawful wife.

The assertion is colored by Reformation phraseology and ideas. Skelton could not have acknowledged his "marriage" as legitimate without accepting the Lutheran heresy. Since he remained to the end of his life a firm adherent of the old faith and a bitter opponent of the new, Braynewode's account of the deathbed confession must certainly be false. But Mistress Skelton seems substantial.

It is easy to understand why Braynewode was misled into thinking Skelton a Reformer. In many respects Skelton's opinions agreed with those of the heretics. The poet's greatest enemy was Cardinal Wolsey, whose opposition to King Henry's divorce stamped him as the mainstay of Catholicism in England. Like the Reformers Skelton vigorously attacked the abuses of the clergy, particularly of the bishops. He protested that the rulers of the Church were grasping, unlearned, and lazy. Braynewode says that Skelton waged continual warfare against the preaching friars, especially the Dominicans, and the statement is supported by one of the *Merry Tales*,[29] which tells how Skelton refused to permit a friar to preach in his church of Diss. When the friar tried to force his way to the

[27] "Edwardus Braynewode, amator suæ patriæ, collegit, Sui temporis res gestas, li. i. 'Ioannes Skeltonus poeta laureatus.' Atque nonnulla alia. Claruit A.D. 1549." (*Index*, p. 68). In the *Scriptorum Brytanniæ catalogus* (p. 718), Bale says that Braynewode died in 1556.

[28] *Index*, p. 253: "Sub pseudoepiscopo Nordouicensi Ricardo, mulierem quam secreto desponsauerat, vt Antichristi vitaret obprobria, sub concubinæ titulo custodiebat, quam tamen in mortis articulo confitebatur se pro legitima semper tenuisse coniuge."

[29] Tale viii.

pulpit armed with a papal bull, Skelton addressed his parishioners:

Maisters, here is as wonderfull a thynge as euer was seene: you all dooe knowe that it is a thynge daylye seene, a bulle dothe begette a calfe; but here, contrarye to all nature, a calfe hathe gotten a bulle; for thys fryere, beeynge a calfe, hath gotten a bulle of the byshoppe of Rome.

The most influential of Skelton's works was his satire on the government of the English Church, *Colin Clout*. After his death the poem became a model for the pamphleteers of the Reformation, who imitated not only its style and meter but its ideas as well.

But Skelton was no Reformer. In *Colin Clout* he attacked the clergy, but

> Of no good bysshop speke I,
> Nor good preest I escrye,
> Good frere, nor good chanon,
> Good nonne, nor good canon,
> Good monke, nor good clercke,
> Nor yette of no good werke:
> But my recountyng is
> Of them that do amys,
> In speking and rebellyng,
> In hynderyng and dysauaylyng
> Holy Churche, our mother
> (ll. 1097–1107)

Denunciation of evil priests and bishops and opposition to the wandering preachers do not mark Skelton as an adherent of the new religion. His attitude, like that of Colet and More, was typical of English humanists, not of English Reformers.

Nor does lack of celibacy make Skelton a heretic. He may have had a mistress, but he never defended the practice. When, on one occasion, he was accused of loose morality, his only reply was an attack on his critic:

> Lewdely your tyme ye spende,
> My lyuyng to reprehende;

And wyll neuer intende
Your awne lewdnes to amende[30]

Skelton seems to have considered lack of celibacy in a priest a venial sin. He is disturbed because laymen condemn it violently:

Of persons and vycaryes
They make many outcryes;
They cannot kepe theyr wyues
From them for theyr lyues;
And thus the loselles stryues,
And lewdely sayes by Christ
Agaynst the sely preest.
Alas, and well away,
What ayles them thus to say?[31]

But he makes no attempt to prove that it is lawful for priests to marry.

"FOR THE HEALTH OF HIS SOUL"

Concrete proof of Skelton's orthodoxy is found in two incidents recorded in the archives of the episcopal court at Norwich. On December 3, 1509,[32] John Chapman certified before the Consistory Court that one Thomas Pykerell of Diss[33] had been cited to appear to answer certain interrogatories concerning the health of his soul. The complainant was John Skelton, Rector of Diss. The court record does not confide the nature of the disease infecting Pykerell's spirit.[34] The culprit was absent from the proceedings and

[30] "Poems against Garnesche," Skelton, *Works*, I, 120.

[31] *Colin Clout*, ll. 572–80.

[32] Acts of the Consistory Court, preserved at Norwich Cathedral. The record is quoted in full in Appendix III.

[33] A contemporary Thomas Pickerel who was sheriff and mayor of Norwich is mentioned by Blomefield, *An Essay towards a Topographical History of the County of Norfolk*, III, 218, 219; IV, 229.

[34] *Pro animæ suæ salute* was a stock phrase applicable to those charged with any offense against the church, from failure to attend service on holy days to denial of the immortality of the soul. Pykerell may have been as vicious a character as John Mykylborow, otherwise known as John Framyngham. Mykylborow was called before the Norwich Consistory Court by his parish priest in 1511 (Acts,

was therefore declared contumacious. On the fourth of the following January, Pykerell was absolved but was ordered to appear again on the Monday following the Feast of St. Hilary. On that day (January 14) he again failed to appear, and was again pronounced contumacious. Finally, on February 4, the accused man was "suspended," that is, he was forbidden to enter the church.[35]

In 1511 Skelton was involved in another ecclesiastical suit at Norwich[36] On November 6 Master William Dale, who had been instituted rector of Redegrave in March, 1506, came before the court and denied charges which had been made against him. A week later, he answered the allegations in full and was restored to good standing, but he was commanded to appear on the following Friday to satisfy the Bishop with regard to one of the articles. On the day set Dale and one Thomas Revet, evidently his accuser, promised to abide the decision of the court. Bishop Nikke appointed as arbiters Master Simon Dryver, Doctor of Decrees, and Master John Skelton, Rector of Diss. If agreement was not reached within eight days the case was to be brought before the court on the Monday after the Feast of St. Edmund. Evidently Dryver and Skelton were able to settle the affair, for Dale appeared a week later bearing a letter of correction, which was accepted by the Bishop.

The Dale case is of particular interest because it exhibits Skelton as a responsible member of the ecclesiastical com-

---

November 6, 1511). A witness reports that she said to the accused:

"John, come on and lett us goo to churche and here matens this holy day."

He answered, "Nay, so mot I the [*i.e.*, prosper] I had lever be in a melow peretre."

"John, beware for thy soule health."

"Whan thow seest my soule sitt in a hedge cast thow stonys at it," replied the incorrigible.

[35] C. J. Offer, *The Bishop's Register* (London, 1929), p. 222.

[36] Institution Book XIV, fols. 60 k (r.), 60 k (v.), 60 l (v.), 60 o (r.). Skelton's appointment as arbiter appears at fol. 60 l (v.).

munity, in the favor of his supposed enemy, Bishop Nikke. Perhaps the story of the poet's disagreement with the Bishop is pure fiction; perhaps there had been a quarrel followed by a reconciliation. The latter possibility is suggested by the version of the "Alpha and Omega" story which appears in Rastell's *A Hundred Merry Tales*.[37] After Skelton had presented the fowl (they were pheasants according to Rastell, not capons) "all that were by made great laughter, and they all desired the bishoppe to be good lorde vnto him for his merye conceytes: at which earnest entrety, as it wente, the bysshope was contente to take hym vnto his fauer agayne."

But though the affair of William Dale presents a prosperous Skelton, enjoying the respect of his superior, there is an ominous coincidence about it. The immediate predecessor of the wayward Rector of Redegrave was Thomas Wolsey, who had held the parish from June, 1505, until March, 1506.[38] It was in 1512, soon after Skelton had acted as arbitrator in the Dale suit, that the poet gave up the dull security of Norwich to seek his fortune at the court of his former pupil, King Henry VIII. He found what he sought, but he found misfortune, too, imprisonment and fear of execution at the command of Cardinal Wolsey.

[37] Skelton, *Works*, I, lxxiv–lxxv.
[38] Norwich Institution Book XIV, fol. 50.

The Court of Henry VIII

SHORTLY after Henry VIII came to the throne, in June, 1509, Skelton made an attempt to re-enter the royal service. In a list of those pardoned in the amnesty proclaimed in celebration of the new reign, there occurs:[1] "John Skelton, of London, clerk, poet laureate, *alias* late of Disse, Norf., poet laureate and rector of Dysse, 21 Oct. [1509]." Unfortunately, there is no record of the crime for which the pardon was given. Since everyone who was in danger of prosecution for any cause whatever safeguarded his position by entering his name on the roll, it is impossible to guess the reason for Skelton's inclusion. The document does suggest, however, that Skelton was attempting to exchange his Norfolk residence for the greener pastures of the court. Although "late of Diss" need not mean that he had already decided to quit Diss permanently, it is probable that during his visit to London he tried to discover what favor the new king would show him. He is not recorded as present at the trial of his parishioner Thomas Pykerell, in Norwich, in December, 1509, and January, 1510. Perhaps he was waiting for Henry's response to his coronation ode, "A Laud and Praise Made for Our Sovereign Lord the King."[2] The King must have been flooded with such eulogies, for Skelton was but one of a throng, including More, Erasmus, Ammonio, Barclay, André, and Hawes, who pressed forward, offering gifts of poetical congratulation on the enthronement. Besides writing the "Laud and Praise," Skelton presented the King with a manuscript copy of the *Chronique de Rains* which he an-

[1] *Letters and Papers*, I (ed. of 1920), 232.
[2] Skelton, *Works*, I, *ix–xi*. See the illustration on p. 164.

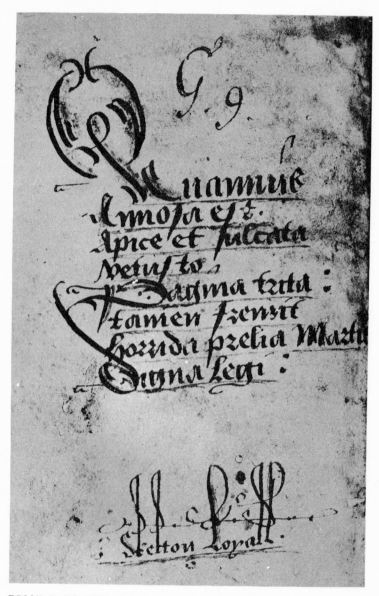

FOLIO i[v] OF SKELTON'S DEDICATION TO KING HENRY VIII
OF A MANUSCRIPT OF *CHRONIQUE DE RAINS*
CORPUS CHRISTI COLLEGE, CAMBRIDGE, MS 432

notated and prefaced with dedicatory verses. (Two pages of the dedicatory matter are reproduced in the illustrations on pages 116 and 174.) In order to remind Henry of his childhood tutor, Skelton also dedicated to him the treatise *Speculum principis*, which he had written years before.[3] What better way of recalling past services? The poet adds an anxious plea for royal favor:[4]

Grant me favor, O Jupiter, God of Trophies, lest I wear away my years at Eurotas.

Skelton Laureate, once royal tutor, soliloquizes mutely with himself, like a man wholly consigned to oblivion or like one dead at heart.

Alas for the faith of gods and men! Why has it happened to me that I should be herded off from the others, that I alone should suffer such misfortune? Royal munificence has not yet deigned to help me, nor has the benevolence of fortune favored me more richly. O Heavens, O Seas [*or* Mary], to whom shall I ascribe this? Shall I blame the gods who perchance are angered with me? No, I will not commit so great a folly. But shall I lightly impute to a great and liberal king a conspicuous failure of generosity? Expel the thought, O best and greatest God, who weighs all things with a just scale in the balance of his inexhaustible generosity . . .

Unfortunately, he had to return to "Eurotas"—*frigidus Eurotas*.[5] Although he was in Westminster in July, 1511,[6] the following November found him in Norwich, acting as arbitrator in the case of William Dale. The Norfolk his-

---

[3] *Speculum*, IX, 29.

[4] *Ibid.*, p. 37: "Tribuat mihi Iuppiter Feretrius ne teram tempus apud Eurotam.

"Skeltonis Laureatus, didasculus quondam Regius, etc., tacitus secum in soliloquio ceu vir totus obliuioni datus aut tanquam mortuus a corde, etc.

"Proh deum atque hominum fidem, vnde hoc mihi quod ego seorsum ab aliis tanto tamque singulari sim fato! Cui nec regalis munificentia nec fortune benignitas adhuc opulentius dignatur aspirare. O celum, o Maria, cui imputabo illud? Ah, imponam ne illud diis iratis forsan mihi. Insaniam tantam non committam. Sed ne imponam ego tanto tamque munifico regi remisse largitatis notabilem labem? Auertat hoc deus optimus, maximus, qui omnia ponderat cum equabilissima lance in statera amplissime largitatis sue . . ."

[5] Ovid, *Amores*, II, 17, 32.   [6] See below, p. 118.

torian, Blomefield, asserts that a house in Diss was in the poet's tenure during 1511.[7] But in 1512 Skelton came again to London.

He probably never returned to his rectory. Not only is there no evidence which links Skelton to Diss after 1511, but it is clear that other priests assumed his duties. In 1515 and 1517 wills were witnessed by one William Bekett or Beget, described as parish priest of Diss.[8] In 1522 a testament was signed by a curate of Diss named William Brakes.[9] A Diss will of 1529, the year of Skelton's death, was witnessed by William Gallyott, priest.[10]

WESTMINSTER

On Saturday, the fifth of July, 1511, the household servant of William Mane, Prior of Westminster Abbey, shopped for dinner. He bought:[11]

Item ij playce	vij	d
Item ij copull soliz	vj	d
Item ij Congger snekes	xiiij	d
Item a syd saltffishe	ij	d
Item ij disches buter	ij	d

The careful accountant records in the margin: "this day at dyner with your maistrchip the Soffrecan and Skeltun the poet with others." This is the first sign of Skelton's association with Westminster, an association that continued until he was buried before the high altar of the parish church of St. Margaret's, Westminster. When the poet

[7] *An Essay towards a Topographical History of the County of Norfolk* (London, 1805), I, 30.

[8] That is, the will of Margaret Bache, Widow of Diss, made on May 6, 1515, and witnessed by "Sir William Beget parish priest" (Norfolk Archdeaconry, Register 1515–1520, 1523, fol. 220), and the will of Roger ffoleser the elder of Diss, made in November, 1517, and witnessed by "Sir William Bekett paresshe prieste of disse" (*ibid.*, fols. 209–10).

[9] Will of Richard Lynd, made on February 5, 1522 (Norwich Consistory Court, Register 1522–1523, fols. 7–8).

[10] Will of John Smyth (Norfolk Archdeaconry, Register 1524–1531, fol. 177).

[11] Westminster Abbey Muniments, 33325, fol. 17. See H. F. Westlake, *Westminster Abbey* (London, 1923), II, 426.

came to Westminster, Braynewode says,[12] he found favor
with John Islip, the abbot of the monastery. Evidence of
that favor is found as early as 1512, for on November 30
of that year Skelton composed an epitaph for the tomb of
Henry VII at Islip's request.[13] In 1516, again at the Abbot's
urging, Skelton wrote an epitaph for Lady Margaret Beaufort.[14] These poems were inscribed on paper or parchment
and hung near the tombs where, almost miraculously, they
remained for more than a century. In 1631 a visitor to the
Abbey described the tomb of Henry VII:[15] "This glorious
rich tomb is compassed about with verses, penned by that
Poet Laureate . . . John Skelton."

In 1518 Skelton wrote still another epitaph for a Westminster burial, but it is extremely doubtful that Abbot
Islip permitted it to be placed near the tomb. The subject of
the "Devout Epitaph on Bedel, Late Belial Incarnate" has
been identified as William Bedell, treasurer and receiver
general of the Lady Margaret and recipient of considerable
favor from Henry VIII.[16] Skelton's description of Bedell as
a scoundrelly priest hater, though contradicted by a pious
and charitable will, may possibly reflect a curious incident
recorded in a letter of the University of Oxford to the Lady
Margaret.[17] An Oxford prostitute had escaped the clutches
of the proctor by running off to Cowley. When she attempted to return to Oxford, she was imprisoned and fined.
For some reason which the writer of the letter could not
understand, the action of the proctor aroused the ire of

[12] Bale, *Index Britanniæ scriptorum*, p. 253.
[13] Skelton, *Works*, I, 178.   [14] *Ibid.*, p. 195.
[15] John Weever, *Ancient Funerall Monuments* (London, 1631), p. 476.
[16] Skelton, *Works*, I, 175. The identification was made by H. L. R. Edwards
who has kindly communicated his discovery to me. It depends on the fact that
Skelton's "In Bedel" appears in Marshe's edition (1568) with the superscription
MDXVIII, the year of William Bedell's death. Mr. Edwards informs me that
Bedell's will was proved in the prerogative court of Canterbury on July 11, 1518,
and that he was buried at the entrance to the Henry VII Chapel in the Abbey.
[17] *Epistolæ academicæ Oxon.*, ed. by Anstey (Oxford Historical Society, 1898),
II, 653–54.

William Bedell. The University protests that it has no desire to anger Bedell, "quem virum pro vestra gracia valde semper complectemur."

Clear evidence of Skelton's residence in Westminster at the time of Bedell's burial is found in a lease preserved among the Abbey muniments.[18] In 1518 the abbot, the prior, and the fraternity of Westminster leased to Alice Newebery the tenement situated on the south side of the Great Belfry, together with all the houses, solars, and cellars thereto appertaining, in which tenement John Skelton, Laureate, was then living [*modo inhabitat*]. In 1529 Skelton was buried in St. Margaret's, the church of the parish in which he lived. And even after his death his words continued to resound in the Westminster records, for some time between 1530 and 1533, the keeper of the Manors scribbled on the dorse of his account book in order to test his pen:[19] "Dame Elyner of Rumyng by her mumyng dumeryng."

The jestbooks confirm the conclusion that Skelton was closely associated with Westminster. It was in the Eagle Tavern in Westminster that the poet first met the famous virago Long Meg.[20] At Skelton's suggestion and because of his promise of new hose and shoes she traded blows with Sir James of Castile and knocked him out. Long Meg's mistress, the hostess of the Eagle, was in love with Skelton, so that Sir James could get no favor from her. In the *Merry Tales* collection Skelton is said to have been imprisoned at Westminster at the command of Cardinal Wolsey,[21] a statement supported by Braynewode's biography.

[18] Register Book II, fol. 146. The date of the lease is August 8, 1518. See Westlake, *Westminster Abbey*, II, 426.

[19] I owe this note to the kindness of Mr. Lawrence E. Tanner, Keeper of the Muniments of the library at Westminster. At the time I visited the library, the document was not available because of the temporary rearrangement necessitated by the coronation ceremony of King George VI.

[20] *The Life of Long Meg of Westminster* (London, 1635). The tales which relate to Skelton are reprinted in Skelton, *Works*, I, lxxxi–lxxxv.

[21] Tale xiv.

The existence of so much evidence which links Skelton with Westminster from 1511 on makes it most probable that he lived there not only in 1518, when Alice Newebery became his landlady, but from his return to London in 1512 until the end of his life, in 1529. It is possible that Skelton chose Westminster as a residence because members of his family lived there. There seems to have been a considerable clan of Skeltons in the parish. Sir Robert Skelton, Vicar of St. Stephen's, Westminster, was mentioned in 1526,[22] and his burial was listed in the parish register of St. Margaret's in 1549.[23] Elizabeth Skelton was christened at St. Margaret's in 1554, and Roger Skylton was buried there in 1563. Skeltons continued to be recorded in the register as late as 1630.

There was congenial company to be found at Westminster, too. The poet's friendship with Islip has already been mentioned. Another resident was William Cornish, musician and deviser of entertainments for both Henry VII and Henry VIII and, like Skelton, a satirical poet.[24] Pietro Carmeliano, the king's Latin secretary, was "residensor" of St. Stephen's, Westminster.[25]

[22] *Letters and Papers*, IV (1), 874.

[23] *Memorials of St. Margaret's Church, Westminster. The Parish Registers, 1539–1660*, ed. by A. M. Burke and H. H. Henson (London, 1914).

[24] The Abbey muniments preserve a great deal of information about Cornish which has not been noticed by his biographers. In 1480–81, he taught the Singing Boys of the Abbey (*W.A.M.* 19087). He leased a tenement from the monastery in 1489 (*W.A.M.* 17887), the rent being reduced from 53 *s.* 4 *d.* to 20 *s.* in consideration of his services to the lessors. In 1497 he was created notary, tabellion, and judge in ordinary (*W.A.M.* 6538). In his notarial function, he recorded the procession of John Islip to receive installation as abbot of Westminster in 1500 (*W.A.M.* 5454).

In 1526–28, clothes for the choir of St. Margaret's were hired from a Master Cornish (transcript of the Churchwardens' Accounts deposited in the Abbey library, Book B, p. 1162), but this Master Cornish may be Dan John Cornyshe, overseer of the foundation of Henry VII (*W.A.M.* 32249).

Cornish's activity as a satirical poet is mentioned in Stow's *Annales* (London, 1615), p. 488. The historian says that Cornish wrote "opprobrious rimes" against Sir Richard Empson. Stow probably refers to the "parable by William Cornishe in ye Fleete," which is found in Marshe's edition of Skelton's collected works.

[25] Transcript of the Churchwardens' Accounts of St. Margaret's, Book B, p. 776 (1516).

There is therefore no evidence for the hypothesis that Skelton lived in Westminster because he required the safety of sanctuary.[26] The Abbey precincts were certainly not populated exclusively by sanctuary men. There is good reason to believe that Skelton took up residence there as early as 1512, and there is no reason to believe that he was in danger of prosecution at that time. In fact, it is probable that Skelton chose to live in Westminster primarily because of its immediate proximity to the royal palace.

SKELTON, *Orator Regius*

In 1512, the year of Skelton's migration from Diss to Westminster, the poet began to use the title *orator regius*.[27] It appears in no poem written before 1512, but in many written after that date. The first piece in which Skelton assumes the appellation was probably composed in May, 1512,[28] and it may be supposed that the honor was conferred on the poet not long before. No document which grants Skelton the title is to be found among the patent rolls. But it is suggested[29] that the eighteenth-century French scholar Du Resnel mentions the missing patent:[30] ". . la patente qui declare Skelton poëte laureat d'Henry viii. est datée de la cinquiéme année de son regne, ce qui tombe en 1512. ou 1513." Although Du Resnel declares Skelton was made Poet Laureate, not *orator regius*, the coincidence of dates is striking. Since neither Skelton nor any of his biographers refers to a laureation ceremony performed by Henry VIII, it seems probable that Du Resnel

[26] It is noteworthy, however, that Alice Newebery's lease did not contain "the usual sanctuary clause" (Westlake, *loc. cit.*) which required the tenant to agree "not to harbour fugitives or malignants beyond one day and one night after due warning" (*ibid.*, p. 424). Perhaps Skelton saw trouble ahead.

[27] This fact is pointed out by H. L. R. Edwards in *PMLA*, LIII, 601–3.

[28] *Ibid.*   [29] *Ibid.*

[30] "Recherches sur les poètes couronnez: poetæ laureati," *Mémoires de littérature, tirez des registres de l'Académie Royale des inscriptions et belles lettres*, X (Paris, 1736), 522. Du Resnel's authority for other information about Skelton is the English historian, Carte, but it is not clear that Carte supplied the patent in question.

was mistaken and that the patent conferred upon Skelton, already Poet Laureate, the title of royal orator.

What a royal orator was is not entirely clear. The equivalence of the words "orator" and "poet" has already been pointed out,[31] and it may be that the appointment designated Skelton official court poet. Skelton's "Calliope,"[32] written after he had got the title of *orator regius*, implies that Henry VIII renewed poetical honors which his father had bestowed. In answer to the query, "Why wear ye *Calliope* embroidered with letters of gold?" Skelton Laureate, *orator regius*, replies that though he is old and somewhat sere, the muse, void of disdain, is fain to retain him in her servitude. Furthermore, a contemporary grammarian, William Horman, credits the poet with the title *vates regius*.[33]

But the word "orator" had another very important meaning. It was the regular term for "ambassador" or "secretary." Giovanni Gigli, ambassador to the Curia,[34] and Jean Mallard, French secretary to Henry VIII,[35] were entitled royal orators. Perhaps the royal office was analogous to that of "university orator," established during this period. The Cambridge statute for the election of an orator, promulgated in 1522, assigns salary and high academic status to the new officer whose primary duty is to write letters in the name of the University to the great of the realm.[36]

The two significant meanings of "orator," that is, "diplomat" and "poet," are by no means without con-

[31] See above, p. 10.   [32] Skelton, *Works*, I, 197.

[33] Bale, *Index*, p. 252.

[34] In MS Cotton Cleo. E III (fol. 142) is a letter "de negotiis à Jo. Giglio regis oratore apud pontificem tractatis" (*Catalogue of Manuscripts in the Cottonian Library* [1802], p. 589).

[35] In MS Bodley 883, *Le Chemin de Paradis*, an illuminated manuscript presented to Henry VIII, Mallard calls himself "son Poete & orateur Francoys" (fol. 7) and "son escripuain" (fol. 6).

[36] *Documents relating to the University and Colleges of Cambridge* (London, 1852), I, 431–34.

nection, however. It has been shown that the ambassadors and secretaries of Henry VII also wrote poems and histories for him. Both functions required training in the disciplines of grammar and rhetoric.

Skelton certainly served the King as a poet, and it is possible that he was also employed as a secretary. He wrote odes to celebrate his country's victories and morality plays to edify the court, engaged in a "flyting" to amuse the king, and composed lyrics to delight him. In the following discussion of his literary activities at the court of Henry VIII, his compositions will be considered according to their kind rather than chronologically.

AGAINST THE SCOTS

The year 1512 found the young Henry VIII deeply embroiled with England's traditional enemies, France and Scotland. Henry VII had attempted to keep the Scots at peace by bestowing his daughter, Margaret, on James IV, but a series of irritations which arose between England and Scotland proved stronger than the ties of royal intermarriage, and in 1512 Scotland and France signed a treaty of mutual aid. In July, 1513, while the French king was busy besieging Milan, Henry VIII crossed the Channel with a powerful army to seek his inheritance of France. James, in accordance with his new agreement with France, but in violation of an older treaty with England, sent a herald to King Henry at his camp near Therouenne, demanding that he desist immediately from attacking France. Before Henry's defiant answer reached Scotland, James struck across the border. He succeeded in taking Norham Castle, and he razed it. But before he had proceeded much farther, he was met by the army of the Earl of Surrey, to whose entirely competent care the defense of England had been entrusted. On September 9, 1513, the armies engaged in battle on Brankston Moor, near Flodden. After a sharp fight the

Scots were utterly routed, and King James was killed together with almost all of his nobility. James's body,
stripped of its armor, was not identified until the following day. Meanwhile events in France had proceeded aus-
piciously for the English. A French attempt to raise the
siege of Therouenne was beaten off in a battle which was
called the Day of Spurs "because they [the French] ran
away so fast on horseback."[37] On August 22 Therouenne
capitulated, and a few days later it was burned and leveled
to the ground. Henry moved on to Tournai, which, rather
than suffer the fate of its neighbor, surrendered after a
short struggle.

While the current of events moved thus rapidly, Skelton, his biographers have assumed, rested in the quiet
backwater of Diss. The hypothesis of his Norfolk residence
has been derived from the superscriptions of two of his
Latin poems, one on the Battle of Spurs and the destruction
of Therouenne: "Chorus de Dis, &c. super triumphali
victoria contra Gallos, &c. cantavit solemniter hoc elogium
in profesto Divi Johannis ad Decollationem," and the other
on Flodden: "Chorus de Dis contra Scottos cum omni
processionali festivitate solemnisavit hoc epitoma xxii die
Septembris, &c."[38] If "chorus" means "choir," and if the
chorus of Diss sang these compositions in the church of
Diss, it seems reasonable to suppose that Skelton remained
in his Norfolk parish while his master fought in France.

But there is something decidedly awkward about the
hypothesis of Skelton's residence at Diss during these high
times. King Henry made no frugal expedition. His entire
court accompanied him, secretaries, entertainers, and
musicians included. One hundred and fifteen members of
the Chapel Royal and five hundred and seventy-nine of the
Chamber crossed the Channel.[39] But a year before, as we

---

[37] *Hall's Chronicle* (1809), p. 550.   [38] Skelton, *Works*, I, 191, 190.
[39] *Letters and Papers*, I (ed. of 1920), No. 2053.

have seen, Skelton assumed the title of *regius orator*, that is, royal spokesman. Carmeliano and Ammonio went with King Henry. Why should Skelton, the master of English eloquence, have been left behind?

There is, in fact, excellent reason for doubting that Skelton remained in Diss in 1513. The "Elogium" on the triumphant victory against the French must have been written on or before the eve of the feast of St. John the Baptist, that is, August 28, when the chorus, according to the superscription, chanted it. If Skelton had given the date in digits, it might be assumed that he or his copyists had erred, but it is most improbable that there was confusion about an important feast of the church calendar. In the course of the poem, Skelton celebrates King Henry's destruction of the walls of Therouenne:

> Henricus rutilans Octavus noster in armis
> Tirwinnæ gentis mœnia stravit humi.

But the decision to destroy the fortifications of the captured city was arrived at only on the evening of August 26.[40] Not even an express dispatched directly to Diss could have brought the news in time for the poem to have been written and sung on August 28. Therefore, neither Skelton nor the chorus of Diss could have been at Diss on August 28, 1513.

What Skelton meant by "chorus of Diss" and what it was doing away from Diss, I do not know. Perhaps the name represents a choir, trained by Skelton during his Norfolk residence, which was taken along on the expedition to augment the royal troupe of singers. Perhaps the word "Diss" stands for John Skelton, and "chorus of Diss" means a division of the King's choristers led by Skelton, the absentee rector of Diss. But unless "profesto Divi Johannis" is an error, the chorus could not have sung of the destruction of Therouenne in Diss church. There is therefore every reason to suppose that Skelton and the chorus

[40] *Ibid.*, No. 2208.

formed part of the magnificent entourage which accompanied King Henry. And a study of Skelton's other writings concerning the wars of 1513 (the "Epitoma" already cited and two versions of an English tirade against the Scots) strengthens this conclusion.

Skelton's poems on the victory of Flodden show a close dependence on the letters sent to King Henry by the Earl of Surrey, the commander of the Northern army. On the night of September 9, just after the battle, Surrey, wearied by the day's toil, hurried off a brief account of his movements to the Queen, who transmitted it to France. The message is not itself extant, but its substance is given in a letter written by an Italian observer in London on September 14.[41] "As yet nothing certain was known of the King [of Scots]; he was supposed to be either dead or a prisoner." Surrey did not mention where the battle had taken place. The only definite news in his dispatch was that after the Scots had advanced twenty miles into England, they had been routed completely. Surrey's letter reached the King at Tournai, on September 15,[42] and it must have been received with rejoicing, for there had been a persistent rumor on the continent that the Scots had won a great victory.

A day or two after the battle Surrey sent a long, detailed account of all the circumstances to the Queen. The messenger carried with him King James's gauntlet and a piece of his coat as sure proof of his death. On September 16 Queen Katherine received this second letter, and immediately sent it off to France. The gauntlet and plaid were dispatched somewhat later on the same day. It was not until September 19 that Surrey's letter reached Tournai; the relics were probably delayed until September 20.[43]

Skelton's first poem on Flodden, the jubilant *Ballad of the Scottish King*,[44] contains passages which must have been

[41] *Calendar of State Papers (Venetian)*, II, Nos. 331, 337.
[42] *Letters and Papers*, I, No. 2391.   [43] *Letters and Papers*, I, Nos. 2268, 2286.
[44] Pynson, n. d., ed. by John Ashton, London, 1882.

written almost immediately after Surrey's first hasty message was brought to King Henry. The poem does not mention the fact that the battle was fought at Flodden, and the only reference to James's fate is the ambiguous

> to the castell of norham
> I vnderstonde ro soone ye cam.
> For a prysoner there now ye be.
> Eyther to the deuyll or the trinite.

It is clear that the *Ballad* must have been written before September 22, for by that date Skelton had heard and recorded full details of the engagement. His "Epitoma contra Scottos," "solemnized" by the chorus of Diss on that day, describes the battle, locates it on Brankston Moor, near Flodden, and declares openly the Scottish king's death: "Scottus Jacobus, obrutus ense, cadit." Besides writing the "Epitoma," Skelton revised the English *Ballad*, inserted his recently acquired information, introduced the whole with a denial of the rumor of a Scottish victory and an invocation to the Muses, and gave the new version the title, *Skelton Laureate against the Scots*.

King Henry received James's gauntlet on September 20; the chorus of Diss celebrated the victory on September 22. The interval acquires significance when one consults Hall's report of the course of events in France. The day after the messenger arrived (Hall misdates the receipt of the gauntlet September 25), fires were lighted throughout the encampment. On the day following,

the tente of cloth of gold was sett vp, and the kynges Chapell sange masse, and after that *Te Deum*, and then the Byshoppe of Rochester [John Fisher] made a Sermond and shewed the deathe of the kynge of Scottes and muche lamented the yll deathe and periurye of him.[45]

The subject matter of the Bishop of Rochester's sermon is

[45] *Hall's Chronicle*, p. 564. There had been a similar celebration in the tent of cloth of gold on September 17, two days after the receipt of Surrey's *first* letter (*Letters and Papers*, I, 2391). On this occasion, the Bishop of St. Asaph preached.

precisely the same as that of Skelton's "Epitoma contra Scottos," which was sung by the chorus of Diss *cum omni processionali festivitate* on September 22. Skelton's poem, a parody on a paschal hymn of Fortunatus,[46] would have been perfectly suited to the occasion which Hall describes. It seems proper to conclude that Skelton's "Epitoma contra Scottos" was written especially for this celebration in the tent of cloth of gold.

There is very little in Skelton's *Ballad of the Scottish King* which could not have been written before even the first news of Flodden reached France. The chief subject of the poem is, not Surrey's victory, but the peremptory message which the herald of the King of Scots delivered to Henry VIII at Therouenne, on August 11, 1513. Skelton's *Ballad* shows an intimate knowledge of the circumstances of the parley. The Scottish messenger, young Sir David Lindsay, declared that the King of England should rest satisfied with having diverted the French king from his expedition against Milan, and demanded that Henry return to England immediately. In MS Harleian 2252 there is a contemporary account of the conversation that ensued:[47]

The kyng stondyng stylle wythe sobyr contenaunce havyng hys hande on hys swerde. sayd haue ye now your tale at an ende. // The harawld of arms seyd nay. / Sey forthe then sayd the kyng. // Syr he [King James] somonyth your grace to be at home in your

[46] The "Epitoma" opens with:
"Salve, festa dies, toto resonabilis ævo,
Qua Scottus Jacobus, obrutus ense, cadit."
Fortunatus' hymn (Daniel, *Thesaurus Hymnologicus*, I, 165–66) begins:
"Salve festa dies, toto venerabilis ævo
Qua Deus infernum vicit et astra tenet."
The old hymn had already been parodied for religious uses in England. Daniel (*op. cit.*, II, 181–85) quotes four "proses" from the *York Processional:* "In ascensione Domini," "In die Pentecostes," "In festo Corporis Christi," and "In dedicatione ecclesiæ," each of which is an imitation of Fortunatus. Fortunatus himself was probably echoing Ovid's celebration of New Year's Day (*Fasti*, I, 87–88):
"Salve, læta dies, meliorque revertere semper
a populo rerum digna potente coli."
[47] Printed in full in Appendix IV.

realme in the defence of hys alye. // Then the kyng anssweryd & sayd. / ye haue well don your message / neverthelesse. hyt becommyth yll a Scotte to somon a kyng of yngelond. / . . . and tell your master that I mystruste not so the ream of ynglond. but he shall haue enowghe to doe when so evyr he begynnythe. / and also I trustyd not hym so well but that I provyded for hym ryghte well. / and that shall he well knowe. / and he to somon me now beyng here for my ryghte and enerytaunce. / hyt wold myche better agreed with hys honowr to haue somonyd me being at home for he knewe well before my comyng hether. that hether wold I come. / and now to send me somons.

The entirely independent account of the same conversation presented by the contemporary chronicler Hall[48] also emphasizes the point that Henry was offended because the Scottish herald had, in effect, served him with a summons *subpœna:* "well said the kyng I will returne to your domage at my pleasure, and not at thy masters somonyng." The first lines of Skelton's *Ballad* clearly reflect the reiteration of the word "summons" in the Harleian manuscript:

> Kynge Jamy / Jomy your. Joye is all go
> ye somm[on]ed our kynge why dyde ye so
> To you no thynge it dyde accorde
> To sommon our kynge your souerayne lorde.
> A kynge a somner it is wonder
> Knowe ye not salte and suger asonder
> In your somnynge ye were to malaperte
> And your harolde no thynge experte[49]

It is evident that Skelton's account corresponds closely to that of the Harleian manuscript. The similarity passes the bounds of chance when the following passage from the Harleian narrative is compared with Skelton's poem:

Tell hym there shalle nevyr Scotte cawse me to retorne my fase. & where he leyethe the frenshe kyng to be hys alye. / hyt wold myche better agreed and becom hym. beynge maryd to the kyng of ynglondes syster. to reconte the kyng of ynglond hys alye.

---

[48] *Hall's Chronicle*, p. 545.

[49] A detail in Hall's account of the interview may explain the last line: "Then the kyng commaunded garter [the English herald] to take hym [Lindsay] to his tente & make him good chere . . . for he was sore apalled."

Says Skelton:

> Trowe ye syr James his noble grace /
> For you and your scottes wolde tourne his face[50]

> Your lege ye layd and your aly
> Your frantick fable not worth a fly,
> [Before the] Frenche kynge, or one or other;
> Regarded ye should your lord, your brother.[51]

These close parallels between the historical account of the interview and Skelton's poem may be explained in any one of several ways. If Skelton was not himself present at the encounter, he must have seen a report of it, probably that which is represented in the Harleian manuscript, little more than a month after the event. But if Skelton was a witness to the proceedings, either of two possible explanations is available. It may be that the King actually used the words which are attributed to him in the Harleian narrative. But although the various accounts of the interview agree as to the substance of the King's speech, they differ widely as to its language. Stenography had not yet appeared in England. Furthermore, the literary quality of the speech recorded in the Harleian manuscript, particularly the clever word play, throws doubt on the hypothesis that the report is a verbatim transcript. A final possibility

---

[50] In the revised version of the poem which is entitled *Against the Scots* (Skelton, *Works*, I, 182–89) these lines appear:
> Trowid ye, Syr Jemy, his nobul grace
> From you, Syr Scot, would turne his face?
>   (ll. 107–8)

The change of "For" to "From" indicates the change in the subject matter of the poem. In the *Ballad*, the chief point is that James tried to divert the English from their attack on France. In the revised poem, Flodden holds the center of the stage.

[51] The last four lines are quoted from *Against the Scots* (ll. 103–6) and not from the *Ballad*. The words "Before the" which apparently slipped out of the revised version have been introduced from the *Ballad*. The parallel passage in the *Ballad* reads:
> "To be so scornefull to your alye /
> your counseyle was not worth a flye.
> Before the frensshe kynge / danes / and other
> ye ought to honour your lorde and brother."

remains. It may be that Skelton, having witnessed the encounter between his master and the herald of the King of
Scots, composed the story which is found in the Harleian
manuscript.

On August 12, the day after the interview, King Henry
confirmed his oral defiance in a letter which the Scottish
herald was to carry to his king. Again the correspondence
of Henry's letter with Skelton's *Ballad* is too close to depend on chance. There are striking parallels, both in idea
and in phrase. In the letter the King of Scots is warned that
he must not trust too implicitly the promises of King Louis
of France. The King of Navarre, relying on his French
alliance, had made war on the Emperor and had lost his
realm as a consequence:[52]

And yf the example of the kyng of Nauarre beynge excluded from
his royalme for assistence gyuen to the Frenche king cannot
restrayne you from this vnnaturall dealynge, we suppose ye shall
haue like assistence of the sayde Frenche kynge as the kyng of
Nauarre hath now: Who is a kynge withoute a realme, and so
the French kynge peaceably suffereth hym to contynue wherunto
good regarde woulde be taken.

In almost the same words Skelton offers the same advice
and drives it home with the same concrete object lesson:[53]

> Of the kynge of nauerne ye may take hede /
> How vnfortunately he doth now spede/
> In double welles now he dooth dreme.
> That is a kynge witou a realme
> At hym example ye wolde none take.
> Experyence hath brought you in the same brake.

[52] Copies of the letter are found in MS Harleian 787, fol. 58; Rymer XIII,
382–83; MS Harleian 2252, fols. 42–43; and *Hall's Chronicle* (1809), pp. 547–48.
The last-named source is here quoted.

[53] The parallel was first drawn by Ashton (*A Ballade of the Scottysshe Kynge*,
pp. 48–49) who concludes, "Skelton evidently saw copies of these letters immediately after their arrival in England—as he makes use of the very phraseology
—'Who is a Kynge withoute a realme,' when speaking of the King of Navarre."
Brie, because he believes that Skelton was at the time a resident of Diss, minimizes
the correspondence, and suggests that both the reference to the King of Navarre
and the verbal parallel are mere coincidence ("Skelton-Studien," *Englische Studien*,
XXXVII (1907), 55–56).

There are further parallels between Henry's letter and Skelton's poem. In both the King of Scots is berated for having chosen a time when Henry was out of England to stir trouble and threaten invasion. In both Scotland is assured that the King of England is supported by Saint George. In both James is accused of treaty breaking and perfidy. And finally the letter asserts that James is a member of a group of malicious "Scysmatyques and their adherentes beynge by the generall counsayll expressely excommunicate and interdicted," while Skelton, in his revision of the *Ballad*, describes the culprit as[54]

> A subtyll sysmatyke,
> Ryght nere an heretyke,
> Of grace out of the state,
> And died excomunycate.

It seems to me that these close and abundant parallels cannot be accounted for as coincidences. Either Skelton saw a copy of the King's letter to James IV or he wrote the letter himself.

Neither the Harleian narrative of Henry's answer to the Scottish herald nor the letter to James can be denied to Skelton on stylistic grounds. The dramatic belligerence of the former and the weightily rhetorical abusiveness of the latter are both literary manners which characterize the poet. Skelton, Poet Laureate, was a proper person to record the King's interview with the representative of Scotland. And it would not be strange if Henry, who employed the humanist scholar Andrea Ammonio to write his Latin letters, should ask the vitriolic Skelton, recently appointed royal orator, to compose a defiance to the King of Scots. The fact that both Henry's answer to the herald and his letter to James IV are found in MS Harleian 2252, a volume containing several of Skelton's poems, is an additional argument for the attribution.

[54] Skelton, *Works*, I, 189.

"WHAT NEWS? WHAT NEWS?"

Skelton's writings on the battle of Flodden, the first of his political poems, are in a sense news reports. The first version of *Against the Scots*, entitled the *Ballad of the Scottish King*, which was dashed off immediately after news of the battle reached France, evidently came to the hands of Richard Pynson, the King's printer, who published it, thus producing what has been called the first printed ballad. There were many other reports of Flodden, both in prose and in verse, which were circulated throughout Europe— some in print, others in manuscript.[55] Pynson himself published at least one other account of the battle, a prose narrative written by a servant of the Earl of Surrey.[56] Whenever an event of international importance occurred, there appeared a similar flood of ballads and prose pamphlets designed to satisfy the popular hunger for news. It is probable, then, that one purpose of Skelton's poems on Flodden was to disseminate information.

In his later political poems Skelton unmistakably shows that his purpose is similar to that of the modern newspaper reporter. The poem which tells "How the doughty Duke of Albany, like a coward knight, ran away shamefully" (1523)[57] begins:

> Reioyse, Englande,
> And vnderstande
> These tidinges newe,
> Whiche be as trewe
> As the gospell

[55] See *Letters and Papers*, I, Nos. 2246–47.

[56] The Pynson edition is not extant, but a contemporary manuscript copy is in MS Additional 29, 506. The title there given reads: "Thordre and behauyoure of the right honourable Erle of Surrey Tresour and Marshal of Englande ayenst the kynge of Scottes and his Inuasions howe the same kynge at the Batayle of Brankston was slayne by the sayd Erle." The author of the pamphlet is "one unworthy / whome it pleased the sayde Erle to haue nyghe aboute hym / aswell in tyme of conclundynge [*sic*] and spekynge of all the premysses / at counsayle and elles where / as at the tyme of the sayde batayle" (fol. 13). On fol. 14 is Carmeliano's epitaph on James IV.

[57] Skelton, *Works*, II, 68–84.

Why Come Ye Not to Court (1522)[58] is punctuated by such lines as:

> What newes, what newes? (l. 230)
> What here ye of Lancashyre? (l. 244)
> What here ye of Chesshyre? (l. 247)
> What here ye of the Scottes? (l. 259)
> What here ye of the Lorde Dakers? (l. 269)

A newspaper is waste paper the day after. Incomplete reports are superseded by fuller and more accurate ones; the new news replaces yesterday's novelty. Unless Skelton was to write a new poem each time a significant happening occurred, he had to devise means of keeping the old report fresh and readable. Skelton's revision of the *Ballad of the Scottish King* illustrates one method of overcoming the difficulty. It is not unlikely that the *Ballad* itself is a revision of an earlier poem, the theme of which was the meeting between the Scottish herald and the King of England.

But bringing up to date by means of revision is a cumbersome process, and applicable only when the new information is an elaboration or a correction of the old. The less closely the new information is related to the old, the more difficult the task of revising the original poem. In order to cope with this difficulty Skelton, in his later political poems, made use of a far more flexible technique. Instead of altering what he had already written, the poet merely added new sections as the news came in. Several of his poems are evidently continuous chronicles of this kind. *Speak, Parrot*, for example, ends in a group of "envoys," each of them dated, constituting a series of fortnightly reports on the current activities of Cardinal Wolsey.[59] In *Why Come Ye Not to Court* two of the added sections are clearly marked by the conclusions of the preceding ones:

> But now vpon this story
> I wyll no further ryme

---

[58] *Ibid.*, II, 26–67.   [59] See below, pp. 165–73.

> Tyll another tyme,
> Tyll another tyme, &c.
>   (ll. 226-29)
>
> Thus wyll I conclude my style,
> And fall to rest a whyle,
> And so to rest a whyle, &c.
>   (ll. 393-95)

And it is clear that the topical references of this poem are
arranged chronologically. The two events discussed at the
end of *Why Come Ye Not to Court*, the election of a mayor of
London and the illness of Cardinal Wolsey, occurred in
late October or early November, 1522, and independent
evidence proves that the poem was completed before November 17 of the same year.[60]

Skelton's political poems are rather more than accounts
of current events. Unlike Skelton, most contemporary re-
porters seem to have been satisfied with presenting the news
in as great detail as possible. The only comments they offer
are the conventional ones: praise of the king's valor, of the
bride's beauty, of the excellence of the feast. But for Skelton, each event demanded a judgment, and each judgment
required expression. When he learned that the body of
King James had lain stripped on the field of battle, he was
not satisfied merely to announce the fact; he must explain
it:[61]

> Out of your robes ye were shaked,
> And wretchedly ye lay starke naked.
> For lacke of grace hard was your hap:
> The Popes curse gaue you that clap.

It is not enough to denounce the popular hatred of the
clergy; Skelton interprets it as a consequence of the proud
insolence of the bishops. Their defects in turn are explained
as the result of too rapid elevation of the low-born. If the
lower clergy are unlearned, it is not a fact merely to be
stated, condemned, or condoned. There must be an ex-

---

[60] See below, p. 163.   [61] *Against the Scots*, ll. 166-69.

planation; in this case, bribed or careless examiners. Skelton's attitude is never that of dispassionate observation. He is a writer of editorials, not a reporter.

Skelton's opinions on foreign politics are extraordinarily simple. He is essentially an isolationist, proud of the force of English arms, but, toward the end of his life, at least, suspicious of the value of exercising them. The Scots are uncivilized and treacherous, the French are proud, and even the Burgundians and the Spaniards, consistently allied to the English throughout the reign of Henry VIII, are unfriendly and untrustworthy partners. Skelton gives no expression to the Tudor dream of reconquering "our inheritance of France," but he does have hope for the subjugation and absorption of Scotland. Thus, at the end of *Against the Scots* occurs:

> Scotia, redacta in formam provinciæ,
> Regis parebit nutibus Angliæ[62]

But Skelton's proud jingoism is tempered by the realization that wars are expensive, that even when victories are gained, the victors gain little in prosperity and happiness:[63]

> For now, syr Trestram,
> Ye must weare bukram,
> Or canues of Cane,
> For sylkes are wane.
> Our royals that shone,
> Our nobles are gone
> Amonge the Burgonyons,
> And Spanyardes onyons,
> And the Flanderkyns,
> Gyll swetis and Cate spynnys,
> They are happy that wynnys;
> But Englande may well say,
> Fye on this wynnyng all way!
> Now nothynge but pay, pay,
> With, laughe and lay downe,
> Borowgh, cyte, and towne.

---

[62] See also *Why Come Ye Not to Court*, ll. 343–66.
[63] *Why Come Ye Not to Court*, ll. 914–29.

MAGNIFICENCE

Skelton's opinions on domestic policy are equally clear and place him definitely with the conservative party. His ideas find their most philosophical and least personal expression in the morality play *Magnificence*, which was written about 1516.[64] Ramsay, the learned editor of the play, has shown very clearly that the character of the title role must have been meant for Henry VIII.[65] Magnificence, heir to enormous wealth (Felicity), is led by Fancy and a host of prettily aliased vices to banish Measure and to misuse Liberty. He is consequently reduced to Poverty, Despair, and Mischief. Only when Magnificence recalls his old counsellor, Sad Circumspection, is he brought by Perseverance into Goodhope and Redress.

If King Henry ever saw the play, he must have recognized himself and found it hard to forgive its author. For, like Magnificence, he had inherited a great fortune from his circumspect father, he had spent lavishly on elaborate and fanciful trivialities, and he had turned off the staid council that had guided his predecessor, in favor of a group of untried young men, chief of whom was Thomas Wolsey, once grammar school teacher and rector of Redegrave and shortly to become the most gorgeous of English cardinals and the most powerful chancellor of the realm.

Skelton thus clearly aligned himself with the party out of favor, the older nobility headed by Surrey (Duke of Norfolk after Flodden) and by the Duke of Buckingham, who inevitably grumbled at their own lack of influence and at the rapid elevation to almost supreme power of a person of humble birth. Perhaps it was because the King had once been Skelton's pupil that the poet dared to teach him, to criticize his extravagance and his choice of favor-

[64] *Magnyfycence*, ed. by R. L. Ramsay, "Early English Text Society [Publications]," E. S., XCVIII (1908), xxv.
[65] *Ibid.*, pp. cviii–cx.

ites, and to warn him of impending downfall. At any rate, Skelton was never one to hold his tongue. When critics caviled at the violence of his attack on the King of Scots, he answered,[66] "Si veritatem dico, quare non creditis mihi?" Those who grudge at the truth, "Percase have hollow hearts." Skelton's heart was sound, and he did not hide it.

Despite the fact that *Magnificence* is a play about the court, there is nothing to prove that it was presented there. But it was written during a period in which Skelton was in royal service, within a year of his poems against Sir Christopher Garnesche, which were composed at the King's commandment. It is probable that some of Skelton's plays were performed before the King, though none except *Magnificence* is extant. Warton[67] declares that he has seen a copy of *The Nigramansir; a morall enterlude and a pithie written by Maister Skelton laureate, and plaid before the king [Henry VII] and other estatys at Woodstoke on Palme Sunday*, printed by Wynken de Worde, in 1504.[68] The plot, which Warton summarizes, concerns a trial of Simony and Avarice before the Devil, as judge. Other dramatic pieces are listed in the *Garland of Laurel*. "Vertu, the sovereign interlude" (1. 1177) is a title which suggests a play like *Magnificence*, dealing with the proper conduct of a sovereign. It has already been suggested[69] that the "comedy *Achademios*" (1. 1184) was a Latin exercise in praise of the University of Oxford written in partial fulfillment of the requirements for the degree of Poet Laureate. "Pageants that were played in Ioyows Garde" (1. 1383) need not have been dramatic at all.[70] But it is clear that Skelton wrote several plays, and it is likely that some of them were performed before royalty.

[66] Skelton, *Works*, I, 189.

[67] *The History of English Poetry* (London, 1840), II, 508-11.

[68] Warton has been accused of having invented the *Nigramansir*. See Ramsay *op. cit.*, pp. xviii–xix (n. 2).

[69] See above, p. 49.   [70] Skelton, *Works*, II, 330-331.

MANNERLY MARGERY MILK AND ALE

Skelton also contributed to the lighter entertainments of the court of Henry VIII. He seems to have written numerous songs, chiefly erotic and humorous pieces. Only one of the "many matters of mirth" which Skelton wrote about Mistress Margery Milk and Ale is extant.[71] It is found with a musical setting by Cornish, the King's musician, in the beautiful Fairfax manuscript.[72] Since the book seems to have been the King's property (it contains several songs written by Henry himself) it is to be supposed that Skelton's lyrical talents were appreciated at court. "Mannerly Margery," a burly song about a simple, but not too sweet, rustic lass can scarcely be classed as edifying. Mistress Anne, another of the poet's song subjects, seems to have had the advantage of Margery in beauty and sophistication, if in nothing else. The *Garland* catalogue (ll. 1240–44) mentions a poem about some venison and wine that was to have been sent to the lady, but never reached its destination. The last we hear of the romance, if romance there was, is recorded in "Womanhood, Wanton, Ye Want,"[73] in which Anne is accused of being mercenary and promiscuous. Apparently there really was a Mistress Anne, for her address is given:

> To mastres Anne, that farly swete,
> That wonnes at the Key in Temmys strete.[74]

Numbers of other light pieces which are listed in the *Gar-*

---

[71] *Garland of Laurel*, ll. 1198–1204.

[72] MS Additional 5465, fol. 109; Skelton, *Works*, I, 28–29.

[73] Skelton, *Works*, I, 20–21.

[74] Brie (*Englische Studien*, XXXVII, 29–30) ascribes to Skelton an unsigned song about Mistress Anne scribbled on the fly leaf of Trinity College, Cambridge, MS R. 3. 17. The song must be in the hand of its author, for it contains what are clearly author's corrections. The handwriting, however, bears no resemblance to the Skelton autographs which appear in Corpus Christi College, Cambridge, MS 432 and in Public Record Office MS E. 36–228, pp. 67–69. Since the only reason for thinking the poem Skelton's is that it is addressed to a lady named Anne, I must doubt the validity of the attribution.

land catalogue have been lost. One regrets the disappearance
of "The ballad of the mustard tart" (l. 1245), the "Epito-
mes of the miller and his jolly mate," (ll. 1411–17), "Of
lovers' testaments and of their wanton wills," (l. 1496),
"The repeat of the recule of Rosamund's bower," (l. 1390)
and the "Mourning of the maple root" (l. 1377).

Of serious love lyrics, however, there is a scarcity. One,
couched in marvellously ornate language, complains bit-
terly of a separation.[75] Another,[76] written "at the instance
of a noble lady," bears the burden, "wher I loue best I
dare not dyscure!" But the prettiest of Skelton's lyrics are
to be found in the *Garland of Laurel*. The ladies of the train
of the Countess of Surrey had honored the poet by weaving
a wreath of laurel for him, and he reciprocated by presenting each of them with an appropriate eulogy. Of these, the
poem to Margaret Hussey:

> Mirry Margaret,
> As mydsomer flowre
>   (ll. 1004–5)

is the best known. But the one addressed to little Mistress
Isabell Penell is more reminiscent of the gentle Skelton of
Philip Sparrow:

> By saynt Mary, my lady,
> Your mammy and your dady
> Brought forth a godely babi! . . .
>
> It were an heuenly helth,
> It were an endeles welth,
> A lyfe for God hymselfe,
>   To here this nightingale,
> Amonge the byrdes smale,
> Warbelynge in the vale,
> Dug, dug,
> Iug, iug,
> Good yere and good luk,
> With chuk, chuk, chuk, chuk!
>   (ll. 973–1003)

[75] Skelton, *Works*, I, 25–26.   [76] *Ibid.*, I, 27.

It is a little difficult to reconcile the writing of these trivia with Skelton's reputation for solid learning. The explanation may lie in part in the fact that music was considered an essential part of the grammar school curriculum, and consequently, that skill in music was required of grammarians. Carmeliano, who served Henry VIII both as Latin secretary and as king's luter, illustrates the association between the arts. Skelton, too, had knowledge of music, for in the *Bowge of Court*, Harvy Hafter begs the poet:

> Wolde to God, it wolde please you some daye
> A balade boke before me for to laye,
> And lerne me to synge, Re, my, fa, sol!
> And, whan I fayle, bobbe me on the noll.
>
> (ll. 256–59)

Song writing, therefore, was a justifiable occupation for a Poet Laureate. As for the frivolity and indecency of some of his poems, Skelton offers a rather thin excuse:[77] "The white appeareth the better for the black." That is, the cause of virtue is advanced by the portrayal of vice in its true colors. The explanation may possibly serve for *Elinor Rumming*, but it can hardly be stretched to cover *Philip Sparrow* and the songs about Margery and Anne.

Skelton, in fact, was caught in the eddy between two literary currents. He had been brought up in the tradition which conceived literature to be a means of propagating virtue, and it was this tradition that dominated the English Renaissance of the early Tudor period. But there was another humanist tradition, that which took literature to be a means of giving pleasure. Traces of the more liberal approach are to be found in Skelton's time. There is no great moral lesson to be learned from Thomas More's jest of the Sergeant and the Friar. But neither he nor Skelton was able to justify the merely pleasant muse. It was not until Wyatt and Surrey that it became proper to write learnedly for pleasure alone.

[77] *Garland*, l. 1237.

Sober Alexander Barclay, imbued with a passionate hatred for Venus and all her works, could not tolerate the spectacle of a learned poet descending to matters of mirth and love. At the end of his translation of the *Ship of Fools* (1508) he adds proudly:[78]

> Holde me excusyd: for why my wyll is gode
> Men to induce vnto vertue and goodnes
> I wryte no Iest ne tale of Robyn hode
> Nor sawe no sparcles ne sede of vyciousnes
> Wyse men loue vertue, wylde people wantones
> It longeth nat to my scyence nor cunnynge
> For Phylyp the Sparowe the (Dirige) to synge.

According to the bibliographer, Bale, Barclay wrote a book *Contra Skeltonum*.[79] It is no longer to be found. But scattered through Barclay's works are numbers of denunciations of laureate poets who write ribald, erotic songs. To some extent, these reflect a current reaction against frivolous rhetoricians who employed their high art for the low purposes of amusement. Since Barclay's writing is largely translation, it may be dangerous to accept such passages as representing his opinion of Skelton. Nevertheless, it seems to me probable that even when Barclay was imitating Æneas Silvius or Baptista Mantuanus, his tirades against laureate poets were aimed particularly at the English author of *Philip Sparrow*. The following, for instance, depends upon Mantuan, but it is largely expanded, and the additions seem to be directed at Skelton:[80]

> Then is he decked as Poete laureate,
> When stinking Thais made him her graduate.
> When Muses rested, she did her season note,

[78] Edited by Jamieson (Edinburgh, 1874), II, 331.
[79] Bale, *Index*, p. 19.
[80] *The Eclogues of Alexander Barclay*, ed. by Beatrice White, "Early English Text Society [Publications]," O.S., CLXXV (1928), 165. The corresponding Latin of Mantuan:

> "Hi se nescio qua mentis leuitate poetas
> Esse uolunt postquam triuialibus ora cicutis
> Applicuere. sibi applaudunt: sua carmina iactant."

And she with Bacchus her camous did promote:
Such rascolde dra[n]es[81] promoted by Thais,
Bacchus, Licoris, or yet by Testalis,
Or by suche other newe forged Muses nine
Thinke in their mindes for to haue wit diuine.

Whether or not this was intended as an attack on Skelton,
it seems likely that Skelton took it so. For in the *Garland
of Laurel*, Skelton's account of his own laureation by the
Countess of Surrey, in 1523, it is Bacchus who welcomes all
the poets and orators of antiquity to the celebration. And
in the same poem we are told that round the laurel tree
there danced

the nyne Muses, Pierides by name;
Phillis and Testalis . . .

(ll. 680–81)

It sounds as though Skelton is accepting the challenge and
flaunting his immorality. Also included in the *Garland* is an
attack on the "jangling jays" who "discommend" the
innocent *Philip Sparrow* and shame poor Jane Scroupe
(ll. 1261–1375). A few lines before this invective, Skelton
clearly echoes Barclay's sneering

It longeth nat to my scyence nor cunnynge
For Phylyp the Sparowe the (Dirige) to synge.

Skelton cites some of his light poems, and then says:

To make suche trifels it asketh sum konnyng,
In honest myrth parde requyreth no lack

Suche problemis to paynt it longyth to his [Skelton's] arte

(ll. 1235–36, 1246)

SIR CHRISTOPHER GARNESCHE AND GORBELLIED GODFREY

Although Barclay and Skelton disliked each other, they
also shared an object of dislike. In the first eclogue of his

[81] The text reads *drames* which the editor of the *Eclogues* glosses "dramas, plays."
But it seems probable that the word should be "dranes," *i.e.*, "drones," as in
Skelton's "dronken dranes" (Skelton, *Works*, II, 222).

Miseries of Courtiers (written *c.* 1513), Barclay strikes at a scurrilous fellow named Godfrey Gormand:[82]

> . . . Godfrey Gormand lately did me blame.
> And as for him selfe, though he be gay and stoute,
> He hath nought but foly within and eke without.
> To blowe in a bowle, and for to pill a platter,
> To girne, to braule, to counterfayte, to flatter,
> He hath no felowe betwene this and Croydon,
> Saue the proude plowman (Gnato) of Chorlington.

It seems likely that this objectionable Godfrey Gormand was Gorbellied (Fat) Godfrey, a scribe who, in the name of his master, Sir Christopher Garnesche, carried on a flyting with Skelton about 1514.[83] The correspondence in the dates of the attacks and in the names and characteristics of the two Godfreys is so close that there can be little doubt of the identification. Possibly Godfrey Gobelive, the merrily vicious and abusive dwarf of Hawes' *Pastime of Pleasure* (1508), also represents the stout scribe.[84] Unfortunately, further information about Godfrey is lacking.

Godfrey's patron, Sir Christopher Garnesche, a scion of a well-known Norfolk family, served Henry VIII in the capacity of gentleman usher and sergeant of the Tents.[85] He must have distinguished himself in the fighting in France, for immediately after Tournai was taken Henry VIII dubbed him knight. A few years later Garnesche was able to give a thoroughly romantic proof of his chivalry.

[82] *Op. cit.*, p. 29.

[83] The date is established by H. Stearns, in *Modern Language Notes*, XLIII (1928), 518–23.

[84] Ian Gordon (*London Times Literary Supplement*, Nov. 15, 1934, p. 795), noting the resemblance between Godfrey Gobelive and Gorbellied Godfrey, suggests that Hawes may have been Garnesche's scribe and that Skelton used the name of the character Hawes had created in order to attack him. But since Hawes evidently disapproves of Godfrey Gobelive, it seems to me more likely that both Skelton and Hawes are attacking the same person.

[85] Most of the available information about Garnesche is summarized by Stearns, *loc. cit.* A few additional items may be found in the Addenda volumes of the *Letters and Papers* series.

The King's sister, Lady Mary, on her way to marry King Louis of France, had a very rough Channel crossing,

with great ieopardy at the entryng of the hauen, for the master ran the ship hard on shore, but the botes were redy and receyued this noble lady, and at the landyng Sir Christopher Garnyshe stode in the water and toke her in his armes, and so caryed her to land . . .[86]

According to Skelton (only his side of the quarrel is recorded), Sir Christopher "rudely reviled" him in the King's hall, calling him a knave.[87] Why Garnesche did so, Skelton does not say. A possible clue to their conflict is the circumstance that both Garnesche and Skelton may have been employed in the same government bureau. Garnesche held the office of sergeant of the Tents during the early years of the reign of Henry VIII. Skelton's "Laud and Praise Made for Our Sovereign Lord the King" is found in his own handwriting in an account book devoted to records pertaining to that department.[88] At any rate, Skelton much resented being called a knave, and responded with an outburst of poetical abuse to which Garnesche or his scribe Godfrey replied. The bout continued for several rounds. It seems that the King acted as referee in the encounter, for each of Skelton's poems is subscribed "By the King's most noble commandment," and each bears a title drawn from the language of the tilt yard: "Skelton Laureate Defender against Lusty Garnesche Well Beseen Christopher Challenger." Just how earnest the quarrel was, it is difficult to determine. Undoubtedly it was the occasion of much mirth for the King and his court, and surely, too, at least one of the combatants was conscious of its entertaining aspects. Nevertheless, it is difficult to dismiss the affair as a conventional poetic game of abuse. No man in Sir Christopher's position could have laughed gaily at Skelton's cannonad-

[86] *Hall's Chronicle*, p. 570.
[87] "Poems against Garnesche," Skelton, *Works*, I, 116.
[88] Public Record Office MS E. 36–228, pp. 67–69.

ing. Skelton's attacks include sneering references to Garnesche's recent knighthood, to his ancestry, his appearance, his morals, and his new affluence. Scribe Godfrey (whom Skelton suspects of being the author of Garnesche's replies) is abused for his lack of ingenuity in thinking up epithets and for daring to insult a Poet Laureate. It is a pity that Garnesche's poems have disappeared, for they would surely have thrown a revealing, if unflattering, light on Skelton's life. But from Skelton's defensive answers it is possible to rescue some information. That the poet was at the time in the service of the King is proved by Sir Christopher's threat to slash Skelton's coat of green and white, the colors of the royal livery.[89] Skelton's morals were impeached, and his family was disparaged. The epithets "scald" (scabby) and "mad" were applied to him.[90]

With such literary exercises, weighty and trivial, edifying and entertaining, Skelton, *orator regius*, busied himself:

> Thus passyth he the tyme both nyght and day,
> Sumtyme with sadnes, sumtyme with play[91]

It is difficult to estimate how much of his writing was done in the official capacity of court poet. Only the invectives against Garnesche are expressly asserted to have been written "at the King's most noble commandment." Probably, the poems on Flodden and many of the songs were also composed at the King's request. Perhaps *Magnificence* had a court presentation. But, as I will try to show in the following chapters, the Skelton who returned from Diss could never again restrict himself to the narrow bounds appropriate to an *orator regius*.

[89] Skelton, *Works*, I, 124.   [90] *Ibid.*, I, 120, 128, 130.   [91] *Garland*, ll. 1423–24.

The Grammarians' War

D URING the reign of Henry VII, when Skelton first entered royal service, humanist learning was rare among Englishmen. Foreigners were employed as secretaries and ambassadors; they delivered lectures in the humanities at Oxford and Cambridge. But as soon as it was recognized that rhetorical learning was a key to court favor, the development of English humanism proceeded apace. Under Henry VIII the proportion of alien scholars dwindled markedly. Ruthall, Pace, and John Clerk could speak admirably at the Curia; Thomas Wolsey, Chancellor of England, had once been usher at Magdalen and could write his own Latin letters. A crowd of bright young scholars, many of them boasting knowledge of Greek, dimmed the glory of the first English humanists.

It was inevitable that the rapid growth of the new learning in England should cause disturbance. Keen competition led to continual bickering among the adepts of the rhetorical discipline. The riots of the "Trojans" and the "Greeks" which occurred at Oxford are among the several possible illustrations.

In 1519 there arose a violent grammarians' war in which Skelton participated. The immediate occasion was the publication of rival Latin phrase books, both called *Vulgaria*, by William Horman, head master of Eton, and by Robert Whittinton, a Poet Laureate of Oxford. Until 1519 the field of printed Latin grammars in England had been largely dominated by the works of John Stanbridge (1463–1510), Fellow of New College. His *Vulgaria*[1] was

[1] *The Vulgaria of John Stanbridge and The Vulgaria of Robert Whittinton*, ed. by Beatrice White, "Early English Text Society, [Publications]," O. S., CLXXXVII (1932).

widely used in England, even in so progressive an institution as Colet's school of St. Paul's. In 1519 a new edition
of his book was published, perhaps under the editorship
of his disciple, Whittinton.[2] During the same year Horman
produced a far larger and more elaborate *Vulgaria*, which he
printed at his own expense and undertook to sell himself.[3]
Evidently it usurped the place of Stanbridge's book at St.
Paul's, for it is introduced with commendatory poems by
William Lily, then head master, and by John Rightwise,
then submaster of Colet's foundation. In order to meet the
competition Whittinton prepared a new *Vulgaria*, which
was printed in 1520. Moreover, he answered the challenge
directly. On the door of St. Paul's he hung an epigram for
all the boys to see:[4]

Bossus
Doctrine est censor cantatus Lilius. Ohe
  Hunc licitatorem Cherylus alter habet
Mercibus at nostin quibus. Ipsi vix sibi querunt
  Quas pueri Hormani (noscito cunta) nugiferis
Merx sua scin quanti datur? Octo octussibus. Eheu.
  Lais cara nimis dat penitere procis

Whittinton hits the arrogance of Lily (who had brought
his Greek all the way from Rhodes) and sneers at the high
price of Horman's elaborate treatise. His own *Vulgaria*,
which was considerably shorter, must have been less
expensive.

The epigram fixed to the door of St. Paul's led to a
quarrel between Lily and Horman on the one hand and
Whittinton on the other. The chief documents of the
controversy are two curious volumes, the *Antibossicon* of
William Lily and another *Antibossicon* by Horman, both
printed by Pynson, in 1521. The titles are explained by
Whittinton's assumption of the name "Bossus," perhaps
chosen with reference to the "boss" of Billingsgate, a

[2] *Ibid.*, p. xix.   [3] *Ibid.*, p. xxv.
[4] The epigram is included in Lily's *Antibossicon* (Pynson, 1521), Sig. A8.

bear-shaped fountain erected by Richard Whittington, the
famous lord mayor of London. The name proved a boomer-
ang: Lily's book is illustrated with a woodcut of a bear
being attacked by six dogs, and the first of the attacks on
Whittinton included in the volume is a celebration of the
nuptials of "Bossa," the bear of Billingsgate (a district
already notorious for abusive language), and "Bossus,"
her perfect mate, the stony-headed, insolent Whittinton.
There is nothing to be gained from a detailed account of
Lily's poems, since they consist for the most part of an
impeachment of the grammatical correctness of Whittinton's poems in abuse of Lily. One section is devoted to
Whittinton's proud boast of his possession of the laurel.[5]
Lily points out that the Romans honored their poets, not
with the laurel, which was reserved for conquerors, but
with the ivy. Horman's *Antibossicon* is no more edifying. It
includes a poetical epistle from Horman to Lily, an "invective letter" from Whittinton to Horman, a letter from
Robert Aldrich (another master at Eton and contributor of
a commendatory poem to Horman's *Vulgaria*), and finally
"Apologeticon Hormani ad protouatem bifarium," which
forms the bulk of the book. The "Apology" is in two sections—the first, Horman's defense of himself; the second, a
detailed examination of his rival's grammars, particularly
the *Vulgaria*, in which Horman gleefully points out Whittinton's slips.

There are several other contributions to the quarrel
which have not previously been noticed. The most important is *Antilycon in defensionem Roberti Whitintoni in
florentissima oxoniensi Achademia Laureati / contra quendam
Zoilum suæ grammaticæ oblatrantem sub lyci prosopopeia*,
printed by Wynken de Worde on January 5, 1521.[6] Aside

[5] Sig. E 4–F 1.

[6] An apparently unique copy of this pamphlet is preserved in the library of the
Duke of Devonshire, who has kindly permitted a photostatic copy to be made.
The copy has been deposited in the library of Columbia University. It is with per-
mission of the Duke of Devonshire that I quote from the book.

from a few pieces quoted in the *Antibossicons* of Lily and
Horman, the *Antilycon* is all that remains extant of Whittinton's part in the controversy. The object of the attack
is apparently Lily:

> Se scire solum hoc inquit ille Socrates
> Se nescium. sed hic (sua est quæ inscitia)
> Quid scire se non arrogat? scientulus
> Græcissat. vnde cuique se scientiæ
> Antistitem putat. vel hunc Apollinem.
> Doctos tot inter quos fouet terra anglica
> Est censor ecquis?[7]

As Lily attacks Whittinton under the allegory of a bear, so
Whittinton abuses Lily under the figure of a wolf. The
book includes Whittinton's invective against his critic, a
dialogue between the Reader and the Wolf, another between the Laurel and Pallas, and a complaint of the Nine
Muses. It is most obscurely written, evidently in imitation
of the allusive manner of Persius.

Another document of the quarrel is an epigram written
by a pupil of Lily, John Constable, which was published
in 1520 under the title "In Bossum Liliomastigem:"[8]

> Heus subito tacuit / vidit sua carmina Bossus
>   Quum vicijs toties stulta scatere malis.
> Quunque pari nequeat conatu vincere vatem /
>   Suppudet: et versus iam negat esse suos.
> Euome de anguineo libeat si pectore virus:
>   Nil nocet egregio perfida lingua viro.

A third fragment of the controversy may possibly be
represented by "The Maryage of London Stone and the
Fayre Pusell the Bosse of Byllyngesgate." This anonymous
poem is appended to the second edition (*c.* 1522) of the also

---

[7] Sig. A 1. Lily refers sneeringly to the *Antilycon* in the second section of his
Antibossicon (Sig. C 1.).

[8] *Ioannis Constablii Londinensis et artium professoris epigrammata.* Ex officina
Richardi Pynsonis / nonis Septembris [1520]. Cum priuilegio a rege indulto.
Sig. D 2.

anonymous *Treatyse of This Galaunt*.[9] If "Whittinton" be
substituted for "London Stone," the piece becomes perfectly parallel to Lily's epithalamium on the marriage of
"Bossus" and "Bossa." The author asks that the reader
rejoice at the marriage of London Stone, "He that in
sclaunder / ony wyll dysclose," and remarks that the
wedded pair form a perfect match. The date and the substance of the poem strongly suggest that it relates to the
war of the grammarians. And it is not impossible that the
piece was written by Lily himself.

Although the controversy is in major part both abusive
and trivial, there is an important educational problem involved. One group of grammarians held that the best
method of teaching Latin was by "imitation" of classical
examples; the other minimized the value of imitation and
insisted that "precepts," grammatical rules, were the essential basis of instruction. Horman's *Vulgaria* is a loose
topical arrangement of a large number of Latin sentences,
quoted or adapted from classical authors, together with
English translations. It was intended, obviously, that the
student compare his own translation of the Latin with
Horman's English. The topical arrangement facilitated the
preparation of themes, for if the student was ever in need
of an apt quotation on any subject, all he had to do was to
leaf the pages of his *Vulgaria*. The process of learning was
therefore primarily a matter of "imitation." Whittinton's
book, on the other hand, is divided, not topically, but in
accordance with the grammatical principles illustrated. At
the head of each section is a grammatical rule, or "precept,"
which is followed by a series of examples, in both Latin
and English versions, by which the rule is driven home.
The examples are sometimes culled from the classics, but
more frequently they are Whittinton's own. The introduc-

[9] Wynken de Worde, n. d. "The Maryage of London Stone" is reprinted in
W. C. Hazlitt, *Early Popular Poetry of England* (London, 1866), III, 161–63.

tion to his *Vulgaria* makes explicit the contrast between his method and that of Horman.[10] He denounces the stupid insolence of those teachers who put imitation before precept, who lead their unfortunate pupils into the immense labor of blindly reading and aping the classics without providing them first with instruction in grammar. Boys so taught can cheat their parents by a display of flashy scraps of erudition, but any competent examiner will discover their ignorance in a few moments of questioning.

To such strictures Horman replies with equal ill temper.[11] A few precepts are certainly necessary for the beginner, but classical excellence can be attained only by the imitation of classical authors. Whittinton's abominable Latin style is proof that teaching by precept leads to unfortunate results. A fuller statement of Horman's position is contributed by Colet, the founder of St. Paul's School.[12] If a man wishes, he says,

to vnderstande latyn bokes, and to speke and to wryte the clene latyn, let hym aboue all besyly lerne & rede good latyn authours of chosen poetes and oratours, and note wysely how they wrote and spake, and studi alway to folowe them: desyryng none other rules but theyr examples . . . For redyng of good bokes, diligent informacyon of taught maysters, studyous aduertence & takynge hede of lerners, heryng eloquent men speke, and fynally [b]esy imitacyon with tongue and penne, more auayleth shortly to gete the true eloquent speche than al the tradicions, rules, and preceptes of maysters.

The difference between Horman and Whittinton is the same as that which had split Colet's friendship with Linacre some years before.[13] Whittinton, like Linacre a conservative humanist, believes that before good Latin can be achieved there must be a sound foundation of grammar. Horman is willing to concede that some grammatical

---

[10] *Op. cit.*, pp. 33–34.   [11] For example, *Antibossicon*, Sig. G 7.
[12] Colet's *Æditio*, quoted in J. H. Lupton, *A Life of John Colet* (London, 1887), pp. 291–92.
[13] See S. Knight, *The Life of Dr. John Colet* (London, 1724), pp. 135–39.

instruction is necessary, but he places his emphasis on the imitation of the classics. His students memorize fewer rules than Whittinton's and begin reading much earlier. The controversy resolves itself, therefore, into something very much like the modern quarrel between those who advocate the so-called "direct method" of teaching languages and those who believe that a long preparation of grammatical study cannot be dispensed with.

Skelton threw himself into the quarrel on Whittinton's side. In *Speak, Parrot*, written in 1521,[14] when the controversy was at its height, there occurs a passage clearly commenting on the grammarians' war (ll. 181-87):

> *Plauti* in his comedies a chyld shall now reherse,
>   And medyll with Quintylyan in his Declamacyons,
> That Pety Caton can scantly construe a verse,
>   With *Aveto in Græco*, and such solempne salutacyons,
>   Can skantly the tensis of his coniugacyons;
> Settynge theyr myndys so moche of eloquens,
> That of theyr scole maters lost is the hole sentens.

Skelton is even more conservative in his educational theory than Whittinton. He agrees with his brother in the laurel in condemning the slurred treatment of grammar and the hasty introduction to the classics which mark the practice of Horman and his sympathizers. But he goes further. Himself a student of eloquence, he feels that the trend toward glorification of expression as opposed to content has gone too far. Rhetoric has been allowed a weedy growth, at the expense not only of grammar, but also of logic and the other liberal arts (ll. 171-73):

> Tryuyals and quatryuyals so sore now they appayre,
> That Parrot the popagay hath pytye to beholde
> How the rest of good lernyng is roufled vp and trold.

Particularly is this true with respect to the new enthusiasm for Greek, a movement of which Lily is an outstanding

[14] See below, pp. 161 ff.

representative. Skelton is by no means an opponent of the study of Greek. But he feels that the young scholars who boast a knowledge of the language are interested only in reading the Greek classics and writing in imitation of them. Such learning has little justification, Skelton believes. Expression for the sake of expression has no value. A language is useful primarily for what it can convey (ll. 147–52):

> For *aurea lingua Græca* ought to be magnyfyed,
> Yf it were cond perfytely, and after the rate,
> As *lingua Latina*, in scole matter occupyed;
> But our Grekis theyr Greke so well haue applyed,
> That they cannot say in Greke, rydynge by the way,
> How, hosteler, fetche my hors a botell of hay!

There is also a bit of sniping at no less a person than Erasmus (ll. 158–59):

> For they scrape out good scrypture, and set in a gall,
> Ye go about to amende, and ye mare all.

The lines clearly refer to the second edition of Erasmus' text of the New Testament in which Jerome's Latin was "amended" by reference to the Greek.

Aside from the passages in *Speak, Parrot*, none of Skelton's contribution to the literature of the grammarians' war remains. Yet it is clear that he was further involved. In 1519 Whittinton published a long ode in praise of Skelton in a volume which includes poems addressed to the King, to Wolsey, and to Sir Thomas More.[15] Though the elegant eulogy of Skelton runs to 136 lines, carefully wrought as an acrostic,[16] it contains very little information.

---

[15] *Opusculum Roberti Whittintoni in florentissima Oxoniensi achademia laureati.* At the end, "Expliciunt Roberti whitintoni Oxonie Protouatis Epygrammata: vna cum quibusdam Panegyricis Impressa Londini per me wynandum de worde. Anno post virgineum partum. M. CCCCCxix. decimo vero kalendas Maij."

[16] The first letters of the hexameters read:
"Quæ Whitintonus canit ad laudes tibi, Schelton,
Anglorum vatum gloria, sume libens."
The poem is reprinted in Skelton, *Works*, I, xvi–xix.

The statements that Skelton had been made Laureate at Louvain and that he was a famous rhetorician exhaust the biographical matter. It must be concluded that Whittinton did not know Skelton personally at the time, that he addressed the eulogy to him because Skelton was a brother Laureate and in court favor. But perhaps the eulogy stimulated a friendship which led Skelton to take Whittinton's part in his quarrel with Lily and Horman.

That Skelton did attack Lily directly is learned from a note contributed by William Horman to Bale's notebook.[17] Horman declares that Skelton wrote an invective against Lily of 64 verses, beginning: "Vrgeor impulsus tibi Lille retundere dentes." An epigram which Lily wrote against Skelton remains extant. It was translated by Fuller:[18]

> With face so bold, and teeth so sharp,
> Of viper's venome, why dost carp?
> Why are my verses by thee weigh'd
> In a false scale? may truth be said?
> Whilst thou to get the more esteem
> A learned Poet fain wouldst seem,
> Skelton, thou art, let all men know it,
> Neither learned, nor a Poet.[19]

Skelton's part in the grammarians' war is interesting chiefly because it shows that his educational tenets were consistent with his opinions on other subjects. A conservative in politics and religion, he was also suspicious of newfangled methods of teaching. Although he was an

[17] Bale, *Index*, pp. 252–53.
[18] *Worthies* (*Norfolk*) (1662), p. 257; Skelton, *Works*, I, xxxviii. The Latin reads: "Lilii Hendecasyllabi in Scheltonum ejus carmina calumniantem.
> Quid me, Scheltone, fronte sic aperta
> Carpis, vipereo potens veneno?
> Quid versus trutina meos iniqua
> Libras? dicere vera num licebit?
> Doctrinæ tibi dum parare famam
> Et doctus fieri studes poeta,
> Doctrinam nec habes, nec es poeta."
[19] Wood declares (*Athenæ*, I, 34) that Lily wrote another piece against Skelton:
> "*Apologia ad* $\begin{cases} Joh.\ Skeltonum \\ Rob.\ Whittington \end{cases}$"

adept of the humanist discipline of rhetoric, he did not believe that rhetoric was the whole of learning. His attitude toward Greek was similarly conservative. He granted that it was a golden language, but denied that it had value apart from its useful applications. For Skelton, eloquence remained the handmaid of virtue and religion.

Speak, Parrot[1]

> For in this processe Parrot nothing hath surmysed,
> No matter pretendyd, nor nothyng enterprysed,
> But that *metaphora*, *allegoria* with all,
> Shall be his protectyon, his pauys, and his wall.
>
> (ll. 205–8)

THE WALL of metaphor and allegory that Skelton built around his *Parrot* perhaps served to keep off the pursuivants of his archenemy, Cardinal Wolsey; certainly it has proved a formidable obstacle to the comprehension of the reader of today. Most of Skelton's commentators have avoided the poem. Those who have tried to elucidate it have restricted themselves to notes on scattered passages. There has been but one reasoned attempt to understand *Speak, Parrot* as a whole,[2] and since that argument derives from what I believe to be an erroneous date, it arrives at no satisfactory conclusion.

The difficulty of *Speak, Parrot* resides, first, in the protective confusion in which Skelton shrouded it. Intentional obscurity was fashionable in Renaissance satire, but in the case of *Speak, Parrot* it was more than a convention;

[1] The substance of this chapter and of the following one was originally published in *PMLA*, LI (1936), 59–82, 377–98. It is reprinted here by permission of the publisher. As they now appear the chapters have been divested of discussion of the work of earlier investigators and are restricted to exposition of my own theses. The reader who wishes to compare the interpretations of other students of Skelton with that here presented is referred to my original publication in *PMLA*. Certain other changes have been made, partly as a result of the discussion between Mr. H. L. R. Edwards and myself which was published in *PMLA*, LIII (1938), 601–22. These changes include a strengthening of the central argument with new evidence discovered by Mr. Edwards and myself and an elimination of such debatable passages as add nothing to the primary theses. I have also included some additional matter designed to round out the discussion.

[2] J. M. Berdan, " 'Speke, Parrot;' An Interpretation of Skelton's Satire," *Modern Language Notes*, XXX (1915), 140–44. The same author's "The Dating of Skelton's Satires," *PMLA*, XXIX (1914), 499–516, also contains relevant material.

it was a device calculated to answer an acute need. For, as the following discussion purports to prove, the poem was a direct onslaught on the most powerful man in England, Cardinal Wolsey. If Skelton wished to keep his head, he had to guard his speech.

A second difficulty depends upon the fact that the poem was probably not written as a unit, nor circulated as a unit. It dealt with current affairs, and as events succeeded each other Skelton added to his original composition, and he probably deleted what was no longer timely. That he did so seems the best explanation of the fact that *Speak, Parrot* is found in two almost entirely different versions, one represented by the early editions,[3] the other by a manuscript of the Harleian collection.[4]

The printed text opens with a description of Parrot, his habitat, natural endowments, and learned accomplishments. He is many languaged and much in favor with the ladies. There follow thirteen stanzas (ll. 52–142), clearly satirical in intent, but otherwise not clear at all. Then commences an attack on the new academic trend to Greek, and a lament on the decay of the *trivium* and *quadrivium* —in short, of all sound learning. A prayer for the "suffrage ornate" of "rhetoricians and orators in fresh humanity," and several stanzas on Parrot's attribute of immortality bring the poem to a close.

The manuscript version breaks off at line 59 of the printed text, just at the beginning of the satirical section. It contains nothing of the body of the printed poem save a few lines of the conclusion. But it continues beyond that point to form the only text for a substantial section of added matter, which is composed chiefly of a group of discrete compositions: "Lenuoy primere," "Secunde Lenuoy," "Le dereyn Lenveoy," "Lenvoy royall," "Le

[3] *Here after folweth certayne bokes compyled by mayster Skelton*, in several undated editions, and *Pithy pleasaunt and profitable workes of maister Skelton*, Marshe, 1568.
[4] MS Harleian 2252, fols. 133–39.

Popagay sen va complayndre," an attack on the "franticness" that "doth rule," and a poem of ten stanzas declaring that such evils have never been seen "since Deucalion's flood." Interspersed among these are various smaller parcels and some lines of Latin verse.

For convenience, the poem as a whole may be split into two gross divisions, the first including the text as it appears in the printed versions, the second consisting of the added matter which appears only in the manuscript.[5]

The modern reader has an additional obstacle to his comprehension. When the poem was first circulated, the issues which it touched were alive and ready to the intellect. A single telling word would then have constituted a sufficient key to a particular subject of current talk. Although, it is true, the enormous collection of *Letters and Papers of the Reign of Henry VIII* makes it possible for the student to immerse himself in the affairs of the period, it cannot supply him with the emphasis and the meaning which those affairs had for the early sixteenth century. But aside from this difficulty, one which is inevitable to the study of all ancient political writings, the interpretation of *Speak, Parrot* has been particularly confused because the poem lacks a date. Since the satire is cautiously obscure, it is dangerous to attempt to date it on the basis of topical allusions alone. Attempts to assign a date to the poem on such evidence have resulted in widely varying conclusions. An allegory intended to describe a given political situation will often fit a dozen other situations as well. Unless an accurate date can be determined before the allusions are examined, therefore, no interpretation of so obscure a poem as *Speak, Parrot* can be accepted as valid.

[5] There is some difficulty in indicating the precise point of the division. Lines 269–79, which, in the early printed versions, follow line 237 and close the poem, appear in the manuscript following lines 238–68. Lines 238–68 consist of a love song composed by Parrot at the request of Galathea. This song is found only in the manuscript. For a discussion of the intermediate section, lines 238–79, see *PMLA*, LIII, 601 ff., sec. 2 (1).

SKELTON'S CALENDAR

At this impasse, Skelton himself takes a hand. Mindful of the hardships of posterity, he scatters through the second part of *Speak, Parrot* certain hints as to the time of writing. Characteristically, he makes the interpretation of these hints as difficult as he can. The dates run:

1. Penultimo die Octobris, 33° (Lenuoy primere)
2. In diebus Novembris, 34 (Secunde Lenuoy)
3. 15 kalendis Decembris, 34 (Le dereyn Lenveoy)
4. Kalendis Decembris, 34 (after l. 355)
5. 34 (after l. 373)
6. 34 (end of the poem)

Surely "33" and "34," occurring as they do in connection with month and day, represent years in some system of chronology. But no system in common use accounts for them.[6]

At the end of Skelton's *Why Come Ye Not to Court*, there again occurs the mysterious numeral "xxxiiii." Fortunately this fact does not add further difficulty to what is already difficult enough. For *Why Come Ye Not to Court* is by no means so obscure a poem as *Speak, Parrot*. Political characters appearing under their own names are freely and openly criticized. The air of timely comment throughout the poem: "What news, what news?" (l. 230), "What hear ye of the Scots?" (l. 259), "Is Master Mewtas dead?" (l. 784), gives the impression that the satire was written almost immediately after the events it discusses. The first datable allusion in *Why Come*, to Wolsey's mission to Calais (July–November, 1521), does appear to designate an event considerably earlier than the rest. However, it is placed definitely in the past tense:

[6] "That these figures may refer to the year of the century is impossible, because Skelton died in 1529; that they may refer to the year of the reign of Henry VII is equally impossible, because he was on the throne but twenty-three years." Berdan, *Early Tudor Poetry* (New York, 1920), p. 176. Chronologies based on the regnal year of Henry VIII or on the poet's age offer no better solution.

> The countrynge at Cales
> Wrang vs on the males:
> Chefe counselour was carelesse
>   (ll. 74-76)

In contrast, the "What news?," "What hear ye?" vein
marks mention of events of summer and fall of 1522:
Surrey's expedition against the French coast from July to
October of that year (ll. 150-65), the French attack,
which, it was supposed, was forming at Montreuil (ll. 374-
75), the activities of the wardens of the Northern marches
(ll. 269-96), and the election of a goldsmith, Sir John
Mundy, as mayor of London (ll. 897-911). Mundy's election, the latest event mentioned in the poem,[7] occurred on
October 28, the old Lord Mayor's Day.

The bearing of this discussion upon the date of *Speak,
Parrot* is obvious. For if the "xxxiiii" with which *Why
Come Ye Not to Court* concludes be taken as a designation of
the time of events transpiring in October, 1522, the tan-
talizing "Penultimo die Octobris, 33" following "Lenuoy
primere" of *Parrot* must mean October 30, 1521. The following temporal indications: "In diebus Novembris, 34,"
"15 kalendis Decembris, 34," and "Kalendis Decembris,
34" are then susceptible of two interpretations. The change
from "33" to "34" may represent the passage of a year,
which would place the composition of that part of *Speak,
Parrot* following line 301 in late 1522. But internal evidence
forbids such a conclusion. "Lenuoy primere," thus removed from the rest by more than a year, is almost perfectly parallel to "Secunde Lenuoy" and "Le dereyn
Lenveoy," immediately after it in the text. Each requests a
character, whose identity is veiled, to return from over-
seas. Each satirizes that character. Each concludes with a

---

[7] There are allusions to a recent infection of Wolsey's eye in ll. 1178-98. If this
infection is the same as the disease mentioned in certain dispatches among the
Letters and Papers (III, Nos. 2661, 2684), it must have begun to trouble Wolsey
about November 1, 1522.

diatribe on Skelton's detractors, who criticize what they
do not comprehend. And to each is appended the motto
"Morda puros mal desires," followed by the date. Surely
the three envoys cannot plausibly be separated by any ex-
tensive interval. The close sequence of the first four dates,
if we ignore the annual numbers—October 30, in the days
of November, November 17, and December 1—suggests
another interpretation. Skelton's chronological scheme corresponds to no familiar one. His New Year's Day is therefore in all probability neither January 1 nor March 25. Nor
does it celebrate the enthronement of a king. If we are permitted to suppose that it honors some other event, one
which fell between October 30 and "in the days of November," there is no longer any conflict between the dating
and the internal evidence, for the change from "33" to
"34" from the first to the second envoy indicates an interval, not of a year, but of a few days. On this hypothesis
Skelton's numerals resolve themselves thus:

Penultimo die Octobris, 33	October 30, 1521
In diebus Novembris, 34	November, 1521
15 kalendis Decembris, 34	November 17, 1521
Kalendis Decembris, 34	December 1, 1521
34	December, 1521 or early (?) 1522

The whole second section of *Speak, Parrot* gains considerably in unity.

The suggested arrangement does not conflict with a
possible date for *Why Come Ye Not to Court*. The completion
of that poem must precede the end of Year 34, according to
the hypothesis either October 31 or early November, 1522,
and it must follow October 28, 1522, when Sir John Mundy
was inducted into office. If the argument be valid, there is
left a very short period during which the poem must have
been finished.

The group of consequences thus tentatively derived receives striking support from a curious device which follows

Skelton's autograph[8] of "A Laud and Praise Made for Our Sovereign Lord the King,"[9] a panegyric written in honor of the coronation of Henry VIII (June 24, 1509). As the illustration opposite shows, in the loop depending from the "S" of Skelton's motto, "Bien men souient," there are inscribed the numerals "21°." The villainous scrawl flanking the loop probably reads "Deo gratias." This "21°" looks suspiciously of the character of the 33 and 34 found in *Speak, Parrot* and *Why Come Ye Not to Court*. If Year 34 ended in November, 1522, Year 21 ended in November, 1509. Year 21 thus included precisely the period in which Skelton must have written his coronation poem. The dates fit so neatly that there can be little doubt of the correctness of the interpretation offered.

There is another instance of Skelton's use of his calendar. On a dedicatory leaf of the copy of the *Chronique de Rains* which Skelton presented to Henry VIII (Corpus Christi College, Cambridge, MS 432) there occurs a similar "Bien men souien" device, this time with the number "24°" in the loop (see the illustration on page 174). On another leaf of the same dedication, "24°" appears again, now in connection with a scrawled "Deo gratias."[10] The discovery serves as additional evidence for the proposed interpretation of Skelton's calendar. His presentation of the volume must follow June, 1509, for he addressed the book to Henry VIII. Since Skelton does not sign himself *orator regius*, he probably gave the book to the king before May, 1512.[11] If the meaning assigned to 33 and 34 in *Speak, Parrot* and in *Why Come Ye Not to Court* is correct, the 24° of the gift volume must refer to the period, November, 1511–November, 1512.

[8] See Appendix V.
[9] Public Record Office, MS E. 36–228, pp. 67–69; Skelton, *Works*, I, *ix–xi*.
[10] The "Deo gratias, 24°" in the *Chronique de Rains* was first noticed by H. L. R. Edwards (*PMLA*, LIII [1938], 601).
[11] See above, p. 122.

PAGE FROM "A LAUD AND PRAISE MADE FOR OUR SOVEREIGN
LORD THE KING"
PUBLIC RECORD OFFICE MS E36-228, PAGE 69

There is good reason to suppose, therefore, that the second section of *Speak, Parrot* (that in which the calendar numbers appear) was written during the fall of 1521. The clearly distinguishable first section (that which is found in the early printed editions) was probably composed not long before, but it is impossible to date it with precision. Consequently, the second portion of the satire will be discussed first. Since the parcels composing it are quite discrete, there will be no violence done to the structure of the poem if the various dark places are analyzed, not in their actual sequence, but in an order best fitted to show the strength of the present hypothesis.

THE SECOND PART OF *Speak, Parrot*

In the autumn of 1521 Wolsey was at Calais.[12] It is not necessary to enter into the controversy concerning the political motives of the conference which he was attending there, since the intricacy of those motives found no reflection in Skelton's comment. France and the Empire were at war. Henry VIII was formally the ally of both Francis I and Charles V, and on the basis of the treaties of alliance, both monarchs demanded his military aid. Henry, either because he did not feel ready to declare himself or, more doubtfully, because of a genuine desire to keep the peace, persuaded the warring rulers to agree to a conference over which Cardinal Wolsey, acting for the King of England, was to preside. Accordingly Wolsey left Dover for Calais on August 1, 1521, with an elaborate entourage—so elaborate, in fact, that Secretary Pace requested the Cardinal to send back some of the courtiers to repopulate the empty halls of the King's palace. *Monsieur le médiateur* played the difficult diplomatic game as he could, listened to the extravagant demands of both parties, cajoled, haggled, and

---

[12] The material for this summary is taken largely from Brewer's introduction to Vol. III of *Letters and Papers, Foreign and Domestic, of the Reign of Henry VIII* (London, 1867) and from the documents of the period included in that volume.

threatened. But it became more and more apparent to which side English policy really leaned. Wolsey, on some slight pretext, left the French ambassadors to twiddle their thumbs at Calais, while he spent three weeks at Bruges in conference with Emperor Charles, arranging details for a royal marriage and plans for a combined attack on France. English gentlemen appeared in the Emperor's army at the siege of Ardes. There was an exodus of English students from Paris. Of course the conference did not succeed, if success would have meant the attainment of a truce. Wolsey returned to England on November 28, 1521, having accomplished nothing more tangible in the way of peace than a temporary agreement safeguarding the fishing fleets of the three nations. Henry, in consideration of his chancellor's unusual expenses, endowed him with the revenues of the rich abbey of St. Albans and tried to secure his election as pope on the death of Leo, in December, 1521. The following year, England and France were at war.

It is in the period of this conference that the present hypothesis places the first three envoys (ll. 280–345) of the second part of *Speak, Parrot*. Each of these envoys requests the person to whom it is addressed to return over the sea. The fourth envoy is dated "Kalendis Decembris, 34"—if the reasoning be correct, shortly after Wolsey's departure for England—and neither in this nor in later sections is the plea for a homecoming repeated. The correspondence[13] seems sufficiently striking to justify the following reconsideration of some of the obscurities of the poem.

1. "Our sullen Sir Sydrake" of "Le dereyn Lenveoy" is told that

> . . the maters he mellis in com to small effecte;
> For he wantythe of hys wyttes that all wold rule alone;
> Hyt is no lytyll bordon to bere a grete mylle stone
>
> (ll. 328–30)

---

[13] Independently noted by I. A. Gordon, in *London Times Literary Supplement*, February 1, 1934, p. 76.

Skelton adds that this "senator"

> . . . may now come agayne as he wente,
> *Non sine postica sanna*, as I trowe,
> From Calys to Dovyr, to Caunterbury in Kente
>   (ll. 338–40)

This is exactly the itinerary which the Cardinal followed when he "went."

> And thus honorably accompanied he rode through London the .xxv. day of Iuly . . . Thus passed he to Cantorbury where tharchebishop, and the bishop of Cantorbury and other places [prelates?] receiued him in pontificalibus. . . . the .viii. day of Iulye he came to Douer: the xx. day he and thother Lordes with their retinues toke passage, & ariued at Calayce in safetie. . . .[14]

Calais to Dover to Canterbury would have been the route taken by the Cardinal had he "come as he went."

2. "Sullen Signor Sadoke" is the subject of "Secunde Lenuoy."

> With porpose and graundepose he may fede hym fatte,
>   Thowghe he pampyr not hys paunche with the grete seall:
> We haue longyd and lokyd long tyme for that,
>   Whyche cawsythe pore suters haue many a hongry mele:
> As presydent and regente he rulythe every deall.
>   (ll. 309–13)

When Wolsey went to Calais he took that indispensable instrument, the great seal of England, with him. So much inconvenience was caused that Pace, Henry's secretary, found it necessary to write to the Cardinal asking that the seal be sent back with the Master of Rolls, for the lack of it had postponed the Michaelmas term, with consequent injury to the King's revenue.[15] Mention of Wolsey's possession of the seal is not omitted from the chronicles:

---

[14] *Hall's Chronicle* (1809), pp. 624–25.—The dates are clearly wrong, but the itinerary is given correctly. The Cardinal was at Canterbury on July 31, at Dover, August 1, and at Calais, August 2 (*Letters and Papers*, III, Nos. 1453, 1458).

[15] *State Papers* (*Henry VIII*), I, 70–71.

It is to suppose the Emperor knewe of the Commission geuen to the sayd Cardinal, whiche had the kynges power as if his grace had been present, and also had the great seal with him, which had not been seen before.

Duryng the continuaunce of the Cardinall in Calayce all writtes and patentes wer there by him sealed and no shyriffes chosen for lacke of his presence.[16]

The scarcity of grants listed in the *Letters and Papers* for the months of the Calais conference[17] shows what slender meals the poor suitors digested. While Wolsey gorged on porpoise and grampus, all England suffered from lack of the seal.

3. "Lenuoy primere" is considerably the most difficult of the three sections here supposed to allude to the Calais conference. Parrot is told (ll. 282–91) to persuade "Jerobesethe" "home to resort,"

> For the cliffes of Scaloppe they rore wellaway,
>   And the sandes of Cefas begyn to waste and fade,
>   For replicacion restles that he of late ther made;
> Now Neptune and Eolus ar agreed of lyclyhode,
> For Tytus at Dover abydythe in the rode;
>
> Lucina she wadythe among the watry floddes,
>   And the cokkes begyn to crowe agayne the day;
> *Le tonsan de Jason* is lodgid among the shrowdes,
>   Of Argus revengyd, recover when he may;
>   Lyacon of Libyk and Lydy hathe cawghte hys pray:

"Cefas" is the key. Every educated person of Skelton's time would have known that it occurs in the Bible as another name for Saint Peter.[18] The verse must then read, "The sands of Saint Peter. . ."—probably a place name. Many localities are so designated. But there is a "Saint Peter's" in France which was also known as "Dampierre-lez-Dunes" (Saint Peter of the Dunes), from its situation

---

[16] *Hall's Chronicle*, pp. 625, 627.

[17] *Letters and Papers*, III; No. 1531 (August): 3 grants; No. 1621 (September): 6 grants; No. 1725 (October): 8 grants; No. 1818 (November): 6 grants. In July, the month before the trip to Calais, there were 38 grants (No. 1451).

[18] John i. 42; I Cor. i. 12; iii. 22; ix. 5; xv. 5; Gal. ii. 9.

on a sandy moor. There is also a village on a sea coast bluff (Cap Blanc-Nez) variously called "Scales," "Scala," and in French "Escalles," "Ecailloux," and "Escailles" (meaning "oyster" and perhaps "scallop"). Both Saint Peter's and Scales are in the environs of Calais—Saint Peter's was later joined to it, and Scales is only eight miles away.[19] "There" of "replication restless that he of late there made" refers both to "Cefas" and to "Scaloppe," that is, to Calais, a town Skelton could not have openly named at that time without immediately being accused of attacking the Cardinal, but to which he might allude under these veiled names of its neighbors. At Calais in the course of this conference there were many "restless" answers. Perhaps the one here involved is that of Wolsey to the French ambassadors on October 16, in which the Cardinal threatened France with the antagonism of the civilized world if his terms for a cessation of hostilities were not accepted, pointed to the compliance of Henry VIII with the wishes of Francis in the matter of the truce with the Scots, and bewailed the expense in time and money entailed by his embassy.[20]

"Le tonsan de Jason" provides another clue to the topic of the envoy. For contemporaries of Skelton the expression must have meant the Order of Jason's Fleece, probably the most famous and influential of the knightly societies of the day. The order was in effect the highest council of Burgundy, and even the Emperor Charles had to explain his actions to its assembly. When Charles visited England in 1522, the golden fleece was the theme of the pageants set about London in his honor.[21] Moreover, the fleece was used as a metaphor for the Low Countries in an anonymous poem

[19] *Dictionnaire topographique du Département du Pas-de-Calais* (Paris, 1907), *s.v.* Saint-Pierre-lez-Calais, Escalles.

[20] *Letters and Papers*, III, No. 1683.

[21] See C. R. Baskervill, "William Lily's Verse for the Entry of Charles V into London," *The Huntington Library Bulletin*, IX (1936), 1–14.

written about the same time: "A king to wear a Flemish fleece, all Saxons shall it rue."[22] The "tonsan" is therefore a figure for Charles V, the head of the order.

A third point of reference for the reconstruction of "Lenuoy primere" is the name "Lyacon" in line 291. It appears a second time in *Speak, Parrot*, in line 393, where it almost certainly stands for Wolsey. Dyce supposes, and it seems reasonable to suppose, that the word should be "Lycaon."[23] The evil king whom Jupiter turned into a wolf connotes viciousness and opposition to majesty, and at the same time provides opportunity for a pun on the cardinal's name: "lycaonta marinum," "maris lupus," that is, "wolf-sea."[24] Line 428 of *Parrot* speaks of "His wolf's head" which "gapeth over the crown," certainly a reference to the cardinal and probably intended as another phonetic equivalent of "Wolsey."

The combination of Calais ("Scaloppe" and "Cefas"), Charles V ("*Le tonsan de Jason*"), Wolsey ("Lyacon"), and the date in October can scarcely be set in any situation other than the meeting of 1521. But the meaning of the envoy remains obscure. Parrot is to request Wolsey to return home. Calais is in terror (mock terror, it may be assumed) at his latest "replication." Neptune and Eolus are in concord; that is, the channel is calm. The moon is set; day dawns. Wolsey, the great ambassador, has circumvented the wily Charles V. He is even bringing home Jason's fleece in the shrouds of the Argo.[25] The wolfish Chancellor, whenever he may "recover" (return?), has caught

[22] Furnivall, *Ballads from Manuscripts* (London, 1868–72), I, 316.

[23] Skelton, *Works*, II, 345.

[24] *Decastichon*, following *Why Come Ye Not to Court.*

[25] Dyce's punctuation has no MS justification and must be ignored. The MS has a faint dot after "Argus," in line 290, which suggests:

    Le tonsan de Jason is lodgid among the shrowdes
    Of Argus. Revengyd, recover when he may,
    Lyacon of Libyk and Lydy hathe cawghte hys pray:
                                    (ll. 289–91)

what prey he desires from France and from the Empire. As in lines 307–8 of "Secunde Lenuoy" and throughout "Le dereyn Lenveoy," Skelton is mocking Wolsey's inefficacy as a diplomat and his failure to achieve anything in his very expensive mission.[26]

It is to be noted that in each of the three messages just discussed Wolsey is addressed under a highly virtuous name. "Jerobesethe" ("Lenuoy primere") is Gideon, heroic leader of Israel's hosts. "Sadoke" of "Secunde Lenuoy" is a Biblical high priest. "Sydrake" ("Le dereyn Lenveoy"), chief adviser to King Boccus in a popular fable,[27] converts the heathen king to Christianity and instructs him on every imaginable topic. Wolsey too is leader of the nation, chief cleric, and most intimate counselor of the king. The sarcasm implicit in Skelton's choice of names is obvious.

The first three envoys, then, so similar in general structure and appearance, were written within a period of three weeks and bear a single message, "Come home, Wolsey, from Calais. You are wasting your time and ours; you are causing trouble and expense."

4. Galathea remarks:

I compas the conveyaunce vnto the capitall
  Of ower clerke Cleros, whythyr, thydyr, and why not hethyr?
For passe a pase apase ys gon to cache a molle,
  Over Scarpary *mala vi*, Monsyre cy and sliddyr:
Whate sequele shall folow when pendugims mete togethyr?

(ll. 405–9)

These lines occur late in the poem, in a section marked "34" with no indication of month. Since they follow a section dated "Kalendis Decembris, 34" (l. 355), it may be assumed that they were written after December 1, 1521,

---

[26] Another explanation of the meaning of "Lenuoy primere" is offered by Edwards, *PMLA*, LIII (1938), 617–18.

[27] *The history of kyng Boccus & Sydracke*, translated from the French by Hugh of Caumpeden, printed *c*. 1510.

and in view of the close temporal succession of those added pieces the dates of which are more specifically given, not long after December 1. Dyce notes the probability of an allusion in line 407 to Secretary Pace.[28] Even more clearly the preceding line plays on the name of John Clerk, the scholar who carried Henry's *Assertio septem sacramentorum* to the Pope. The word "capital" usually refers to Rome, and the mention of Mount Scarpary (in Tuscany) makes certain that the "pendugims" (whatever they were) were to meet in the Imperial City.

Shortly after December 2, 1521, Henry sent Richard Pace to Rome, where, in company with John Clerk, he was to strive for the election of Wolsey as successor to the late Pope Leo. Parrot's answer (ll. 428–30) to the question as to what would happen when the cardinals met is therefore not without point:

Hys woluys hede, wanne, bloo as lede, gapythe over the crowne:
  Hyt ys to fere leste he wolde were the garland on hys pate,
  Peregall with all prynces farre passyng hys estate

The papal crown must be the garland referred to, and this unit of the poem was therefore written before news of the choice of Cardinal Tortosa on January 9, 1522, reached England.

5. That much of the conclusion of *Speak, Parrot* alludes satirically to the Cardinal is immediately obvious. There is criticism of Wolsey's political policies, of his extravagance, his proud building of Hampton Court, his strict administration of petty laws, his treatment of the monasteries, his "hatred" of the Church. So bold a bragging butcher; so mangy a mastiff cur, the great greyhound's peer; so much of "my lord's grace," and he so graceless— these have never been seen before. The denunciation, no longer shrouded in metaphor and allegory, rises to its climax in the stanza (ll. 498–504):

[28] Skelton, *Works*, II, 347.

So myche raggyd ryghte of a rammes horne;
  So rygorous re[u]elyng in a prelate specially;
So bold and so braggyng, and was so baselye borne;
  So lordlye of hys lokes and so dysdayneslye;
  So fatte a magott, bred of a flesshe flye;
Was nevyr suche a ffylty gorgon, nor suche an epycure,
Syn[s] Dewcalyons flodde, I make thé faste and sure.

One of the few obscure lines in this section: "So many
swans dead, and so small revel" (l. 482), is readily explained by the 1521 date. The crest of the Staffords, the
family of the Duke of Buckingham, is described: "Out of a
coronet or, a swan's head & neck between 2 wings elevated
argent, the bill gules."[29] It is traditional satiric technique
to represent a character by his heraldic cognizance. In May,
1521, Buckingham was executed for treason, and many of
his contemporaries laid his fall to the malice of Wolsey.

Sufficient evidence, I believe, is afforded by the foregoing analysis of the second part of *Speak, Parrot* to confirm
the 1521 date assumed on the basis of the "xxxiiii" at the
close of *Why Come Ye Not to Court* and the "Deo (21°)
gratias" following the eulogy of Henry VIII. This means
that 1521–22 is thirty-four years after the beginning of
Skelton's chronological system. Since Year 33 ends between "Lenuoy primere" (October 30, 1521) and "Secunde
Lenuoy" (the days of November, 1521) something must
have occurred between October 30, and November, 1488,
of enough importance to warrant the establishment of a
special calendar, still in use after thirty-four years. No
event of historic significance falls within the required
period. One is led, therefore, to search among happenings
which might have been sufficiently important to the poet
personally, without finding reflection in the chronicles.

In a previous chapter,[30] it has been shown that 1489 was
the year in which Skelton first appeared as a poet of the court

[29] Doyle's *Baronage*, *s.v.* "Buckingham."
[30] See above, p. 63.

of Henry VII. During that year he composed three poems on occasions of national importance. In June, 1489, Caxton spoke of him as having been lately created Poet Laureate. November, 1488, therefore, may well have been the date of a significant event in Skelton's life. Perhaps it was the beginning of his service to the kings of England. Perhaps it marked the date of his laureation at Oxford. If either hypothesis is correct, Skelton's calendar system took its origin from the beginning of his recognized poetical career.

THE FIRST PART OF *Speak, Parrot*

There is a sharp break between the first and second parts of *Speak, Parrot*. The second part, which appears only in the manuscript, has already been discussed. Of the first part, none is to be found in the manuscript except the introduction (ll. 1–59) and a few of the closing lines (ll. 230–37). It is a whole in itself, certainly not the most coherent of wholes, but complete with a beginning and an end obviously so designed.

Clearly, it was written before "Lenuoy primere" (October 30, 1521). But it is difficult to define the early limit. The lament over the victory of the Greeks at the universities (ll. 146–70) indicates a date later than 1519, when a royal letter ended the interference of the "Trojans" with the students of the new learning.[31] A similar *terminus a quo* is hinted by the lines:

For they [the Greeks] scrape out good scrypture, and set in a gall,
Ye go about to amende, and ye mare all.

(ll. 158–59)

This must refer to Erasmus' *New Testament*, probably not the first edition (1516), for that retained the Vulgate Latin, but the second (1519), which introduced new readings from the Greek into the Latin text ("scraped out good Scripture").

After introducing the poem with a description of Parrot

[31] J. B. Mullinger, *University of Cambridge* (Cambridge, 1873), I, 526.

FOLIO ii^r OF SKELTON'S DEDICATION TO KING HENRY VIII
OF A MANUSCRIPT OF *CHRONIQUE DE RAINS*
CORPUS CHRISTI COLLEGE, CAMBRIDGE, MS 432

and some lines of praise for the King and Queen, the poet
passes to a warning of the dangers of too much boldness.
Discretion, he says, is the mother of noble virtues all. But

> . . . reason and wyt wantyth theyr prouyncyall
> When wylfulnes is vycar generall.
> *Hæc res acu tangitur*, Parrot, *par ma foy:*
> *Ticez vous*, Parrot, *tenez vous coye.*
>
> (ll. 55–58)

Who is "willfulness" and why must Parrot be mum? We
are told in *Why Come Ye Not to Court* (ll. 102–106):

> For wyll dothe rule all thynge,
> Wyll, wyll, wyll, wyll, wyll,
> He ruleth alway styll.
> Good reason and good skyll,
> They may garlycke pyll

The context of the lines from *Why Come* shows unmistakably that it is Wolsey that rules.

This first intimation of the subject of the following
satire is borne out by the next stanza (ll. 59–65):

> Besy, besy, besy, and besynes agayne!
> *Que pensez voz*, Parrot? what meneth this besynes?
> *Vitulus* in Oreb troubled Arons brayne,
> Melchisedeck mercyfull made Moloc mercyles;
> To wyse is no vertue, to medlyng, to restles;
> In mesure is tresure, *cum sensu maturato;*
> *Ne tropo sanno, ne tropo mato.*

"*Vitulus* in Oreb," the calf shaped from the melted ornaments of the rebellious Israelites on Mount Horeb, finds a
parallel in the "Conflatus vitulus" of the "Decastichon
virulentum in galeratum lycaonta marinum," a Latin
epigram appended to *Why Come Ye Not to Court*. "The wolf
of the sea with the cardinal's hat" is there called many
strong names, of which "golden calf" is one. The term is
also found in the second part of *Speak, Parrot* (l. 347, l. 349,
and after l. 373) where it clearly applies to the hated

Cardinal. Skelton's fondness for it probably depends on the double significance of the word: as Satan, or false idol, and as a reminder of the butcher's trade of Wolsey's father. Since the calf troubled Aaron's brain, and since Moloch was merciless,[32] Parrot must be most discreet. He must mingle his wisdom with madness.

> Aram was fyred with Caldies fyer called Ur;
>   Iobab was brought vp in the lande of Hus;
> The lynage of Lot toke supporte of Assur;
>   Iereboseth is Ebrue, who lyst the cause dyscus.
>   Peace, Parrot, ye prate, as ye were *ebrius:*
> Howst thé, *lyuer god van hemrik, ic seg;*
> In Popering grew peres, whan Parrot was an eg.
>   (ll. 66–72)

The first line of this stanza serves to show that Skelton uses "allegoria" in its most common medieval sense, that of allegorical interpretation of the Scriptures. The verse seems quite meaningless. But it echoes the Biblical "And Haran died before his father Terah in the land of his nativity, in Ur of the Chaldees" (*Gen.* xi. 28). The strange form in which the line appears in *Speak, Parrot* is explained by a medieval comment on the quotation from Genesis:[33]

Ur means *fire* . . . that is, [they were burned] in the fire of the Chaldees. And the Chaldees reverence fire as God. As the Chaldees relate, Terah together with his children was cast into the fire by them because he refused to worship it. In this fire, Haran was consumed.

Haran, then, died in the fire called Ur because he would not worship a false god. The next line calls up the suffering Job underwent in the land of Huz because he would not succumb to the wiles of the devil. "The lineage of Lot took support of Assur" is quoted from the eighty-second psalm (Vulgate enumeration). It means, according to the traditional interpretation, that the spirits of evil conspire to-

[32] *Speak, Parrot*, l. 395: "Moloc, that mawmett, there darre no man withsay."
[33] *Commentarius in Genesin Angelomi Luxoviensis monachi*, Migne, *Patr. Lat.*, Vol. CXV, col. 168. The translation is mine.

gether for the attack.[34] But "Jereboseth is Hebrew, who list the cause discuss." And Jerubbesheth, in Hebrew, means "striver against the thing of shame"—a euphemism for Jerubbaal, "striver against Baal" (again the false idol). Pieced together, the lines of the stanza first warn Parrot of the dangers of opposing evil, then exhort him nevertheless to remain steadfast to his purpose, and finally enjoin him again to "whist."

The attack now (ll. 75–77) becomes more direct.

> The iebet of Baldock was made for Jack Leg;
> An arrow vnfethered and without an hed,
> A bagpype without blowynge standeth in no sted:

Skelton is expressing a pious wish: the gibbet of Baldock is a fit place for Jack Leg and is as useless without him as an arrow without a head. Again a parallel passage may be cited from *Why Come Ye Not to Court:*

> Suche a prelate, I trowe,
> Were worthy to rowe
> Thorow the streytes of Marock
> To the gybbet of Baldock:
> (ll. 950–53)

The solution is found in Mandeville's *Travels.* We are informed that "þat cytee of Baldak was wont to ben cleped Sutis & Nabugodonozor founded it. And þere duelled the holy prophete Daniel. ."[35] This city is Susa, or Shushan, and the gibbet is of course the high gallows on which was hanged Haman, prime minister of King Ahasuerus and betrayer of the Jews. The allusion was considered so neat for chancellors of Henry VIII that after the fall of Wolsey it was applied to his protégé Thomas Cromwell:

> Iff this A-man wer hanged, then der I well say
> this Realme then Redressyde full sone sholde be.[36]

[34] Peter Lombard, *Commentarius in Psalmos*, Migne, *Patr. Lat.*, Vol. CXCI, col. 783.

[35] "Early English Text Society [Publications]," O.S., No. CLIII, 27.

[36] Furnivall, *Ballads from Manuscripts*, I, 308: "An Exhortacyon to the Northe, A.D. 1536," ll. 109–10.

The next stanza is a mixture of sense and nonsense, but enough of the former may be identified to render undoubted the subject of its reference.

> Ic dien serueth for the erstrych fether,
> Ic dien is the language of the land of Beme;
> In Affryc tongue byrsa is a thonge of lether;
> In Palestina there is Ierusalem.
> Colostrum now for Parot, whyte bred and swete creme!
> Our Thomasen she doth trip, our Ienet she doth shayle:
> Parrot hath a blacke beard and a fayre grene tayle.
>
> (ll. 80–86)

The key line is "In Affryc tongue byrsa is a thonge of lether." "Byrsa" had a very specific meaning for the contemporaries of Skelton. It represented the highly ornamented bag or purse in which the great seal was always carried[37] and so, by easy metaphor, the lord chancellor, keeper of the seal. "Ic dien" and the "ostrich feather" of the lines immediately preceding this are at present the particular badge of the Prince of Wales, but their use then was not so clearly specialized.[38] At no date conceivable for the poem was there a Prince of Wales. If the symbol may be taken as referring to the crown, the contrast between "Ic dien serveth for the ostrich feather" and "byrsa" as a "thong of leather" suggests the relative mildness of the king as opposed to the strength and ferocity of his chief minister. Henry is content to serve, while Wolsey tyrannizes over England.[39]

The poem proceeds into a passage of great obscurity:

> Parot can say, Cæsar, ave, also;
> But Parrot hath no fauor to Esebon:
> Aboue all other byrdis, set Parrot alone.

[37] *Oxford English Dictionary, s.v.* "burse."

[38] Henry VIII used the feathers and motto on stained glass in the Tower of London. See Nicholas Harris Nicholas, "On the Badge and Mottoes of the Prince of Wales," *Archæologia*, XXXI (1846), 370.

[39] The question "Why come ye not to court?" makes this point. Compare also *Speak, Parrot*, ll. 132, 348–51, 399–404, 423.

Ulula, Esebon, for Ieromy doth wepe!
   Sion is in sadnes, Rachell ruly doth loke;
Madionita Ietro, our Moyses kepyth his shepe;
   Gedeon is gon, that Zalmane vndertoke,
   Oreb *et* Zeb, of *Judicum* rede the boke;
Now Geball, Amon, and Amaloch,—harke, harke!
Parrot pretendith to be a bybyll clarke.

O Esebon, Esebon! to thé is cum agayne
   Seon, the regent *Amorræorum*,
   And Og, that fat hog of Basan, doth retayne,
   The crafty *coistronus Cananæorum*;
And *asylum*, whilom *refugium miserorum*,
Non fanum, sed profanum, standyth in lyttyll sted:
Ulula, Esebon, for Iepte is starke ded!
                   (ll. 112–28)

The attack on the meaning of this passage must be made
from the flank. To Skelton's readers the foregoing verses
would undoubtedly recall their Biblical sources. These are
two. First, there are the stories which may be grouped
under the name Heshbon, references to which are found
throughout the Old Testament. Sihon, king of the Amor-
ites, was evicted from Heshbon, his chief city, by Gideon.
Shortly afterward his neighbor and ally, Og, king of
Bashan, was also defeated and slain. Heshbon thus became
a city of the Israelites, who ruled until they in turn were
overthrown by the Philistines. The second source is the
eighty-second psalm, which is described in the Douay and
authorized versions as "a prayer against them that oppress
the church." The psalm warns of the conspiracies of the
enemies (among whom are Gebal, Ammon, and Amalek)
and prays that they may be overcome as were the Midian-
ites, Oreb and Zeb and Zalmunna.

Two Heshbons are sharply distinguished in medieval
allegory. The first is the city under the rule of the heathen:

When we see a person living in infamy of life and error of religion, do not hesitate to say of him, "Behold, this is the city of Heshbon under the rule of King Sihon."[40]

The victory of Gideon is a victory of the sword of the Spirit and the darts of the Word of God. A new city rises on the ashes of the old:

> It is not the custom of the sons of Israel to leave demolished the cities which they have destroyed. Having undermined and overthrown a man's evil thoughts and impious dispositions, they replace what they have destroyed in his heart with good thoughts and pious dispositions. They will implant the doctrine of truth, propound respect for religious usage, teach ordinate living, and inculcate reverence and integrity of conduct. And then, indeed, those who speak in parables [*ænigmatistæ*] will say amongst themselves, "Come, let us build Heshbon, which was the city of Sihon."[41]

In Skelton's poem this second Heshbon has given way to the first. Alas, cries Parrot, Gideon and Jephtha and Moses are here no longer to defend the forces of the good. The lack of such heroes has turned the city "that was Sihon's" again into the hands of that evil king. All is lost; Parrot alone has courage enough to say that he "hath no favor to Esebon."

As "Esebon" is the heart of these stanzas, so the determination of its specific meaning lays bare their essential structure. In the eighty-second psalm the object of the attack of Gebal, Ammon, and Amalek is traditionally understood to be the Christian Church. The Abbot Wolbero,[42] commenting on a passage in the Song of Songs, and Hraban,[43] in an alphabetical catalogue of allegorical symbols

---

[40] Rabanus Maurus, *Enarrationes in Librum Numerorum libri tres*, Migne, *Patr. Lat.*, Vol. CVIII, col. 723. The translation is mine.

[41] *Ibid.*—Note that the Biblical verse (Num. xxi. 27) reads, "Venite in Hesebon, ædificetur et construatur civitas Sehon," and that therefore the expression "quæ fuit civitas Seon" represents Hraban's emphasis.

[42] Wolbero, *Commentaria in Canticum Canticorum*, Migne, *Patr. Lat.*, Vol. CXCV, cols. 1231–32.

[43] Rabanus Maurus, *Allegoriæ in Sacram Scripturam*, Migne, *Patr. Lat.*, Vol. CXII, col. 917.

to be found in the Scriptures, both assert that Heshbon signifies the Church. The sorrowful Rachel is another figure for the Church (the index in Migne[44] lists thirteen instances of such interpretation). Skelton tells us that one of the evils that has befallen Heshbon on the second coming of Sihon is that asylum, once the sacred refuge of the miserable, now "standeth in little stead." The subject of the poet's lament is, therefore, the evil state of the ecclesiastical system and the cowardliness of the clergy, who, unlike such heroic ancients as Thomas à Becket (the contrast is drawn in *Colin Clout*, ll. 162–74), fail to maintain their rights against the onslaught of the enemy.

There is no need to seek for historical personages to attach to each of the names which Skelton used. The people of Israel had many titles for their one adversary; the satirist considers his not less worthy. The Caesar whom Parrot will not flatter with an "ave," who has caused the decay of the ancient prerogatives of the Church, who from Scarpary to Tartary is known to rule the ring, who is Sihon and Og and Judas Iscariot, can be none but Cardinal Wolsey.

The satire of the first part of the poem up to this point now forms a fairly lucid thought sequence. It is dangerous for Parrot to fight against the cardinal-chancellor, the evil enemy of Church and State—would that he were hanged. If Parrot mind his safety, he must mind his tongue. Yet Parrot is a brave bird, and he will speak his speech. Let there be no foolhardiness though; let the accusations and the curses be made with discretion, allegorically, and confused with meaningless patter. For the adversary is powerful and merciless.

If Thomas Wolsey may be found lurking in so many lines of *Speak, Parrot*, it cannot be altogether rash to look for his presence even in those parts of the poem which seem on first examination not concerned with him. The attack

---

[44] *Patr. Lat.*, Vol. CCXIX, col. 249.

on the over-emphasis of Greek in the university curricula
(ll. 146–87) is straightforward enough. Manifestly, it is a
statement of Skelton's position in the current controversy
between the "Trojans" and the "Greeks." But it is difficult to believe even Skelton guilty of the entire inconse-
quence implied by the acceptance of this section at face
value only. The connecting link is provided quite naturally
by the fact that Wolsey had set himself up as a patron
of the Greeks. In 1519 or 1520 he founded a professorship
of the language at Oxford. Mullinger describes the consequences:[45]

Then, even to the dullest intellect, the whole question of this
new lore assumed another aspect. The Trojans suffered sorely
from numerous defections, and ultimately disbanded. Priam,
Hector, and Paris retired into private life. It began to be understood that Greek was the road to favor at court and to prefer-
ment, and consequently probably, after all, a laudable and
respectable branch of learning.

If Wolsey's action was significant enough so to settle the
long-standing scholastic controversy, it is surely not a
long leap to the conclusion that Skelton, in a poem concerned mainly with the cardinal, was directing particularly at him his satire on the too-zealous proponents of
the new learning.

    In the stanzas concluding the first part of the poem
(ll. 209–29), we are told that "Parrot is no churlish
chough" (the Cornish chough appears in Wolsey's coat of
arms), but Skelton's "own dear heart"; that its beak has
been burnished by Melpomene; that when Parrot is dead,
it, like man's soul, will never putrefy; and that Parrot
was created by Him who "made you of nothing by his
majesty."

    The original of Parrot may be found in Boccaccio's
Genealogia deorum:[46]

[45] Mullinger, *The University of Cambridge*, I, 526.
[46] Book IV, chap. xlix. The translation is mine.

Of Psyttacus, Son of Deucalion

Psyttacus, son of Deucalion and Pyrrha (so Theodontius says) having been steeped in the learning of his grandfather, Prometheus, went to Ethiopia where he was much venerated. When he had reached a great age, he prayed that he might be removed from human affairs. Yielding to his entreaties, the gods transformed him into the bird which bears his name. I believe that the origin of this myth is the renown of his name and his virtue, which endures perpetually green for this venerable dead man, just as those birds are green.

Parrot of *Speak, Parrot*, then, is Psyttacus, son of Deucalion. Both are wise, both free from decay, both associated with Lybia. One was divinely created, the other, divinely metamorphosed. Naturally Parrot is able to compare these bad times with those "since Deucalion's flood" (1. 442)—Deucalion was his father! Moreover, this Parrot, son of Deucalion, must be none other than the laureate poet, John Skelton. Does not Skelton assert, "Parrot is my own dear heart"? Like the bird whose plumage remains everlastingly green and like the ancient whose virtuous fame endures perpetually, the poet is able to say of himself:

> Eterno mansura die dum sidera fulgent
> Equora dumque tument hec la[ur]ea nostra virebit.
> Hinc nostrum celebre et nomen referetur ad astra
> Undique Skeltonis memorabitur alter adonis[47]

Thus Psyttacus serves Skelton's purpose perfectly. The poet uses Parrot as he uses Colin Clout, a mouthpiece by means of which he is enabled to speak strong language, yet remain legally irresponsible.

So read, *Speak, Parrot* becomes a little less like "feathers in the wind." The first part achieves at least a semblance of unity, consisting of an introduction of Parrot, a compli-

---

[47] These verses are found under an absurdly youthful portrait entitled "Skelton Poeta," at the beginning of the 1523 edition of the *Garland of Laurel*. This cut is the same as that for *April* in *The Kalendar & Compost of Shepherds*. Skelton was about 63 years old at the time; so the portrait must represent his eternally enduring fame rather than his person.

ment to the King and Queen, a veiled satire on their chief minister, and a conclusion embodying a description of the method of the poem and a suggestion of the identity of the speaking bird. The second part is simply a series of more or less discrete envoys or afterthoughts appended to the poem itself in the fashion of the three Latin pieces added to *Why Come Ye Not to Court*, and like those pieces finding place by virtue of its compatibility in purpose with the poem preceding it. And the purpose is the same as that of *Why Come:* to attack Cardinal Wolsey with all the resources of vituperative expression at the poet's command.

Indeed, throughout this argument, *Why Come Ye Not to Court* has been much used in elucidation of the meaning of the more obscure earlier poem. The close correspondence in date, theme, and verbal material of the two satires is immediately arresting and of itself turns the attention to their essential difference in tone. This change is not one of intensification of motive, for the attack on Wolsey in *Parrot* is at least as virulent as that in *Why Come*. But in the later poem the mouthpiece is dropped. Skelton speaks in his own person. Here is no metaphor, no allegory, no "*ticez vous*, Parrot," no intermingling of lines of nonsense to mislead the Cardinal's bloodhounds. And Skelton's development from the whisperer of 1521 to the Jeremiah of 1522 seems adumbrated even in the course of the few months covering the composition of the second part of *Speak, Parrot*. The obscurity shrouding the meaning of "Lenuoy primere" shields progressively less the intent of later sections. No contemporary could have doubted the identity of the "chief cardinal" who "carries a king in his sleeve."

In *Speak, Parrot*, therefore, Skelton fired the opening gun of the battle which brought him both his greatest misfortune and his strongest claim to enduring renown.

The Quarrel with Wolsey

AT THE height of his powers Skelton met the greatest of his opportunities. As a professed satirist his task was to denounce evil. His philosophy defined as evil that which exceeded the mean and overturned established order. Wolsey, the excessively proud, the upstart innovator, was the very embodiment of all that Skelton thought vicious. A more cautious man might have stood by and grumbled; Skelton burst forth into violent and increasingly plain-spoken denunciations, which culminated in the brilliant invective of *Colin Clout* and *Why Come Ye Not to Court*. That Skelton behaved as he did justifies his life as a satirist. For in this conflict he proved himself, not an ill-tempered brawler who struck where he could safely strike, but a spirited critic willing to stake his life for the freedom of his tongue.

The evidence bearing upon the course of events in Skelton's quarrel with Wolsey is scant and unsatisfactory. The interpretation of that evidence is therefore sketchy and liable to substantial shifts with each slight increase of factual knowledge. These, briefly, are the elements that must be considered in any reconstruction of the story.

1. The morality *Magnificence* which, its latest editor believes, is directed at Wolsey.[1]

2. *Speak, Parrot*, an obscurely written invective against Wolsey.

3. *Colin Clout*, apparently a general satire on Church government, which includes several passages clearly criticizing Wolsey.

---

[1] *Magnyfycence*, ed. by R. L. Ramsay, "Early English Text Society [Publications]," E. S., XCVIII.

4. *Why Come Ye Not to Court*, a bitter and undisguised assault on Wolsey.

5. *Garland of Laurel*, which mentions *Speak, Parrot* and *Colin Clout*.

6. "Lautre Enuoy" to the *Garland of Laurel*, which dedicates the *Garland* to the King and to Cardinal Wolsey.

7. "Lenuoy" to *The Doughty Duke of Albany*, another dedication to Wolsey.

8. *A Replication against Certain Young Scholars*, written at Wolsey's request.

9. Bale's statement that Skelton died in sanctuary at Westminster.[2]

Here is material that proves that Skelton was at one time an antagonist and at another a dependent of Cardinal Wolsey. The story of Skelton's life, as it is usually told, is based chiefly on the biography in Bale's *Scriptorum illustrium maioris Britanniæ catalogus*. Bale asserts that Skelton died a sanctuary man at Westminster because his writings had angered Wolsey. The poet's burial at St. Margaret's bolsters the statement. Therefore it has been generally concluded that those of Skelton's poems which attack Wolsey must have been written after those which address the Cardinal as a patron, for, as Dyce puts it, "Wolsey might have forgiven the allusions made to him in *Colyn Cloute;* but it would be absurd to imagine that . . . he continued to patronize the man who had written *Why Come Ye Nat to Court.*"[3] The latter part of Skelton's life, then, becomes the tale of a "humble client" of the Cardinal, transformed into his "dearest foe" by some "extraordinary provocation," who died a heroic death at Westminster because of the powerful wrath he had dared to provoke.

The available evidence, however, disturbs the simplicity of the narrative. Dyce himself realized that the

[2] Bale, *Scriptorum catalogus* (Basle, 1559 [?]), pp. 651–52.
[3] Skelton, *Works*, I, xliv.

Garland of Laurel (published October, 1523) and *The Doughty Duke of Albany* (late 1523), both dedicated to Wolsey, were written after the attacks on Wolsey had begun. In the *Garland of Laurel* catalogue, two of the three major satires on Wolsey, *Speak, Parrot* and *Colin Clout*, are mentioned. In order to preserve the traditional story of Skelton's death in sanctuary, it is necessary to make one of two assumptions: that the dedicatory poems attached to the *Garland of Laurel* and to *The Duke of Albany* do not properly belong to those works but were misplaced by Skelton's first editor, Marshe (1568), or that the versions of *Speak, Parrot* and *Colin Clout* which are mentioned in the *Garland* catalogue actually contained no attacks on Wolsey and that these attacks were incorporated into the poems at a time which followed the writing of the *Garland*.

But a more recent discovery renders either position difficult to maintain. There can be no doubt that the dedication to Skelton's *Replication against Certain Young Scholars* belongs to the poem, since it is included in the first edition of that poem, which was published almost immediately after its writing. Mullinger, the historian of the University of Cambridge, points out that Skelton's *Replication* deals with the abjuration of two Cambridge heretics, Thomas Bilney and Thomas Arthur, on December 8, 1527.[4] This is certainly later than the latest date assignable to any of the poems against Wolsey: *Speak, Parrot, Colin Clout*, or *Why Come Ye Not to Court*. If Skelton died in sanctuary, in 1529, therefore, it must be assumed that the *Replication* represents the poet's unsuccessful attempt to propitiate the angry Cardinal. Yet no such note is struck in the dedication. Instead, Wolsey is spoken of as the patron of the work.

Rather than continue to prop a faltering theory with a group of hypotheses *ad hoc*, it seems better to start from

[4] J. B. Mullinger, *The University of Cambridge*, I, 607–8.

the beginning. There is no strong reason for ignoring the dedicatory envoys to the *Garland of Laurel* and to *The Duke of Albany*. It is true that the *Garland* dedication does not appear in the first edition of that poem. It is first found in the collected edition of Skelton's works which was issued in 1568. But it is not therefore necessary to assume that the editor of the 1568 edition carelessly misplaced it. Nor can any such criticism be alleged against the envoy to *The Duke of Albany*, since there is extant no edition of the poem which antedates that in which the envoy appears. The dedicatory envoys exist, and until they are proved to be valueless as evidence, they must be included in any analysis of the quarrel.

Acceptance of this neglected material together with a reconsideration of the dates and meanings of several of the poems leads to a new interpretation of the story of Skelton's conflict with Wolsey.

Most of the dates of Skelton's writings against Wolsey have been determined. Little criticism can be made of the careful researches of Ramsay, who assigns *Magnificence* to 1515 or 1516.[5] In the preceding chapter, I attempted to show that the latter part of *Speak, Parrot* was composed toward the end of 1521 and that *Why Come Ye Not to Court* was finished in late October or early November, 1522. There is no ambiguity about the reference of *The Duke of Albany* to events in November, 1523. Mullinger's dating of the *Replication* after December, 1527, is beyond doubt. There remain only *Colin Clout* and the *Garland of Laurel*.

THE DATE OF *Colin Clout*

At the latest, *Colin Clout* must have been written before October, 1523, for it is mentioned in the *Garland of Laurel* which was published in that month and year. The early limit, however, is more difficult to define. One section (ll.

---

[5] "Early English Text Society [Publications]," E.S., XCVIII, xxv.

376–438) consists of an attack on those in power in the Church for their treatment of the monasteries. At first sight the poet seems to be alluding to Wolsey's program of dissolution of monastic houses which began in earnest in 1524. If no other interpretation were possible, it would be necessary to conclude that the passage in question was added after the *Garland of Laurel* was written and that the composition of *Colin Clout* stretched over a considerable period. But no such conclusion is required. Analysis of the passage shows that the reference is probably, not to the dissolutions of 1524, but to a disestablishment of monastic foundations which took place in 1522.

Skelton's discussion of the monasteries is divided into two sections. In the first the poet declares that the harsh treatment accorded the monks is making them

> . . . . fayne
> For to tourne agayne
> *In secula seculorum,*
> And to forsake theyr corum,
> And *vagabundare per forum*
> (ll. 376–80)

This was a common complaint *before* the breaking up of the monasteries began.[6] The satirist then turns to the nuns, with whom the prelates are "now" beginning "the self same game." They "must" (not "are fain to") leave their abodes. Skelton attacks the bishops for destroying the nunneries:

> Ye do them wrong and no ryght
> To put them thus to flyght;
> No matyns at mydnyght,
> Boke and chalys gone quyte;
> And plucke awaye the leedes
> Evyn ouer theyr heedes,
> And sell away theyr belles,
> And all that they haue elles:
> Thus the people telles,

[6] See Polydore Vergil, *Historia Anglica* (1603), pp. 1661–62.

> Rayles lyke rebelles,
> Redys shrewdly and spelles,
> And with foundacyons melles,
> And talkys lyke tytyuelles, ·
> How ye brake the dedes wylles,
> Turne monasteris into water milles,
> Of an abbay ye make a graunge
>   (ll. 406-21)

In 1521–22 dissolution of monastic houses occurred for the first time in fourteen years. Two religious foundations were dissolved—Bromehall and Lillechurch, both establishments for nuns.[7] Among the chief temporal assets of the former was a water mill.[8] Not only is there no reason for doing violence to the unity of *Colin Clout* by assigning this part of it to 1524, but also the emphasis on nunneries and the mention of a water mill seem to prove that it was written sometime in 1522. The proposed position of *Colin Clout* close to *Speak, Parrot* (late 1521) and *Why Come Ye Not to Court* (late 1522) is strongly supported by the numerous verbal and thematic correspondences among the three satires.

THE DATE OF THE *Garland of Laurel*

The catalogue in the *Garland of Laurel* includes both *Speak, Parrot* and *Colin Clout*. If late 1521 is accepted as the date of *Speak, Parrot*, the early limit for the composition of the *Garland* is defined. The late limit is provided by the date of publication of the *Garland*, October, 1523. It seems unlikely that the writing of the three Wolsey poems was interrupted by the composition of the *Garland*, a work entirely alien in character, containing, as will be shown, an apology for previous satires. One inclines, therefore, to place the *Garland* after *Why Come Ye Not to Court* (late 1522). Since some time must be allowed for the process of publica-

---

[7] F. A. Gasquet, *Henry VIII and the English Monasteries* (London, 1888), I, 63–65.

[8] *Letters and Papers*, III, No. 2080.

tion, it may tentatively be concluded that the *Garland* was written in late 1522 or in early 1523.

There is strong support for this conclusion. The *Garland* opens with a stanza specifying the situation of the stars at the time Skelton walked in the Forest of Galtres and dreamed his dream:

> Arectyng my syght towarde the zodyake,
>   The sygnes xii for to beholde a farre,
> When Mars retrogradant reuersyd his bak,
>   Lorde of the yere in his orbicular,
>   Put vp his sworde, for he cowde make no warre,
> And whan Lucina plenarly did shyne,
> Scorpione ascendynge degrees twyce nyne

The most significant clue in this bundle of astronomical information is "Mars retrogradant." Mars retrogrades once every twenty-five and one-half months approximately (the interval between retrograde periods is not constant). According to a calculation which a student of astronomy[9] was good enough to perform for me, Mars "reversed his back" on December 3, 1520, and again on January 22, 1523. The *Garland* was therefore written either during the winter of 1523 or before 1521, that is, before *Colin Clout* and *Speak, Parrot*, both of which it mentions.

There is but one difficulty in accepting the later date. When the dreamer of the *Garland* wakes at the close of his vision, he observes Janus in the heavens, making his almanac for the New Year. But January 22 is rather late for a New Year's greeting ("Good luck this new year! the old year is past"). A calculation of the movements of Mars done for H. L. R. Edwards[10] brings the retrogradation a little closer to January 1, for it places the beginning of the planet's reversal at January 14 or 15. It is very likely that for his information as to planetary movements Skelton

[9] Dr. J. Wolf, of the faculty of Physics at the College of the City of New York.
[10] *PMLA*, LIII (1938), 608–9.

relied on the inaccurate astronomical tables of his time rather than on direct observation. This probably explains the failure of the calculations to jibe precisely with Skelton's date.[11] But an additional bit of information provided by Edwards seems to put the matter beyond doubt. Skelton's "whan Lucina plenarly did shyne" must mean that the moon was full. And the moon was full on January 2, 1523.[12]

The probable dates of those of Skelton's poems which bear in some way on his quarrel with Wolsey may now be summarized: *Magnificence*, 1515 or 1516; *Speak, Parrot*, late 1521; *Colin Clout*, 1522; *Why Come Ye Not to Court*, autumn, 1522; *Garland of Laurel*, January, 1523; *Duke of Albany*, late 1523; and *Replication*, 1528.

One significant observation leaps immediately from the list. In the space of somewhat more than a year were written all three poems containing violent attacks on Cardinal Wolsey. These poems are followed by another group of three, each of which is dedicated to the Cardinal. This in turn suggests two inferences. First, from its position in the sequence, *Colin Clout*, cannot be merely what it appears to be, a general satire on Church conditions farced with occasional attacks on Wolsey. Second, the *Garland*, composed so soon after the most ripping and most open of the invectives, must in some way betray their existence and perhaps also the reason for their cessation.

THE SATIRE OF *Colin Clout*

Colin Clout, unlike *Speak, Parrot*, does not attempt to reveal truths to the initiate while hiding them from the lay. The meaning of the poem is not wrapped in puns and conundrums. Nevertheless, it is difficult to grasp the satirist's full purpose. Numerous digressions confuse his mean-

---

[11] For another explanation of the discrepancy, see *ibid.*, p. 610.

[12] *Ibid.*, p. 609. For further evidence in support of the January, 1523 date assigned to the *Garland*, see *PMLA*, LI, 386–90.

ing. Skelton is the wrathful man, intent upon his chosen adversary, yet quick, too, to belabor every annoying passer-by. Furthermore he has not yet given up caution entirely. Skelton makes no criticisms himself; under the pseudonym of Colin Clout he merely reports what people are saying. Finally, the structure of the poem hides another safeguard, one that allows Dyce to say that "Wolsey might have forgiven the allusions made to him in *Colyn Cloute.*" That trick may be uncovered only by an analysis of the poem.

Colin Clout begins, logically enough, with a statement of subject matter. The author proposes to treat of the disagreement between clergy and laity (ll. 47–70). He proceeds to report the accusations made by the commons against the great prelates. They are proud, neglectful of their flocks, oppressive, careless of the rights of the Church, ungenerous, cowardly, slothful, and ignorant. They eat meat in Lent. They do not properly examine candidates for the priesthood. They give evil advice to the King. They oppress the monks and disestablish the nuns. But punishment awaits them (ll. 71–487).

Next, Colin briefly recounts clerical criticism of the lay. The commonalty is infected with heretical notions. When they condemn the clergy, they condemn it too generally (ll. 488–580).

What is the explanation of the prevalent hatred of the clergy? The layman has discovered that because the prelates have "come up of naught" they are inordinately proud. Bishops are deaf to these murmurs; they listen only to flatterers. They leave enlightenment to the poor doctors, whereas, if they preached they could easily become "lanterns of light." "Wax" doctors (those who have their degrees through influence, not through study) and itinerant friars cause distrust of the Church. The bishops can curb these creatures, but they are too busy building royal mansions and looking at lewd tapestries (ll. 581–981).

Thus everyone carps at the Church. The condition cannot continue always, for one man cannot forever rule the King. If the people talk so, there must be something in what they say. Bishops ought to mend their ways. They should not be angry with Colin; it betrays them. But they heed no correction. They threaten to punish Colin. They will not even allow this book to be printed (ll. 982–1249).

The satire, in short, seems general enough. It is peculiar only in that it stresses so strongly the evils of the great prelates instead of proceeding in orderly fashion, criticizing class by class. But closer examination reveals the similarity of *Colin Clout* to its chronological neighbors, *Speak, Parrot* and *Why Come Ye Not to Court*. The "bishops" are almost invariably one bishop. That one is Wolsey.

At every turn the satirist's meaning shows itself. When the few good prelates are censured for cowardice, it is because they are

> . . . loth to hang the bell
> Aboute the cattes necke,
> For drede to haue a checke
> (ll. 163–65)

They fear to "shoe the mockish mare." When "some" of the bishops are denounced as luxurious, they are described as riding on mules, bedecked in gorgeous garments (ll. 309–22), a description that tallies perfectly with Cavendish's famous picture of Wolsey proceeding to court. They give counsel against the common weal (ll. 360–61). Who was in a position to give such counsel? "Some of you do eat in Lenten season flesh meat" (ll. 205–6). In Lent, 1522, to the great disgust of the people, Wolsey promulgated a dispensation easing the rigors of the rule, perhaps because he himself, being poor in health, had asked for and secured a similar privilege from the Pope.[13] They oppress the

---

[13] Polydore Vergil, *Historia Anglica*, p. 1698; *Letters and Papers*, III, Nos. 634, 647, 676.

monks. All the religious of England murmured at the
stringency of Wolsey's visitations. Sometimes Skelton
loses the thread of his plurals. When it is prophesied that
"they" will be punished, the punishment falls only on

> . . . one
> That shuld syt on a trone,
> And rule all thynges alone
>   (ll. 475-77)

The proud prelates take it upon them to rule "both king
and kaiser" (l. 606). They have forgotten their pauper
origins, but they may trip so "that all the world may say,
come down, in the devil way" (ll. 671-72). Instead of
controlling itinerant friars, they spend their time "building
royally their mansions curiously" (ll. 936-37). Only Wolsey, the upstart butcher's son who ruled England and built
Hampton Court, can fit the description. Skelton again
forgets his plural:

> Sqyre, knyght, and lorde,
> Thus the Churche remorde;
> With all temporall people
> They rune agaynst the steple,
> Thus talkynge and tellyng
> How some of you are mellyng;
> Yet softe and fayre for swellyng,
> Beware of a quenes yellyng.
> It is a besy thing
> For one man to rule a kyng
> Alone and make rekenyng,
> To gouerne ouer all
> And rule a realme royall
> By one mannes verrey wyt
>   (ll. 982-95)

Finally Colin declares that ᴛhe prelates refuse to be corrected, that to all criticism they answer,

> How darest thou, daucocke, mell?
> How darest thou, losell,

Allygate the gospell
Agaynst vs of the counsell?
(ll. 1162–65)

And Wolsey was chief of the Council.

Colin Clout, then, is a bitter attack on Thomas Wolsey, thinly curtained with the appearance of medieval class satire. It is Wolsey in his capacity of ruler of the Church that is the particular subject of the poem. In the same year Skelton wrote *Why Come Ye Not to Court*, an invective directed, not against "Cardinal" Wolsey, but against "Chancellor" Wolsey, the governor of the realm. There is no curtain, however thin, which obscures the meaning of *Why Come Ye Not to Court*. The three attacks on Wolsey, *Speak, Parrot* (late 1521), *Colin Clout* (1522), and *Why Come Ye Not to Court* (late 1522) progress from extraordinary obscurity to outspoken denunciation. The last poem constitutes the climax of Skelton's greatest quarrel.

Suddenly, Skelton's battle against the powers ceased. There are no more tirades against Wolsey. A bare month or two after the climactic *Why Come Ye Not to Court*, Skelton wrote the *Garland of Laurel*, as peaceful and unvenomed a work as he was capable of producing. Surely this poem, which constitutes an estimate of the labors of a lifetime, must give some evidence of the recent turmoil, perhaps even hint a reason for the abrupt change in tone.

THE ALLEGORY OF THE *Garland*

The *Garland of Laurel* was written at Sheriff-Hutton in Yorkshire, a castle which the King had granted to the Duke of Norfolk for life. The immediate occasion of the poem was the gift of a silken chaplet, embroidered with laurel leaves, flowers, and birds, which was bestowed upon Skelton by the Countess of Surrey, wife of the Duke's son. The *Garland* is not, however, merely a grateful acceptance of the honor. It is a justification of Skelton's right to the laurel and consequently a justification of his poetical career.

In broad outline, the structure of this allegorical poem is clear enough. Skelton dreams that he is the subject of a disputation between Pallas and the Queen of Fame. The Queen of Fame admits that Skelton is a learned disciple of Pallas, but she nevertheless questions his right to renown. He cannot be famous, she says, unless he has written deserving works. All the great poets and orators, both of antiquity and of modern times, are summoned to the court of Fame in order to pass judgment on Skelton's merit. The three English classics, Gower, Chaucer, and Lydgate, urge Skelton forward (that is, inspire him), first to the pavilion of Pallas (academic study), and then to the court of Fame. At the command of the Queen of Fame, Occupation (her registrar) reads a list of Skelton's works. When she has finished the catalogue, a triumphant shout from the scholarly throng welcomes the poet to renown.

Into this allegory, there is interpolated an episode of considerable biographical interest. When Skelton arrives at the palace of Fame, he is warmly greeted by Occupation. She has met the poet previously on two occasions:

> Of your aqueintaunce I was in tymes past,
>   Of studyous doctryne when at the port salu
> Ye fyrste aryuyd; whan broken was your mast
>   Of worldly trust, then did I you rescu;
>   Your storme dryuen shyppe I repared new,
> So well entakeled, what wynde that euer blowe,
> No stormy tempeste your barge shall ouerthrow.
>
> (ll. 540–46)

Before Occupation begins to read from the catalogue of Skelton's works, she escorts him on an allegorical journey. They come to a field, surrounded by a great wall of flint (l. 568). Occupation bids the poet walk on the wall, but warns him that it is slippery and dangerous. Skelton sees a thousand gates, representing the "issues and ports of all manner of nations." Over the gate of Anglia stands a crowned leopard, fierce of countenance. Below is an evil horde of dicers, card players, hypocrites, bawds, rioters, and flatterers, crowding and pushing one another as each attempts to win fame. A sudden blast of gun fire grievously wounds many of them and disperses the rest. A mist covers the scene, and for a time Skelton, frightened by the vision, remains in darkness (1. 650).

When the cloud lifts, Skelton and his mentor find themselves in a pleasant arbor, amid flowers and singing birds: "It was a new comfort of sorrows escaped." In the garden there is a laurel tree in which the phoenix nests. The Muses and the Dryads dance about. Jopas lifts up his voice in noble song; he tells of the course of the moon, of the origin of man, of the passing of the seasons, and

> . . . he browght in his songe
> How wronge was no ryght, and ryght was no wrong
> (ll. 703-4)

And Skelton points out that this delightful garden is situated on the estate of the Countess of Surrey (ll. 766-70). With this revelation the meaning of the episode becomes entirely clear. The vision of the gate of Anglia and the crowned leopard is an allegory of the English court and the King. The despicable rout represents the courtiers who haunt the King's palace, seeking place and glory. Skelton, too, has walked in the treacherous court. But it is a dangerous path to renown, as the slippery foothold and the blast of gun fire testify.

In contrast, life as a servant of the Countess of Surrey is peaceful and civilized. The lady appreciates learning, and rewards the learned. No crowd of jostling courtiers surrounds her.[14] Her household indeed provides a safe haven. And Occupation asks:

[14] The pleasure of the place is not entirely without alloy, however. Occupation points out an unpleasant fellow, Envious Rancor, who "sets men afighting and

How say ye? is this after your appetite?
  May this contente you and your mirry mynde?
Here dwellith pleasure, with lust and delyte;
  Contynuall comfort here ye may fynde,
  Of welth and solace no thynge left behynde;
All thynge conuenable here is contryuyd,
Wherewith your spiritis may be reuyuid.

(ll. 707–13)

The meaning of the allegory, then, is that Skelton has given up the royal court for the household of the Countess, whose "clerk" he has become (l. 777). It was Occupation who introduced him to both spheres of activity. She brought him to the court when he first arrived at the fruition of his studies. And when his storm-driven ship was in danger of sinking, that is, when his quarrel with Wolsey had carried him almost to the brink of ruin, Occupation led him to the solace of the Countess' household.

In addition to the visions there are other indications in the *Garland of Laurel* of the recent crisis in Skelton's life. Of particular interest are the references to the poet's invectives against Wolsey in the catalogue read by Occupation. Occupation describes some of Skelton's works; to others she grants only passing mention. The descriptions always tally with the poems as we know them—with two striking exceptions: *Speak, Parrot* and *Colin Clout*. Although the third of the Wolsey group, *Why Come Ye Not to Court*, was composed immediately before the *Garland*, it is omitted outright.

The following is Occupation's description of *Speak, Parrot:*

Item the Popingay, that hath in commendacyoun
Ladyes and gentylwomen suche as deseruyd,
And suche as be counterfettis they be reseruyd

(ll. 1188–90)

---

sits himself still" (ll. 720–65). The culprit's real name, given in a number cryptogram, is Rogerus Stathum. He may have been a relative of Geretrude Statham, one of the ladies who helped weave Skelton's garland (ll. 1038–61).

Colin Clout is buried in a group of light pieces:

> Also the Tunnynge of Elinour Rummyng,
>   With Colyn Clowt, Iohnn Iue, with Ioforth Iack;
> To make suche trifels it asketh sum konnyng
>   (ll. 1233–35)

Of course, *Parrot* is not a eulogy of gentlewomen, nor is *Colin Clout* a "trifle." It is clear that Skelton desires to hide the significance of these satires. He wishes to claim them as his compositions, but he is not willing to admit that they are attacks on Wolsey. Perhaps Skelton feels that he can actually falsify the intention of *Speak, Parrot*, since the meaning of the poem is so carefully hidden. *Colin Clout* wears the disguise of general satire and may pass as a "trifle." But about *Why Come Ye Not to Court* there can be no mistake. However much it may hurt to omit an important poem from the list of the works of the Laurel, Skelton finds it expedient to ignore *Why Come Ye Not to Court* completely.

The poet's mood at the time he wrote the *Garland* is more clearly illuminated by Dame Pallas' explanation of Skelton's failure to write against vice:

> And if so hym fortune to wryte true and plaine,
>   As sumtyme he must vyces remorde,
> Then sum wyll say he hath but lyttill brayne,
>   And how his wordes with reason wyll not accorde;
>   Beware, for wrytyng remayneth of recorde;
> Displease not an hundreth for one mannes pleasure;
> Who wryteth wysely hath a grete treasure.
>
> Also, to furnisshe better his excuse,
>   Ouyde was bannisshed for suche a skyll,
> And many mo whome I cowde enduce;
>   Iuuenall was thret parde for to kyll
>   For certayne enuectyfys, yet wrote he none ill,
> Sauynge he rubbid sum vpon the gall;
> It was not for hym to abyde the tryall.
>
> In generrall wordes, I say not gretely nay,
>   A poete somtyme may for his pleasure taunt,

Spekyng in parablis, how the fox, the grey,
  The gander, the gose, and the hudge oliphaunt,
  Went with the pecok ageyne the fesaunt;
The lesarde came lepyng, and sayd that he must,
With helpe of the ram, ley all in the dust.

Yet dyuerse ther be, industryous of reason,
  Sum what wolde gadder in there coniecture
Of suche an endarkid chapiter sum season;
  How be it, it were harde to construe this lecture;
  Sophisticatid craftely is many a confecture;
Another manes mynde diffuse is to expounde;
Yet harde is to make but sum fawt be founde.

                                    (ll. 85–112)

Now this highly interesting passage cannot really constitute an explanation of why Skelton never wrote satire—
we know, and his audience must then have known, that
he had written much. It must, therefore, explain why the
flow of diatribe has suddenly stopped. First, the old poet
assures us, such efforts are not worth while; they do not
pay. Furthermore, they are dangerous. Was it for Juvenal
to "abide the trial?" It is perhaps permissible to "taunt"
from the cover of beast fable or other "color," but people
are likely to misunderstand such "an endarked chapter."
To those who have supported him in his fight against
Wolsey, Skelton apologizes for his defection. To the party
in power he says, "Perhaps you have misunderstood me.
After all, is not *Speak, Parrot* a praise of virtuous ladies,
and *Colin Clout* a trifle of honest mirth?"

"TO MY LORD CARDINAL'S RIGHT NOBLE GRACE"

Skelton is now engaged in covering up the traces of his
recent attacks, in minimizing their importance, in claiming
that they have not been properly taken. The explanation
for this change of heart is to be found in the much-neglected
envoys, one to the *Garland of Laurel*, the other to *The
Doughty Duke of Albany*. The *Garland* envoy is not, it is true,

included in the first edition of the poem. But it has been concluded that the *Garland* was written in 1523. A strikingly similar envoy is attached to *The Duke of Albany*, also written in 1523. The two dedications strongly support each other. Surely it is racking the long arm of coincidence to assume that Editor Marshe, in 1568, fortuitously so placed these supposedly stray pieces. It seems more probable that the *Garland* envoy was omitted from the 1523 edition because Skelton did not wish to make public the reason for his sudden capitulation. The two messages must be examined closely.

Envoy to the *Garland of Laurel:*

Ad serenissimam Majestatem Regiam, pariter cum Domino Cardinali, Legato a latere honorificatissimo, &c.

Lautre Enuoy

Perge, liber, celebrem pronus regem venerare
Henricum octavum, resonans sua præmia laudis.
Cardineum dominum pariter venerando salutes,
Legatum a latere, et fiat memor ipse precare
Prebendæ, quam promisit mihi credere quondam,
Meque suum referas pignus sperare salutis
Inter spemque metum.

Twene hope and drede
My lyfe I lede,
But of my spede
Small sekernes;
Howe be it I rede
Both worde and dede
Should be agrede
In noblenes:
Or els, &c.

Envoy to *The Doughty Duke of Albany:*

Skelton Laureat, obsequious et loyall. To my lorde cardynals right noble grace, &c.

Lenuoy.

Go, lytell quayre, apace,
In moost humble wyse,

> Before his noble grace,
>> That caused you to deuise
>> This lytel enterprise;
> And hym moost lowly pray,
>> In his mynde to comprise
> Those wordes his grace dyd saye
> Of an ammas gray.
> *Ie foy enterment en sa bone grace.*

Within one year after *Why Come Ye Not to Court*, Skelton, obsequious and loyal, wrote a poem at the request of Cardinal Wolsey! It is not difficult to supply the explanation. In the *Garland* envoy the poet declares that he lives "between hope and dread." The "dread" must have been the threat of such punishment as that accorded to Ovid and Juvenal. It is probable that Skelton was forced to hide himself in sanctuary to escape Wolsey's anger.[15] But there was "hope" as well as "dread." Both envoys remind Wolsey of a conversation in which there was talk of a prebend (the "amice grey" of the dedication to *The Duke of Albany* was a hood of grey fur worn by canons and holders of prebends). "Don't forget your promise," begs Skelton.

One need not condemn the poet too harshly for accepting the bribe. Wolsey was everything; Skelton was nothing. For daring to oppose the Cardinal, so exalted a personage as the Duke of Buckingham had been beheaded. Skelton had risked his life when he set down Wolsey's vices in bold, stabbing rhyme, each verse bearing a signature as unmistakable as John Hancock's. He had been caught, and he was forced to recant. In the dedication to the *Replication against Certain Young Scholars* (1528), written five years after the envoys to the *Garland* and to *The Duke of Albany*, Skelton again humbled himself before his former adversary, again spoke of Wolsey as his patron. As for Wolsey, he seems to have refrained from harsh treatment of learned men and of authors who attacked him. Perhaps,

[15] See pp. 205–7.

too, Skelton's long association with the King urged the Cardinal toward a peaceful rather than a violent solution.

Yet there are signs that relations between the two never became entirely sweet. Perhaps the "merry tale" of Skelton's encounter with the Cardinal after his imprisonment catches something of the spirit of the poet's surrender:[16]

On a tyme Skelton did meete with certain frendes of hys at Charyng crosse, after that hee was in prison at my lord cardynals commaundement: & his frende sayd, I am glad you bee abrode amonge your frendes, for you haue ben long pent in. Skelton sayd, By the masse, I am glad I am out indeede, for I haue ben pent in, like a roche or fissh, at Westminster in prison. The cardinal, hearing of those words, sent for him agayne. Skelton kneling of hys knees before hym, after long communication to Skelton had, Skelton desyred the cardinall to graunte hym a boun. Thou shalt haue none, sayd the cardynall. Thassistence desirid that he might haue it graunted, for they thought it should be some merye pastime that he wyll shewe your grace. Say on, thou hore head, sayd the cardynall to Skelton. I pray your grace to let me lye doune and wallow, for I can kneele no longer.

Indeed, it seems that shortly after the submission recorded in the *Garland* envoy, Skelton circulated a witticism that Wolsey could not have taken kindly. The circumstances are recorded by Hall:[17]

And in this season [May, 1523], the Cardinall by his power legantyne, dissolued the conuocacion at Paules, called by the Archebishop of Cantorbury, and called hym and all the clergie, to his conuocacion to Westminster, which was neuer seen before in England, wherof master Skelton a mery Poet wrote.

> *Gentle Paule laie doune thy swearde:*
> *For Peter of Westminster hath shauen thy beard.*

And there is reason to believe that despite the humble dedication to the *Replication* (1528), Skelton secreted in the body of that poem a last blow at his most hated enemy.[18] Skelton wrote no poems in praise of the Cardinal. As for

[16] Tale xiv.   [17] *Hall's Chronicle*, p. 657.   [18] See below, pp. 217–19.

Wolsey, it appears that he failed to keep his promise of the "amice grey." There seems never to have been another open break, however. The quip about Convocation is not a serious attack, and the lines in the *Replication* which may contain a hostile reference to Wolsey are cautiously ambiguous.

SANCTUARY AT WESTMINSTER

The only reason for denying a peaceful last six years to the aging poet is the statement in Bale's *Scriptorum catalogus* that because of his invectives against the Cardinal, Skelton was forced to flee to sanctuary at Westminster, where he died, *captivitatis suæ tempore*. This is puzzling. If it is accepted, it forces the conclusion that there occurred a new outbreak between Skelton and Wolsey, with new invectives, which have disappeared without trace. The evidence cannot be disregarded merely because it complicates the proposed reconstruction of the story of the quarrel. But there is more cogent reason for discarding it.

Bale himself had no independent knowledge of Skelton. The note on Skelton in the first (1548) edition of Bale's catalogue[19] is restricted to:

> Skeltonus poeta laureatus, sub diuerso genere metri edidit, *Anglica carmina.*   *li. plu.*

In the course of the decade which elapsed before the publication of the next edition of his work, Bale acquired new information about Skelton from William Horman and Edward Braynewode. Using Braynewode's contribution as a base, Bale compounded the item on Skelton which appears in the 1559 (?) catalogue. It differs from its sources only in slight elaboration, insertion of transitional phrases, and correction of the Latinity. If Braynewode's words, as recorded in Bale's notebook, be compared with the corresponding passage in Bale's 1559 catalogue, the error in-

---

[19] *Illustrium maioris Britanniæ scriptorum summarium* (Ipswich, 1548), fol. 254.

volved in the description of the manner of Skelton's death becomes patent. The notebook reads:[20]

Ob literas in Cardinalem Wolsium inuectiuas, ad Westmonasteriense asylum confugere pro vita seruanda coactus fuit, vbi tamen sub Islepo abbate fauorem inuenit. Mortuus tandem, in D. Margarete templo ante summum altare conditus est, cum hac scriptione alabastrica . . .

The edition of 1559:[21]

Ob literas quasdam in Cardinalem Vuolsium inuectiuas, ad Vuestmonasteriense tandem asylum confugere, pro uita seruanda coactus fuit: ubi nihilominus sub abbate Islepo fauorem inuenit . . . Vuestmonasterij tandem, captiuitatis suæ tempore, mortuus est: & in D. Margaritæ sacello sepultus. . .

Braynewode says merely that, because of his attacks on Wolsey, Skelton was forced to seek safety in sanctuary. "Finally," he died. But there is no necessary connection between the statements. Bale, observing that the poet not only had been pent in Westminster but was also buried there, makes the very natural mistake of linking the two facts. Moreover, in order to save his reader from any "misunderstanding" he emphasizes the connection between Skelton's imprisonment in sanctuary and his burial at St. Margaret's by adding to "he died" the words "at Westminster in the time of his captivity." Of course, Skelton's interment at St. Margaret's requires no such explanation. He was buried at St. Margaret's because it was the church of the parish in which he resided, not because he was a sanctuary man at the time of his death. Since Braynewode says that Skelton fled to sanctuary because of the anger which his invectives had stirred in Wolsey, it must be concluded that the poet's imprisonment had occurred many years before his death, that is, while he was writing the series of satires which ended in the climactic *Why Come Ye Not to Court*.

If Skelton continued to live in the house which Alice

[20] *Index*, p. 253.   [21] *Catalogus* (Basle, 1559[?]), pp. 651–52.

Newebery leased in 1518,[22] his "imprisonment" meant only
that he was not permitted to leave his home. How long
the imprisonment continued, it is impossible to determine.
Francis Thynne declares that Skelton wrote *Colin Clout* at
the house of Thynne's father, in Kent.[23] If the statement is
true, Skelton's restriction to sanctuary could not have begun before 1522. The recklessly outspoken character of
Why Come Ye Not to Court (which was finished in November,
1522) suggests that this last of the satires against Wolsey
was written during the period of Wolsey's active displeasure and after Skelton had found safety in the asylum
of Westminster. Skelton had lost his liberty, and unless
Wolsey infringed the rights of sanctuary he could lose
nothing more. By December, 1522, the imprisonment must
have ended, for the New Year found Skelton at Sheriff-
Hutton, a member of the household of the Countess of
Surrey.

"BY WHOSE SUGGESTION?"

Though the end of the story is therefore quite clear,
the beginning remains mysterious. Perhaps we may accept
Skelton's own assertion as to the cause of his audacious
assault on the ruler of England:[24]

> Some men myght aske a question,
> By whose suggestyon
> I toke on hand this warke,
> Thus boldly for to barke?
> And men lyst to harke,
> And my wordes marke,
> I wyll answere lyke a clerke;
> For trewly and vnfayned,
> I am forcebly constrayned,
> At Iuuynals request,

---

[22] See above, p. 120.
[23] *Animadversions upon Chaucer's Works*, "Early English Text Society [Publica-
tions]," O. S., IX, 10.
[24] *Why Come Ye Not to Court*, ll. 1199–1214.

> To wryght of this [gromys][25] gest,
> Of this vayne gloryous best,
> His fame to be encrest
> At euery solempne feest;
> *Quia difficile est*
> *Satiram non scribere.*

It would have been difficult, indeed, for Skelton to refrain from writing invectives against Cardinal Wolsey. Personal jealousy undoubtedly played a part. Wolsey, a grammarian like himself (though Skelton had little respect for Wolsey's scholarly attainments[26]), of birth as low, or possibly more humble, had become second only to the king in England. But it is more just to emphasize a less selfish reason for Skelton's antipathy. For Wolsey embodied the negation of all that Skelton thought valuable and important.

Skelton's philosophy of the golden mean appears in his first writings. Wit and Will are opposed in the elegy on the Duke of Northumberland. In the Diodorus translation Skelton warns the nobility against pursuit of extravagant follies.[27] For Skelton, Wolsey was the personification of excess. So the poet describes him in *Why Come Ye Not to Court*:

> Ther vayleth no resonynge,
> For wyll dothe rule all thynge,
> Wyll, wyll, wyll, wyll, wyll,
> He ruleth alway styll.
> (ll. 101-4)

> To hasty of sentence,
> To ferce for none offence,
> To scarce of your expence,
> To large in neglygence,
> To slacke in recompence,
> To haute in excellence,

[25] *Works:* "glorious." The word has apparently slipped up from the following line. "gromys" is substituted from the copy of *Why Come Ye Not to Court* in MS Rawl. C. 813.
[26] *Why Come Ye Not to Court*, ll. 505-32.   [27] See p. 64.

To lyght [in] intellegence,
And to lyght in credence;
Where these kepe resydence,
Reson is banysshed thence,
And also dame Prudence,
With sober Sapyence.

(ll. 3–14)

In 1501, when Wolsey was a mere domestic chaplain to the Archbishop of Canterbury, Skelton had tried to impress on his princely pupil the necessity for personal rule, for self-reliance, rather than a policy of dependence on an advisory council. When he rededicated *Speculum principis* to the young Henry VIII (*c.* 1510), he added an emphatic warning at the close: "Regem te calleas. Regere. non Regi."[28] At that time Wolsey had already become king's almoner, and his power was rapidly growing. By 1521, when *Speak, Parrot* was written, Skelton's worst fears had been realized. Henry was king in name only; Wolsey ruled the roost. Skelton's warning of 1510 now became a passionate plea for a cause all but lost:[29]

Non annis licet et Priamus sed honore voceris:
  Dum foveas vitulum, rex, regeris, Britonum;
Rex, regeris, non ipse regis: rex inclyte, calle;
  Subde tibi vitulum, ne fatuet nimium.

God amend all,
  That all amend may!
Amen, quod Parott,
  The royall popagay.

And in *Why Come Ye Not to Court:*

Why come ye nat to court?—
To whyche court?
To the kynges courte,
Or to Hampton Court?—

---

[28] Photostat of MS Additional 26787 made by the Modern Language Association of America (Collection of photographic facsimiles, No. 27). Salter misprints "regie" (*Speculum*, IX, 37).

[29] *Speak, Parrot*, ll. 348–55.

> Nay, to the kynges court:
> The kynges courte
> Shulde haue the excellence;
> But Hampton Court
> Hath the preemynence
>   (ll. 398–406)

The upstart butcher's son has seized supreme power and is overturning the realm of England with his willful excess. And so, until Wolsey is tamed Skelton resolutely refuses to come to court:[30]

> For age is a page
> For the courte full vnmete,
> For age cannat rage,
> Nor basse her swete swete:
>   But whan age seeth that rage
> Dothe aswage and refrayne,
> Than wyll age haue a corage
> To come to court agayne.

It may be that despite his own statement of the case Skelton attacked Cardinal Wolsey because he was urged to do so by a powerful patron. Color is lent to the supposition by the fact that shortly after *Why Come Ye Not to Court* was written Skelton became the servant of the Countess of Surrey. Her father-in-law (the Duke of Norfolk) and her husband were the foremost representatives of the old nobility in England. Although the elder Howard headed the English army at Flodden and the younger led a successful naval raid on the French coast and turned back the forces of the Scottish protector, they bore little sway in the King's council. Wolsey was all-powerful, and Wolsey cared little for military prowess or for ancient name. Nevertheless, the Howards never openly broke with the man they must have hated. In fact, the Duke of Norfolk acquiesced in the judgment of treason against the Duke of Buckingham, who did dare to offend my Lord Cardinal. Norfolk's letters to Wolsey are almost subservient. How-

[30] *Why Come Ye Not to Court*, ll. 31–38.

ever, it would have been good generalship, indeed, for him
to undermine his enemy by hiring the pen of a satirist
whose skin was considerably less valuable than that of the
greatest noble in England.

But aside from the *Garland*, which was written after
Skelton's attacks on Wolsey had ceased, there is little
evidence to show that Skelton received support from the
Howards. It is true that the Flodden poems celebrate the
English commander responsible for the victory and that
the younger Howard also receives hearty praise for his
military activities. But the eulogies need not have been
patronage bred, for the Howards were remarkably successful generals, and Skelton could not have written of English
victories without extolling the leaders of the English
forces. If I understand the allegory of the *Garland* correctly,
Skelton's attachment to the household of the Countess
had begun but shortly before the poem was written. Nor is
there any indication that he continued to serve her, since
the recipient of the dedications of Skelton's last two poems,
The Duke of Albany and the *Replication*, is, not the Countess,
but Wolsey.

In outline, at least, the tale of Skelton's greatest quarrel
is now clear. Whether motivated by personal pique, conflict of opinion, or the urging of a patron, Skelton wrote a
group of poems in 1521–22 constituting a crescendo of
attacks upon the most feared person of the realm, Cardinal
Wolsey. Then the attacks abruptly ceased. A few months
after the last, because of danger so imminent that he was
forced to seek sanctuary and because of the promise of a
bribe, Skelton capitulated. Thereafter, Wolsey became his
patron, and Skelton's last two poems were written under
the Cardinal's auspices. Bale's statement that Skelton died
in hiding at Westminster is apparently erroneous. It is
both pleasanter and more probable to suppose that the last
years of the turbulent poet's life were spent in peace.

The Last Years

THE PRESUMABLY untroubled years between Skelton's capitulation to Wolsey and his death in 1529 are represented by two poems only, *The Doughty Duke of Albany* (late 1523) and *A Replication against Certain Young Scholars Abjured of Late* (1528). The former celebrates the frustration of an attempt by the Duke of Albany, the Scottish protector, to invade England. After reporting the retreat of the Scots, Skelton proceeds to denounce their cowardice and perfidy and then launches into a eulogy of Henry VIII. In contrast to the brilliance and vivacity of *Colin Clout* and *Why Come Ye Not to Court*, *The Duke of Albany* seems uninspired and turgid. The chief interest of the poem lies in the fact that it marks Skelton's return to activities connected with the royal court after the turmoil of his quarrel with Wolsey and the idyllic interlude of his service in the household of the Countess of Surrey. As the envoy of the poem unmistakably declares, Skelton wrote the poem at Wolsey's request and hoped that his labors would be rewarded.

A Replication against Certain Young Scholars, also written at Wolsey's suggestion,[1] is a far more interesting piece. It is an invective against certain heretics of Cambridge who abjured their errors and carried fagots to Paul's Cross (a symbolic burning) on the feast of the conception of the Virgin:

> For ye were worldly shamed,
> At Poules crosse openly,
> All men can testifye;
> There, lyke a sorte of sottes,

[1] Skelton, *Works*, I, 206: "necnon præsentis opusculi fautore excellentissimo . . ."

Ye were fayne to beare fagottes;
At the feest of her concepcion
Ye suffred suche correction.

(ll. 62–68)

On the feast of the conception (December 8), 1527, Thomas
Bilney and Thomas Arthur, both Cambridge men, bore
fagots to Paul's Cross as a token of their renunciation of
heresy.[2] Unquestionably these are the scholars whom
Skelton attacks. The identification is corroborated by a
comparison of the charges against Arthur and Bilney with
Skelton's indictment of the young heretics of the poem.
Bilney and Arthur were accused of having preached
"against images, pilgrimages, and praying to Saints as
mediators."[3] Skelton, likewise, denounces the abjured
scholars for teaching "howe it was idolatry to offre to
ymages of our blessed lady, or to pray and go on pyl-
grimages, or to make oblacions to any ymages of sayntes
in churches or elsewhere."[4]

Despite the plural address of the title it is probable that
the *Replication* was directed particularly against Bilney.
Arthur confessed his errors and abjured without protest.
After his humiliation at St. Paul's, he is heard of no more,
and it is to be supposed that he faithfully kept his promise
to avoid the heresies of which he had been found guilty.
Bilney, on the other hand, proved a more difficult case for
the authorities. Although he was convicted on the evidence
of more than twenty witnesses, he refused to confess that
he had preached heresy.[5] "At last, though he still declined
to confess his error, he felt it politic to abjure, and so great
favour was shown him by his judges that they admitted
him to penance without any confession of his fault."[6] After

---

[2] The identification of these heretics with Skelton's scholars was first proposed
by J. B. Mullinger, *The University of Cambridge* (Cambridge, 1873), I, 607–8. The date
of the ceremony is given in *The Acts and Monuments of John Foxe*, ed. by S. R. Cattley
(London, 1832), IV, 632.

[3] J. Gairdner, *Lollardy and the Reformation* (London, 1908), I, 393.

[4] Skelton, *Works*, I, 209.   [5] Gairdner, *op. cit.*, p. 396.   [6] *Ibid.*, pp. 396–97.

a period of penitential imprisonment, he was released. But
he failed to keep his oath. Soon afterward he began preaching again, at first secretly and later openly. It was not long
before he was haled before the ecclesiastical court at Norwich. In 1531 he was burnt at the stake as a relapsed heretic.

The following lines are therefore applicable only to
Bilney, not to Arthur:

> And yet some men say,
> Howe ye are this day,
> And be nowe as yll,
> And so ye wyll be styll,
> As ye were before.
> What shulde I recken more?
> 　Men haue you in suspicion
> Howe ye haue small contrycion
> Of that ye haue myswrought:
> For, if it were well sought,
> One of you there was
> That laughed whan he dyd pas
> With his fagot in processyon;
> He counted it for no correction,
> But with scornefull affection
> Toke it for a sporte,
> His heresy to supporte;
> Whereat a thousande gased,
> As people halfe amased,
> And thought in hym smale grace
> His foly so to face.
> 　　　　　(ll. 176-96)

And Skelton's ominous warning proved a true prophecy:

> . . . mende your myndes that are mased;
> Or els doutlesse ye shalbe blased,
> And be brent at a stake,
> If further busynesse that ye make.
> 　　　　　(ll. 293-96)

Skelton shows an intimate knowledge of the interroga-
tions which took place in 1527, of the arguments that
passed between the accused and their inquisitors. Since the

trial was held in the Chapter House at Westminster, a few steps from Skelton's home, it may be suspected that he was present at the questioning. The poet's active interest in the suppression of heresy is evident from his citation of Thomas Pykerell, in 1509, and his appointment as arbitrator in the case of William Dale, in 1511. It has recently been pointed out[7] that a Master Skelton was a witness to the abjuration of Thomas Bowgas, a Colchester fuller, who rejected his heretical beliefs at the London residence of the Bishop of Norwich in 1528.[8] If this Master Skelton was Skelton, the poet, it becomes very likely that he was also a witness to Bilney's trial in the preceding year.

The *Replication* exhibits Skelton fighting by the side of Sir Thomas More for the extirpation of heresy. In March, 1528, Tunstall, Bishop of London, granted More special licence to keep Lutheran books in order that he might write answers to them.[9] The first product of this commission was the *Dialogue concerning Heresies*, which, though written in 1528, was not published until the following year.[10] The entire first half of the treatise, from the very beginning to chapter vii of Book III, is devoted to Bilney and his errors. A comparison of More's *Dialogue* with Skelton's *Replication* reveals a striking contrast and a striking similarity. More wrote a lengthy, leisurely prose discussion; Skelton, a brief invective in torrential rhyme. More's work is cool and reasonable; it searches every angle of the argument and leaves no possible objection unanswered. Skelton's reasoning is overwhelmed by the strength of his emotion. But the resemblance between the two works is quite as remarkable. Both were written at the request of prelates concerned in the affair, the *Dialogue* at the suggestion of Tunstall, who presided at the trial, the

[7] By H. L. R. Edwards, *PMLA*, LIII (1938), 610.
[8] Strype, *Ecclesiastical Memorials* (London, 1822), I (ii), 58.
[9] Gairdner, I, 510; Wilkins, *Concilia*, III, 711–12.
[10] R. W. Chambers, *Thomas More* (London, 1935), p. 254.

Replication at the instigation of Wolsey, who had questioned Bilney on a previous occasion. Neither author refers to Bilney by name: Skelton speaks of "certain young scholars," and More denounces "the man ye write of."[11] Both point out that Bilney's rejection of saint worship as idolatry ignores the acknowledged distinction among the categories of *dulia* (honor due to man), *hyperdulia* (honor due to creatures greater than man, like angels and saints), and *latria* (honor due to God alone).[12] In both treatises Bilney is attacked for perfidy and insincerity.[13] More and Skelton agree that Bilney has been treated with excessive moderation. More suggests that it was improper to have admitted him to penance without confession;[14] Skelton believes that he should have been required to confess publicly in the very places where he had uttered his heresies.[15] Finally, both writers feel called upon to defend themselves against the charge that as poets they had no business to dabble in matters theological.[16] It seems likely, therefore, that the *Dialogue* and the *Replication* form part of an officially inspired concerted attempt to destroy the heretical movement in England with the weapon of eloquence.

Skelton's apology for poetry occurs at the end of the *Replication:*

> Ye saye that poetry
> Maye nat flye so hye
> In theology,
> Nor analogy,
> Nor philology,
> Nor philosophy,
> To answere or reply
> Agaynst suche heresy.
> (ll. 306–13)

---

[11] More himself identifies the abjured heretic of the *Dialogue* in the preface to the *Confutation of Tyndale's Answer.*

[12] *Replication*, ll. 275–91; *Dialogue*, Book II, chap. xi.

[13] *Dialogue*, Book III, chap. vii.   [14] Book III, chap. v.

[15] Lines 197–211.   [16] *Replication*, ll. 300–408; *Dialogue*, Book I, chap. xxiii.

In response Skelton advances the arguments commonly proposed by Renaissance poets in defense of their discipline. Did not Jerome say that the psalms of David constitute the Christian analogue of the lyrics of Simonides? Skelton declares that he has treated of the nature and function of poetry in a former work, *The Book of Good Advertisement.*[17] He presents a summary of its conclusions. God, who dwells within laureate poets, instills into their compositions a mysterious energic effect of heavenly inspiration. And it is the Holy Ghost,

> Which is God of myghtes most,
> That he our penne dothe lede,
> And maketh in vs suche spede,
> That forthwith we must nede
> With penne and ynke procede,
> Somtyme for affection,
> Somtyme for sadde dyrection,
> Somtyme for correction
>
> (ll. 384–91)

With this assertion of the high mission of poetry Skelton closes his last poem.

Although the dedication of the *Replication* is as extravagantly humble and eulogistic as Wolsey could have desired, there is at least a suspicion that in the body of the poem Skelton could not resist the opportunity to take a privy dig at his old enemy. Bilney, who is described as a "pauper" in the Cambridge records,[18] must be the subject of the following lines:

> I saye it for no sedicion,
> But vnder pacient tuicyon,
> It is halfe a supersticyon
> To gyue you exhibycion
> To mainteyne with your skoles,
> And to proue your selfe suche foles.

---

[17] Lines 360–71. The *Garland* catalogue includes (l. 1186):
Item Good Aduysement, that braines doth blame
[18] *Grace Book B (II)*, p. 92 (1520–21).

> Some of you had ten pounde,
> Therwith for to be founde
> At the vnyuersyte,
> Employed which myght haue be
> Moche better other wayes.   Obscurus sarcasmos.
> But, as the man sayes,
> The blynde eteth many a flye:
> What may be ment hereby,
> Ye may soone make construction
> With right lytell instruction;
> For it is an auncyent brute,   Ex fructibus
> Suche apple tre, suche frute.   eorum cognoscetis
> What shulde I prosecute,   eos, &c.
> Or more of this to clatter?
> Retourne we to our matter.
>
> (ll. 140-60)

A curious passage this, and Skelton is a little hesitant in setting it down. Who is the "apple tree" against whom the "obscure sarcasm" is directed? Someone had given the heretic Bilney an exhibition (endowment) of ten pounds for his maintenance at the university, someone who was so powerful that criticism of him might be mistaken for sedition. Nevertheless, Skelton dares to compare the charitable one with the fruit he had nourished. In More's *Dialogue* one of Bilney's benefactors is identified:[19]

This man [Bilney] had also been before [his trial in 1527] . . accused unto the greatest prelate in this realm, who for his tender favour borne to the university, did not proceed far in the matter against him. But . . . dismissed him very benignly; and of his liberal bounty gave him also money for his costs.

There can be no question as to the identity of "the greatest prelate in this realm." When Skelton undertook the task of writing against Bilney, he must have been aware that the man at whose request he was denouncing the heretic had himself nursed and generated the viper. Of course, the passage is cautiously obscure, and Skelton provides himself with an additional safeguard:

[19] *The English Works of Sir Thomas More* (London, 1931), p. 193.

Ye dyde prouoke and tyse,
Oftnar than ones or twyse,
Many a good man
And many a good woman,
By way of their deuocion
To helpe you to promocion,
Whose charite wele regarded
Can nat be vnrewarded.
                    (ll. 132-39)

Nevertheless, it is probable that Skelton's contemporaries remembered the Cardinal's liberal bounty "for his tender favour borne to the university" when they read a "sarcasm" directed against one who had supported the heretic's university career. If they did recognize Wolsey in Skelton's lines, the poet who six years before had been in deadly danger was taking an enormous risk. But there was not much time for Skelton's last indiscretion (if indiscretion it was) to produce its penalty.

On June 21, 1529, Skelton died. Over his tomb in the choir of St. Margaret's, Westminster, was placed the inscription in alabaster:[20] "Iohannes Skeltonus vates Pierius hic situs est animam egit, 21 Junij 1529." Bells pealed; candles were burned.[21] A month later Skelton's successor

---

[20] Weever, *Funeral Monuments*, p. 497; Braynewode, in Bale, *Index*, p. 253. In *Scriptorum catalogus* (1559?), p. 652, Bale adds the words "relictis liberis." Both Weever and Braynewode agree on the shorter form.

[21] Churchwardens' Accounts (biennial) of St. Margaret's, Westminster, 1512–30 (Vol. E. 2, unpaginated, Caxton Hall), *sub fin.*: Receiptis by the sayde Wardens Receyuyd in the second yere of this ther accompte for buryalles obittes and lyghtis as perticuler[l]y folowyth

    Item of M*aster* skelton for iiij tapers   ij^s viiij^d
    Item of hym for iiij torches   iiij^s

Receptys of the belles for knylles and peales This second yere
    Item of M*aster* Iohn skelton for knyll and peales vj^s viij^d

Paymentes leide oute by the saide accomptantes this second yere ffor Ryngyng off knylles and pealles
    Item paid to o*ur* lady brotherhed for M*aster* skelton   xx^d
    Item paid for Ringyng of his knyll and peales   xij^d

I owe this note to the kindness of H. L. R. Edwards. My own readings, which depend on the modern transcript of the churchwardens' accounts kept at the Abbey library, are necessarily less trustworthy.

was instituted rector of Diss.²² The poet left no will.
William Mott, the curate of St. Margaret's, administered
his estate.²³

²² Thomas Clerk was instituted on July 17, 1529, "per mortem naturalem mag-
istri Johannis Skeltoune ultimi Rectoris eiusdem vacantem" (Norwich Institution Book XVII, fol. 9).

²³ Peculiar Court of Westminster, fol. 6, "Bracy."

Reputation and Influence

CAXTON, Erasmus, and Whittinton honored Skelton as a scholar; Puttenham and Pope spurned him as a railing mountebank. The antithesis cannot be entirely resolved by an examination of his works. Between the modern reader and the poet there intervenes the distortion imposed by centuries of rapidly shifting traditions in manners and literature. In order to judge fairly of Skelton it is first of all necessary to consult the judgment of his contemporaries. Their opinions need not govern ours, of course. We cannot live or read by the standards of sixteenth-century England. But neither can we understand Skelton by the rule of the twentieth, nor without understanding evaluate him.

During his lifetime Skelton was reputed a learned rhetorician. The only dissenting voice is that of Lily, whose epigram[1] may be discounted, since it is evidently a reply to an attack. Barclay, another critic, is less concerned with Skelton's scholarship than with his morals. On the other hand, Caxton, Erasmus, and Whittinton form a eulogistic chorus. The universities of Oxford, Louvain, and Cambridge dubbed Skelton "Laureate"; he taught a royal prince and served as royal orator.

It is possible to name specifically the excellence for which Skelton was particularly celebrated. A contemporary poet, Henry Bradshaw, addresses him with respect:[2] "inuentiue Skelton and poet laureate." Invention is one of

---

[1] See above, p. 156.

[2] *The Life of Saint Werburge*, "Early English Text Society [Publications]," O.S., LXXXVIII (1887), 199. Bradshaw calls Skelton "father of eloquence" in a similar invocation in *The Lyfe of Saynt Radegunde* (Pynson, n.d.), edited by F. Brittain (Cambridge, 1926), p. 37.

the most important of the five traditional divisions of
rhetoric: invention (or investigation), arrangement, style,
memory, and delivery. It is concerned primarily with
methods of amplifying themes. The Renaissance rhetorician was deeply interested in padding the bare bones of his
ideas with a plentiful supply of appositive and illustrative
matter. For the purpose of such ornamentation, teachers of
rhetoric supplied their pupils with numerous collections
of proverbs, maxims, apophthegms, fables, examples,
similes, descriptions, and selected quotations. These were
usually arranged topically, so that the pupil, having been
assigned a theme for amplification, needed only to leaf the
volumes and to select what was appropriate. A writer who
could richly dilate his compositions, with or without the
aid of such thesauri, was properly called "inventive."

The literary quality of inventiveness was frequently associated in the Renaissance with the mental characteristic
of ingenuity, or wit. A bright, sharp intelligence made it
possible for the rhetorician to speak copiously on any subject, to decorate his themes not only with the gems of
others but also with those of his own manufacture. More
and Erasmus were constantly singled out as examples of
witty, ingenious rhetoricians, for they had both learning,
which armed them with the sentences of the ancients, and
mental acuity, which permitted them to create their own.
A close student of the subject of Renaissance rhetoric cites
the following passage from John Barclay's *The Mirror of
Minds* as an excellent description of witty men:[3]

Some in private and close discourses excel with a short and sting-
ing wit, ever intent upon the follies of others; the other sort
comes nearer to the dignity of eloquence, and whensoever they
please publicly or at home to discourse, their wit is like a torrent
and their memory doth opportunately prompt them with all
things that they have either seen or read. [The latter, he con-

[3] W. G. Crane, *Wit and Rhetoric in the Renaissance* (Columbia University Press,
1937), p. 96.

tinues] are copious in longer eloquence and fitted continually
with an unexhausted store of words and sentences . . . they never
fail of this pompous plenty of words and sentences.

Even the most cursory examination of Skelton's writings reveals that he was what his contemporaries called a
wit. He possesses an amazing fecundity of words and
matter. He showers synonyms, proverbs, pithy sayings,
and examples. Often, the coherence of his poems is overwhelmed by the torrent of appositives. But the fault depends upon an excess of wit, an inability to restrain the
stream of invention.

There are indications that Skelton's pithy sayings circulated widely in his own time. One of his contemporaries
noted on a flyleaf:[4]

> Master Skeltons docters of cownsell
> Docter Rest and docter quyett
> Docter myrthe and docter dyett

Hall's quotation of Skelton's quip concerning Convocation
has already been noted.[5] But the best proof of Skelton's
reputation as a wit is to be found in the fact that very soon
after his death he became the hero of a considerable collection of jests.

Although Dyce refers to the *Merry Tales of Skelton* as
"that tissue of extravagant figments which was put together for the amusement of the vulgar,"[6] few of the tales
are extravagant, several of them may be entirely true, and
by no means all of the readers of the pamphlet were vulgar.
To dispose of the last point first, it is obvious from Dyce's
own collection of references to Skelton that the *Merry Tales*
were read by highly respectable scholars. John Parkhurst,
Bishop of Norwich and Fellow of Merton College, fash-

[4] M. R. James, *A Descriptive Catalogue of the Manuscripts in the Library of Corpus Christi College Cambridge* (1912), No. 31. The couplet probably derives from the famous *Regimen sanitatis Salerni.*

[5] Page 204.

[6] Skelton, *Works,* I, xxx.

ioned a Latin epigram from one of the stories,[7] and John
Chamber, Prebendary of the Free Chapel of Windsor, used
a tale to illustrate a point in his *Treatise against Jvdicial
Astrologie*.[8] Indeed, the jestbook tradition, of which the
Merry Tales of Skelton is a part, is a rhetorical and scholarly
rather than a vulgar tradition. The most famous of the
Renaissance *facetiæ* was written by Poggio Bracciolini, one
of the most celebrated of Italian humanists. A considerable
section of Castiglione's *Courtier* is devoted to a catalogue of
such anecdotes as may properly be told in good society.
Collections of jests, like the multitude of *Apophthegmata*,
Similia, and *Adagia*, were useful sourcebooks for the
rhetorical ornamentation of themes.

In the present connection it is not necessary to know
whether or not the *Merry Tales of Skelton* is true history.[9] It
is pertinent only to inquire what the existence of the
pamphlet signifies as to Skelton's reputation among his
contemporaries. One method of answering the question is
to set Skelton among the other wits of his time and to assign to him the reputation that they possessed. A second
procedure depends upon an examination of the portrait of
Skelton drawn by the *Tales* themselves.

Erasmus and Thomas More, the foremost figures of
English humanism, were also renowned as jesters. Not only
did they frequently employ merry tales to enliven their
writings, even the most serious of them, but also like Skelton they became the protagonists of numerous anecdotes.
The analogy between More and Erasmus and Skelton is by
no means far-fetched. One jest, for instance, is attributed
both to Erasmus and to Skelton. According to a late sixteenth-century manuscript, Stephen Gardiner once lent

---

[7] Skelton, *Works*, I, lxxix–lxxx, from *Johannis Parkhvrsti ludicra siue epigrammata juuenilia* (1573), p. 103.

[8] Skelton, *Works*, I, lxxx, from *A Treatise against Jvdicial Astrologie* (1601), p. 113.

[9] See above, pp. 108–10.

Skelton a palfrey. Instead of returning it, the poet sent back the following lines:[10]

> Non meministi Quod mihi scripsisti de corpore Christi etc.
> Sic tibi rescribo de tuo Palfrido, credo quod habes, et habes.

Precisely the same quip is said to have been sent by Erasmus to Thomas More.[11] More, too, is associated with Skelton in an anecdote. When Skelton wished to have a witness to the discomfiture of Sir James of Castile by Long Meg of Westminster, he could think of no one more appropriate than the learned author of *Utopia*.[12]

Examination of the *Merry Tales of Skelton* confirms the conclusion that the poet was considered, not a mountebank, but a witty rhetorician. Although a few of the anecdotes are of the rough and tumble variety, most of them turn on a clever retort or a pithy saying. When a dinner companion asked Skelton where Christ was during the forty days before his ascent to heaven, he replied, "he was verye busye in the woods among hys labourers, that dyd make fagottes to burne heretickes, & such as thou art the whych doest aske such diffuse questions."[13] One story depends on an epitaph which Skelton wrote for a knave of Oxford,[14] two contain "quick answers" to Cardinal Wolsey,[15] and one contains a retort to the Bishop of Norwich.[16] Clearly, it is no common clown that appears in the *Merry Tales*, but an astute and sharp-tongued scholar.

Skelton's reputation as a merry scholar who scourged the world's evils even as he jested persisted for fifty years after his death. So Braynewode (*c.* 1550) describes him:[17]

---

[10] Ian A. Gordon, in *London Times Literary Supplement*, September 20, 1934, p. 636, quoting from MS Egerton 2642. But see H. L. R. Edwards in *London Times Literary Supplement*, September 27, 1934, p. 655.

[11] J. A. Froude, *Life and Letters of Erasmus* (New York, 1894), p. 109.

[12] *The Life of Long Meg of Westminster*, chap. iv, reprinted in Skelton, *Works*, I, lxxxiii–lxxxv.

[13] Tale iii.   [14] Tale v.   [15] Tales x and xiv.   [16] Tale vi.

[17] In Bale, *Index*, p. 253. "Facetijs in quotidiana inuentione deditus multum erat, non tamen omisit sub persona ridentis (vt habet Horatius Flaccus) veritatem

He was much addicted to the daily invention of witticisms. Nevertheless, like Horace, he proclaimed truth behind the laughing mask, so openly and sharply, that he seemed another Lucian or Democritus, as is manifest in his works. And although he cleverly dissimulated it, he was not without all judgment in his writings.

In William Bullein's *A Dialogue against the Feuer Pestilence* (1564) is found a similar portrait of the keen-witted rhetorician. Bullein describes a vision of Parnassus, of which the only English residents are Gower, Chaucer, Lydgate, Barclay, Sir David Lindsay, and Skelton:[18]

Skelton satte in the corner of a Piller with a Frostie bitten face, frownyng, and he is scante yet cleane cooled of the hotte burnyng Cholour kindeled againste the cankered Cardinal Wolsey; wrytyng many sharpe *Distichons* with bloudie penne againste hym, and sente them by the infernal riuers *Styx*, *Flegiton*, and *Acheron* by the Feriman of helle, called *Charon*, to the saied Cardinall.

Similarly Churchyard, in a commendatory poem to the collected edition of Skelton's works (1568):[19]

Nay, Skelton wore the lawrell wreath,
    And past in schoels, ye knoe;
A poet for his arte,
    Whoes iudgment suer was hie,
And had great practies of the pen,
    His works they will not lie;
His terms to taunts did lean,
    His talke was as he wraet,
Full quick of witte, right sharp of words,
    And skilfull of the staet

In Grange's *Golden Aphroditis* (1577) Skelton is coupled with Erasmus:[20]

For by what meanes could *Skelton* that Laureat poet, or *Erasmus*

---

fateri, tam aperte ac mordaciter, vt alter videretur Lucianus vel Democritus, vt ex operibus liquet. Neque in scripturis absque omni iudicio erat, quamuis illud egregie dissimularet."

[18] "Early English Text Society [Publications]," E. S., LII (1888), 16.
[19] Skelton, *Works*, I, lxxvi–lxxix.
[20] "Scholars' Facsimiles and Reprints" (New York, n. d.), Sig. N 4.

that great and learned clarke haue vttered their mindes so well
at large, as thorowe their clokes of mery conceytes in wryting
of toyes and foolish theames? as *Skelton* did by *Speake Parrot,
Ware the hauke, The Tunning of Elynour rumming, Why come ye not
to the Court? Phillip Sparrowe,* & such like, yet what greater sense
or better matter can be, than is in this ragged ryme contayned?
or who would haue hearde his fault so playnely tolde him if not
suche gibyng sorte?

William Webbe, one of the earliest of the historians of
English literature, summarizes the judgment of the first
half century after Skelton's death (1586):[21]

Skelton, who writ in the time of Kyng *Henry* the eyght, who as
indeede he obtayned the Lawrell Garland, so may I wyth good
ryght yeelde him the title of a Poet: hee was doubtles a pleasant
conceyted fellowe, and of a very sharpe wytte, exceeding bolde,
and would nyppe to the very quicke where he once sette holde.

An inventive rhetorician, a merry poet, and a sharp satirist. It is not a bad description.

But it was not long after this time that Skelton's reputation underwent an abrupt change. And this is not surprising. It is entirely proper to venerate the classics and to
extol the moderns, but yesterday's moderns (who may be
tomorrow's classics) are today merely out of fashion.
There were additional factors that speeded Skelton's de-
scent into the critics' Avernus. In the late sixteenth century,
English literature was undergoing bewilderingly rapid
changes: new forms had become established, a new vocabulary had taken hold, great poets had appeared. From the
height of Elizabethan attainment Skelton's vigor appeared
rudeness, his learning puerility. Furthermore, the controversies into which Skelton had thrown himself so ener-
getically held little interest for this later age. Critics of his
own time justified his jests, his slang, and the roughness of
his language and versification by reference to the sober
voice behind the mask. They understood that Skelton

[21] G. Gregory Smith, *Elizabethan Critical Essays* (Oxford, 1904), I, 242.

acted the clown in order to express himself vivaciously and safely. But for the later Elizabethans, the serious purpose had disappeared, and all that was left was the vulgar mountebank. In his *Arte of English Poesie* (1589) Puttenham declares that Skelton, "a rude railing rhymer" "(I wot not for what great worthiness) surnamed the Poet Laureate," wrote "more railing and scoffery than became a Poet Laureate: such among the Greeks were called *Pantomimi*, with us Buffons, altogether applying their wits to scurrilities and other ridiculous matters."[22] Francis Meres[23] and Henry Peacham[24] repeat Puttenham's strictures. During the seventeenth century the trumpet blast of Skelton's fame dwindled to a mere whisper concerning the scurrilous author of *Elinor Rumming* and the buffoon of an outworn jestbook.

Sixteenth-century reprints of Skelton's works provide a close index to the course of critical opinion. Within a few years after the poet's death Rastell published *Magnificence*, and as soon as the fall of Cardinal Wolsey made it possible, *Colin Clout* appeared.[25] *Colin Clout*, *Philip Sparrow*, *Why Come Ye Not to Court*, and a collection including *Speak, Parrot, Against the Scots*, *Ware the Hawk*, and *Elinor Rumming* were reprinted frequently during the next three decades. Finally, in 1568, I. S. collected, and Thomas Marshe published the *Pithy, Pleasaunt and Profitable Workes of Maister Skelton, Poete Laureate*, with an introductory poem by Thomas Churchyard. This edition marks the high water of Skelton's popularity among the booksellers. Aside from a few reprints in the 1580's, none of Skelton's works was again published until 1624, when *Elinor Rumming* appeared with

[22] Edited by Willcock and Walker (Cambridge, 1936), pp. 84, 60, 62.

[23] *Elizabethan Critical Essays*, ed. by G. G. Smith (Oxford, 1904), II, 314.

[24] "The Compleat Gentleman" (1622), in Spingarn, *Critical Essays of the Seventeenth Century* (Oxford, 1908), I, 133.

[25] Godfray, n. d. Since Godfray stopped publishing c. 1535, his edition of *Colin Clout* must have followed hard upon Wolsey's collapse. The edition is not recorded either in Dyce or in the *Short Title Catalogue*, but there is a copy at Woburn Abbey.

a portrait of the ale-wife and poems ascribed to "Skelton's ghost" placed fore and aft. The spirit of the dead poet complains[26] that his merry vein

> . . . now nothing fits
> The time's nimble wits:
> My lawrell and I
> Are both wither'd dry,
> And you flourish greene
> In your workes daily seene,
> That come from the presse,
> Well writ I confesse;
> But time will devouer
> Your poets as our,
> And make them as dull
> As my empty scull.

A chronological examination of Skelton's influence upon English writers discloses a pattern similar to that traced by the course of his reputation and by his popularity among the stationers. For a considerable period after his death, as will appear in the following discussion, Skelton was one of the most influential of English authors. He was imitated, chiefly by controversialists, but also by teachers of grammar and by courtly rhetoricians. But as the sixteenth century drew to a close, *Elinor Rumming* replaced *Colin Clout* as the most famous of his works, and the rowdy superseded the witty satirist.

Skelton's influence upon the school drama is clearly marked. The earliest of such productions at present extant is a fragment of a Prodigal Son interlude (*c.* 1530).[27] Not only are there clear echoes of Skelton in the phraseology, but the Skeltonic form itself is borrowed:

> My name is Robyn ren awaye
> An hosteler that maketh the bottels of hey
> Dwellynge the nexte house to the cocoldes horne
> Not farre from the place that your father was borne

[26] At the end of the poem; Skelton, *Works*, II, 157.
[27] *Collections*, The Malone Society (Oxford, 1907), I (1), 29-30.

Iynckyn iumbler
Rafe rumbler
Philyp flumbler
Thomkyn tumbler
Stephyn stumbler
Henry humbler
Martyn mumbler
Benet bumbler
Gwy grumbler
Do dwell verely
with the same man as I

The author of the school interlude, *Thersytes* (1537?), was certainly much impressed by Skelton. He uses Skeltonic passages constantly and shamelessly borrows Skelton's quips. For example, Ulysses' letter to Thersytes is signed:[28]

writinge at my house on Candelmasse daye
Midsomer moneth, the calendars of maye

Skelton Laureate against a Comely Coistroun ends:

Wryten at Croydon by Crowland in the Clay
On Candelmas euyn, the Kalendas of May.

John Grange's *Golden Aphroditis* is a collection of rhetorical posies presented to "the courtlike dames and ladylike gentlewomen," which is similar, in many respects, to Lyly's *Euphues*. It is the more striking, therefore, that Grange should not only praise Skelton[29] but also imitate him. He does not use the Skeltonic form, and, unlike many of Skelton's disciples, he does not copy considerable passages. Nevertheless, he has clearly made a close study of Skelton, and unmistakable echoes abound. Because Grange does not borrow directly from Skelton, citation of parallel passages is a poor method of demonstrating the Skeltonic influence in the *Golden Aphroditis*. A few examples, however, may serve to prove the point. Grange begs the reader:[30]

[28] "Students' Facsimile Edition" (1912), Sig. C 3.
[29] See above, pp. 226–27.   [30] "Scholars' Facsimiles and Reprints," Sig. B 3.

> Marke well my frende this ragged ryme,
> thrust forth the Elderne pith:

Skelton had said:[31]

> For though my ryme be ragged,
> Tattered and iagged. . .
> If ye take well therwith,
> It hath in it some pyth.

"I. G. biddeth his friende A. T. good morrowe"[32] is a poem filled with proverbial scraps from *Speak, Parrot*.

> Speake Parrot I pray thee, may nothing be got?
>
> *Perliez bien ou perliez rien*, you know my minde:

Surely these lines depend on:

> Speke, Parrot, I pray you, full curtesly they say
> (*Speak, Parrot*, l. 15)
>
> *Perliez byen*, Parrot, ou *perlez rien*
> (l. 33)

And there is at least one case of direct copying. Skelton had concluded his "commendations" of Jane Scroupe, the girl who mourned Philip Sparrow, with the lines:

> She is worthy to be enrolde
> With letters of golde.
> *Car elle vault.*

Grange ends a poem in praise of his heroine, A. O., with the identical words:[33]

> A. O.
> *Worthie to be in rolde,*
> *With letters of golde.*
> Car elle vault.

Skelton's greatest influence, however, is to be found in the literature of controversy. The wordy battle stimulated by Reformation and Counter-Reformation is patterned directly after *Colin Clout*. An early example is the poem,

[31] *Colin Clout*, ll. 53–58.   [32] *Op. cit.*, Sig. S 1–S 2.   [33] *Ibid.*, Sig. G 2.

Rede Me and Be Nott Wrothe. It was written by two renegade Observant Friars, William Roy and Jerome Barlow, in 1528, at a time when Skelton was engaged in antiheretical activities. He must have been shocked to see the weapons he had forged turned against his own cause. In *Colin Clout* Skelton had attacked Wolsey for his destruction of the monasteries:

> No matyns at mydnyght,
> Boke and chalys gone quyte;
> And plucke awaye the leedes
> Evyn ouer theyr heedes,
> And sell away theyr belles,
> And all that they haue elles:
> . . . ye brake the dedes wylles,
> Turne monasteris into water milles,
> Of an abbay ye make a graunge
>
> (ll. 408–21)

The authors of *Rede Me and Be Nott Wrothe* claim that the detested Cardinal is as great a heretic as they:[34]

> I am sure thou hast hearde spoken /
> What monasteries he hath broken /
>   With out their fownders consentis.
> He subverteth churches / and chappels /
> Takynge a waye bokis and bells
>   With chalesces / and vestmentis.
> He plucketh downe the costly leades
> That it maye rayne on saynctis heades /
>   Not sparynge god nor oure ladye.
> Where as they red servyce divyne /
> There is grountynge of pigges and swyne /
>   With lowynge of oxen and kye.

But it is not necessary to search for verbal parallels in the mass of poetry which was produced by the religious controversy during the second and third quarters of the century. A large proportion of this very considerable body of literature was written in Skeltonics,[35] and many of the

[34] Arber, *English Reprints* (Westminster, 1895), p. 113.

[35] Dyce (Skelton, *Works*, I, cvii–cxxx) has collected several examples and numerous titles of such pieces. See also E. Bischoffsberger, *Der Einfluss John Skel-*

pieces are little more than centos drawn from *Colin Clout*. Skelton had written to chastise the erring Church, but his matter and meter were employed with more deadly intent by his successors. Spenser's use of the name Colin Clout in his *Shepherds' Calendar* suggests the extent to which Skelton's poem had become associated with matters of religious controversy.

Skelton's polemical example was also followed outside the religious field. In a typically humanist controversy on the excellence of beards,[36] one of the antagonists uses Colin Clout as a pseudonym. *Vox populi, vox dei*[37] is a long complaint in Skeltonics on the poverty of the commons. In 1589 there appeared:[38]

> A Skeltonicall Salutation,
> Or condigne gratulation,
> And iust vexation
> Of the Spanish Nation,
> That in a bravado,
> Spent many a Crusado,
> In setting forth an Armado
> England to invado.

The decline in Skelton's reputation from witty satirist to grinning jackanapes is reflected in the attitude of his later imitators. In the plays of the *Downfall* and *Death of Robert Earl of Huntington afterward Called Robin Hood* (1601), which pretend to be rehearsals prior to performance before Henry VIII, Skelton takes the part of master of ceremonies and acts Friar Tuck. Jonson couples Skelton with another jestbook character, Scogan, and produces them in the masque of *The Fortunate Isles* "in like habits as they lived."[39]

---

tons auf die englische Literatur (Freiburg, 1914) and M. C. Lenthicum, in *Library*, Fourth Series, IX, 169–83.

[36] *The treatyse answerynge the boke of Berdes Compyled by Collyn clowte* (1543), ed. by Furnivall, "Early English Text Society [Publications]," E. S., X (1870), 305–16.

[37] Skelton, *Works*, II, 400–413.

[38] Imprinted at London for Toby Cooke; Skelton, *Works*, I, cxxvi–cxxviii.

[39] "Skelton" is made to quote from *Elinor Rumming*.

In another of Jonson's masques, *The Gipsies Metamorphosed*, the Skeltonic speeches are assigned to The Patrico who is "the orator of the gang, the mock priest."[40] There is a "Merry-mad Letter in Skeltons Rime" in *Hobson's Horse Load of Letters* (1617), and a "Skeltonicall Salutation" in the *Workes* of John Taylor the Water Poet (1630). Toward the end of the seventeenth century John Cleveland wrote "The Old Gill," "a piece of disgusting grossness (suggested by Skelton's Elynour Rummynge)."[41]

Beyond what is obvious in direct borrowings or in the use of the unmistakable verse pattern, it is impossible to estimate the magnitude of Skelton's influence on English literature. It may be that the remarkable freedom and colloquialism of Elizabethan drama and the violent slash and batter of the prose pamphlets owe something to Skelton's example. And it is more than probable that Skelton both borrowed from and contributed to the great underground tradition of popular poetry which ignores the stilted regularity of formal verse, which cares nothing for measure or number, which sings to satisfy no critic but the ear. From the Second Shepherd's Play to the words attached to the modern popular song, that tradition has persisted. It has had few representatives among recognized poets. Histories of literature have given it little discussion, properly so, since the bulk of such poetry is both trivial and stupid. But Skelton, neither trivial nor stupid, rises above the other poets of the tradition, and by his excellence fortifies it. A learned humanist, he discovered a means of expressing himself with the conscious purpose, not of securing praise from brother scholars, but of influencing large numbers of readers and swaying them to his opinion. That he was successful is obvious from the flood of imitative controversial pieces that followed immediately upon

[40] Gifford's edition (1816), VII, 374.

[41] Skelton, *Works*, I, cxxix. Numerous additional examples of Skelton's influence have been collected by Bischoffsberger (*op. cit.*).

his example. And it is hard to believe that the influence of *Colin Clout* was canceled by the snobbishness of a Puttenham or a Pope. What Skelton wrote, a man might repeat to his neighbor and his neighbor to a grandson. For Skelton held to the primary purpose of the study of rhetoric, the purpose to which his learned contemporaries gave continual service, but lip service only. By the force of his poetic genius he tried to scourge, cleanse, and refashion his England.

Perhaps it is his very directness of purpose, his immediate adaptation of means to end, which makes Skelton particularly acceptable to modern taste. A considerable group of English poets, including W. H. Auden, E. K. Blunden, Philip Henderson, Richard Hughes, and Robert Graves, has found Skelton worthy of republication, study, and imitation. Graves represents the attitude of the group:[42]

> For he will not stop
> To sweep nor mop,
> To prune nor prop,
> To cut each phrase up
> Like beef when we sup,
> Nor sip at each line
> As at brandy-wine,
> Or port when we dine.
> But angrily, wittily,
> Tenderly, prettily,
> Laughingly, learnedly,
> Sadly, madly,
> Helter-skelter John
> Rhymes serenely on,
> As English poets should.
> Old John, you do me good!

Weary of the formal prettiness of schoolbook poetry, weary, too, of equally formal and self-conscious "free verse," Graves and the others have found in Skelton a poet

[42] *Fairies and Fusiliers* (New York, 1919), pp. 54–55.

hidebound neither to traditionalism nor to antitraditional-
ism, a poet who had something to say and who found an
effective means of saying it.

What, then, is John Skelton? A passionate man, he
does not permit an unimpassioned judgment. One may be
disgusted by his capering and his posturing, by the ful-
someness of his eulogies and the intemperance of his abuse.
On the other hand, precisely this violence, this lack of
restraint, is his chief poetic virtue. He throws his bitter,
egotistical self unreservedly into everything he writes.
Rhythm, epithet, and concept surge together and force
the reader irresistibly forward. Nor is it a dull, roaring
torrent of verbosity which Skelton pours forth, over-
powering in its bulk, stupid and pointless on analysis.
Skelton does not reiterate blow after blow, hammering
constantly at his target. In his best work he is startlingly,
vitally awake; he smashes here and stabs there, now
openly, again slyly, pounding and thrusting from every
conceivable angle. He is so full of ideas that he rarely has
patience to round them. He caricatures swiftly and then
rushes on, never finishing anything, but ripping the sheet
and starting anew. If the reader dozes, he sees nothing but
the blur of movement.

It is strange that so intemperate a person should have
professed a philosophy of the golden mean. Indeed, his own
description of excess, embodied in the morality *Magnificence*, reads like a criticism of his works. Fancy soliloquizes:

> Nowe to curteys, forthwith vnkynde;
> Somtyme to sober, somtyme to sadde,
> Somtyme to mery, somtyme to madde;
> Somtyme I syt as I were solempe prowde;
> Somtyme I laughe ouer lowde;
> Somtyme I wepe for a gew gaw;
> Somtyme I laughe at waggynge of a straw;
> With a pere my loue you may wynne,
> And ye may lese it for a pynne.

I haue a thynge for to say,
And I may tende[43] therto for play;
But in faythe I am so occupyed
On this halfe and on euery syde,
That I wote not where I may rest.

(ll. 1020–33)

But it is not quite fair to liken Skelton to unbridled, un-principled Fancy. Unbridled he may be, but unprincipled he is certainly not. Throughout his career he fought furiously for the same conservative ends. He demanded that the King rule his own land, that the Church retain its ancient prerogatives, that education keep in view its ultimate purpose, the increase of virtue and religion. Despite the pressure of events, his opinions remained stable. The King's delegation of his power to Wolsey did not turn Skelton into a rebel; the abuses of the Church did not convert him into a Reformer; the excesses of the new humanism did not make him renounce rhetoric and the study of the classics. His philosophy was cool, moderate, considered. Skelton's violence resides, not in his con-clusions, but in his expression of them. If what I say is right, why should I not say it? That is the key to Skelton. Truth, or what he conceives to be truth, overrides all other considerations. If there is a good to be praised, let praise flow over. If an evil exists, stamp on it, pound it down, smash it at all costs. Divine inspiration imposes on the poet the duty of destroying vice and propagating virtue.

[43] That is, "If I may attend . . ."

Appendices

I. BERNARD ANDRÉ'S WORKS

I. Bernardi Andree Tholozatis Poete laureati ac Regii hystorici /
Opera partim completa / partim incompleta sunt hec /.¹

[1] Commentaria in Augustini de ciuitate dei opus ab undecimo
tribus magnis nec adhuc impletum voluminibus. In quibus tam
diuinarum quam humanarum rerum indices sorte litterali / seu
maius vocabularia breuia repperies²

[2] Item deffensio poetarum in dyalogo ad serenissimum
felicissime recordationis Arthurum principem

[3] Ad eundem de [dicendi]³ & scribendi modo elegantia quod
quidam opusculum / Delius orator et poeta egregius⁴ commentatus
est

[4] Ad eundem [grammaticorum]⁵ examen

[5] Ad eundem de Carthagine rapta dyalogus / coram Regia
maiestate henrici septimi recitatus

[6] Ad eundem Atheniensium ac lacedemoniorum legatio /
etiam coram Regia maiestate Henrici 7ᵐⁱ & octaui tunc paruuli
recitata

[7] Ad eundem rationis & sensualitatis / Dyalogus et coram
Regijs maiestatibus recitatus

[8] Ad eundem de Natali suo⁶

[9] Ad eundem de Creatione sua⁷

[10] Ad eundem de Ipsius breui . . . gio

[11] Ad eundem breues sed utiles / ex Cicerone de omni Re
epistole

[12] Ad eundem Obseruationum latine lingue libell[u]s⁸

---

¹ MS Arsenal 418, fol. T.
² A commentary on Augustine is included in MS Arsenal 418. The alphabetical
index which begins on fol. A is headed "Principis Arthuri impensis hec facta
Tabella est In bello loco Anno domini M. c c c c c. Die xvijᵃ Junij et Illustrissimi
Regis nostri Henrici Vij Regni Anno XV composita ab eiusdem Serenissimi Principis
preceptore Bernardo Andree & per manum Suetonij Skern conscripta."
³ MS *discendi*.
⁴ Probably Delius Volscus, perhaps a jesting name for Ægidius of Delft, or
"Egidius Delius Poeta" (see Allen, *Opus epistolarum Erasmi*, I, 234).
⁵ MS *grammaticos*.   ⁶ See *Chronicles and Memorials*, X, 41–42.
⁷ *Ibid.*, pp. 44–46.   ⁸ MS *libellos*.

[13]   Ad eundem de Modo scribendi et dicendi

[14]   Ad eundem Preceptiones Rhetorice

[15]   Ad eundem de Orthographia

[16]   Ad eundem Ars Epistolandi

[17]   Item in Aulum gelium annotamenta

[18]   Item de Carolo francie in Italiam egloge due

[19]   Item in fictos Mecenates Satyra

[20]   Item de vera voluptate dyalogus

[21]   In thebaidem papinii commentarius incompletus

[22]   Siluarum tam latine quam galice libri quinque

[23]   de sillabarum quantitate

[24]   Item Panuagerici non pauci

[25]   Item de generibus nominum

[26]   Artis memorande Epithoma

[27]   Item ad principem Arthurum vocabularium barbarum & latinum

[28]   Item henrici septimi annales[9]

[29]   Philippi Regis castelle[10] in Angliam aduentus

[30]   de morte domini Johannis de gilis Episcopi olim Wigorniensis Elegia

[31]   Item Arthuri principis Epytaphium

[32]   Item Rosarium beate Marie

[33]   Officium immaculate conceptionis Marie christi parentis carminibus ad vesperi horas missam & processionem editum. Ad serenissimam Regiam matrem

[34]   Item ad eandem de festo ui[rgi]nali et presentatione beate marie officium

[35]   Item meditatio in carmine heroico deuotissima super illud stabat mater iuxta crucem &c.

[36]   Item super Andriam et Enuchum familiaris expositio

[37]   Item libellus de omnigenis verborum naturis ad / dominum / henricum daubeney

[38]   Item familiarium epistolarum liber unus

[39]   Item Epigrammaton libri duo

[40]   Item super Eglogas Virgilii secundum 4^{or} sensus expositio admirabilis

[41]   Item hymnorum cristianorum per totum anni circulum libellus unus[11]

[42]   Item annotamenta in plynium

[9] Printed in *Chronicles and Memorials*, Vol. X.
[10] That is, *of Castile*.   [11] Printed in Paris, 1517.

[43] Item sup*er* Eneidem Virgilii in sensu tropologico ex-
posicio non contemnenda

[44] Item sup*er* decem priores libros beati augustini de
ciuitate dei nuper inchoata expositio

[45] Item serenissimi Regis henrici octaui auspicata hystoria

[46] Item ad eundem Epigra*m*maton libellus

II.   MS Royal 16 E xi: "Le Temps de lannee moralize"

Although this volume is unsigned, the dedication renders indisputable the usual ascription to André. The author presents the
book to King Henry VIII on the occasion of the first New Year's
Day of the reign. He begs the young king to retain him in his
service as a historiographer. He declares that he served Henry VII
for twenty-four years (the entire extent of the reign) and that he
wrote annals at the King's commandment. There can therefore
be no doubt of the attribution to André.

III.   MS Royal 12 B xiv: "En ce petit liure sont contenu troys
branlx petitz traictez Lun est a la louange dez tresillustrez et
mes tressouerains le Roy et la Royne dAngleterre.[12] Lautre est
la vie de saincte katherine en metre[13] Le tiers est une moult belle
oraison daristote enuoye au grant roy Alexandre."[14]

It seems probable to me that this volume is also the work of
Bernard André. First, it contains both French and Latin pieces of
the kind that André would be likely to write. Second, the
Oration to Alexander betrays the fact that its author was closely associated with the court of Henry VII (see above, pp. 16–17.)
Third, the *Life of St. Katherine* is said to have been written extempore, the same boast that André makes for his *Hymni Christiani.* Fourth, in the hymn to Henry VIII which opens the
volume, the French is extraordinarily Latinate, just as it is in the
dedication to *Le Temps de lannee moralize*, identified as André's in
Section II of this Appendix. Finally, both volumes apply certain

[12] Fol. 2: "Cy apres sensuit Lexposition du pseaulme huitiesme de dauid aplicque
en leur tresglorieuse louange par chascune lectre de leurs royaulx noms." The
acrostic reads: "Henri huitiesme et Catherine deuxiesme dEspaigne tresillustres
roy et royne de Angleterre et de France et seigneurs dHirlande aulx quelz Dieu
doint sante et longue vie."

[13] Fol. 6: "Vita beate katherine illustris secundum ecclesiasticam Cesarisburgi
hystoriam. Carmi*n*e phalæucyo extemporaliter co*m*posita." The poem consists of
124 Latin hendecasyllables.

[14] Fol. 10: "Aristotelis ad magnum Alexandrum de vite institutione Oratio."

unusual epithets to Henry VIII, epithets which are not to be found in the dictionaries of Godefroy or Littré. *Le Temps de lannee* speaks of the king's "faustissime regne" (fol. 1) and of his "principique haultesse" (*ibid.*). Similarly, the hymn in MS Royal 12 B xiv is addressed to "tresfauste Roy Henri" (fol. 2) and celebrates his "principique maieste" (fol. 3).

IV.   *Salisbury Manuscripts* (Historical Manuscripts Commission) I, 4: "Invocatio de inclyta invictissimi Regis nostri Henrici VIII in Gallos et Scotos victoria per Bernardum Andree poetam regium, cum præfatione ejusdem."

I have not seen this work.

V.   Other compositions of André are listed in the *Dictionary of National Biography* and in Gairdner's introduction to *Chronicles and Memorials*, Vol. X.

II. THE COURT OF REQUESTS

I.   Peter Ottey vs. John Skelton (May 14, 1501)[15]
In causa petri Ottey contra Johannem Skelton respectuatur usque in crastinum ad horam nouenam ante merediem sub spe concordie et datus est terminus eidem Johanni Skelton sub pena xl li ad comparendum coram Reuerendo in xpo patre Ricardo Dunelmensis Episcopo & alijs de consilio domini regis apud london eadem hora nouena si interim concordia nunc factus[16] fuerit in eadem causa inter partes prædictas

II.   Reginald Bray vs. the Prior of St. Bartholomew's (June 10, 1502)[17]
Johannes Skelton comparet coram consilio domini regis uirtute obligacionis in qua prior sancti bartholomei et alij tenentur

---

[15] Act Book of the Court of Requests, Public Record Office, Req. 1-2, fol. 133.
[16] *Sic* MS. Qy. *non facta?*
[17] Act Book, Public Record Office, Req. 1-3, fol. 2. Dyce knew of this case through the abbreviated mention in *Actes, Orders, and Decrees Made by the King and His Counsell, Remaining amongst the Records of the Court, Now Commonly Called the Court of Requests*, 1592, p. 30: "10 Junii apud Westminster Jo. Skelton commissus carceribus Janitoris Domini Regis" (Skelton, *Works*, I, xxvi).

Reginaldo Bray et alijs in ducent*is* libr*is* et committit*ur* carcerib*us*
[ianitoris]¹⁸ d*o*mini reg*is* quo*us*qu*e* pr*i*uilegia d*i*ct*i* pr*i*oris cor*am*
d*i*cto co*n*silio edoceant*ur* et alit*er* sup*er* visu huiu*smo*d*i* stauant*ur*
Et id*e*o decret*um* qu*od* obligac*i*o remane*n*s in custod*i*a maior*is*
ciuitat*is* london delib*e*ret*ur* d*i*cto pr*i*ori aut casset*ur* & c

III. JOHN SKELTON VS. THOMAS PYCKERELL¹⁹

[December 3, 1509, before John Huchons]

Eisd*em* die mensi anno & loco Joh*ann*es Chapman²⁰ certificauit
cor*am* iudice se vigore mandati siu*e* citat*i*o*n*is p*er* eu*m* exhibit*i*
p*er*empt*er* citasse Th*o*m*am* pykerell de dys ad comparend*um* isti*s*
die & loco ad re*s*pond*e*nd*um* cert*is* art*i*clis siu*e* interrogatorijs
co*n*cernend*is* an*i*me sue salute ad promoc*i*onem m*a*g*is*tri Joh*ann*is
Skelton r*e*ctor*is* ib*id*em eid*em* obijciend*i*. Et quia no*n* comparuit
ideo d*o*min*u*s pr*o*nunciauit eu*m* contumacem²¹ postea absolut*us*
est dictus Thom*a*s iiij die Januarij per d*o*minu*m* offic*ialem* et
h*a*bet ad comparend*um* die lune post festum hillarij

[January 14, 1510]

In Skelton con*tra* pykerell pr*æ*conisat*um* no*n* compa*ruisse*
d*o*min*u*s igit*u*r ad petic*i*o*n*em pronu*n*ciauit eum co*n*tumacem

[February 4, 1510]

In Skelton con*tra* pykerell pykerell *s*u*s*pen*s*us

IV. THE KING OF ENGLAND AND THE
SCOTTISH HERALD²²

The mesage that was don by lyon²³ scottysshe herald to *t*he kyng
owr sou*e*rayn lord kyng herry the viiij^th when he laye at the
sege of Turwyn by the seyd herald and the answere of the kyng
to hym ayen an*n*o 1513

---

¹⁸ MS *genitoris.*

¹⁹ Act Book of the Consistory Court, preserved at Norwich Cathedral.

²⁰ Later rector of Chatbery (Act Book, February 5, 1522).

²¹ "[Contuma]x est, qui tribus edictis propositis vel uno pro tribus, quod vulgo peremptorium appellatur, litteris evocatus præsentiam sui facere contemnit" (quoted from Hermogenes in *Thesaurus Linguæ Latinæ* [1906–09], *s. v.*).

²² MS Harleian 2252, fol. 41.   ²³ *lyon* is written over *Ilay.*

The xith day of Auguste An*n*o 1513. the kyng w*ith* many of
hys nobyll lordys. beyng in hys ryche tente./ was browght to
hym the herawld of the kyng of Scotte*s*. the whyche dyd hys
message in effecte as folow*eth*. // pleas hyt yo*u*r nobyll grace. //
the kyng of Scotte*s* my souerayng lorde reco*m*mende*s* hy*m* unto
yow. / and has comaundyd me to shewe yo*u*r nobyll grace that
ye haue here entryd in to the grounde of the kyng of ffraunce.
and leyd sege to hys towne of turwyn by the space of ij^e monthes
and more unfawghtyn w*ith* to yo*u*r grete hono*u*r more ov*er* Syr
by reason of yo*u*r entre cawsythe the kyng of ffraunce to retorne
and call backe hys armye from myllen and hother p*ar*tys of
Italye to the grete hynderans of hys enherytans there. / wherfor
he thynkythe hyt ryghte co*n*uenyent yn as myche as ye haue had
yo*u*r wyll and apytyd in *thi*s doyng. / that ye now returne home
agayne. in to yo*u*r awne realme w*ith* owte makyng ony forther
warre. // and so knelyd stylle and seyd no moo wordys. // The
kyng stondyng stylle wythe sobyr co*n*ten*au*nce havyng hys
hande on hys swerde. sayd haue ye now yo*u*r tale at an ende. //
The harawld of arms seyd nay. / Sey forthe then sayd the kyng. //
Syr he somonyth yo*u*r grace to be at home in yo*u*r realme in the
defence of hys alye. // Then the kyng anssweryd & sayd. / ye
haue well don yo*u*r message / nev*er*thelesse. hyt beco*m*myth yll
a Scotte to somon a kyng of yngelond. / for hyt hathe byn sene
that the kyng of Scotte*s* hathe byn somonyd to com to the
p*ar*leamente of the kyng of ynglond. // and tell yo*u*r mast*er* that
I mystruste not so the ream of ynglond. / but he shall haue
enowghe to doe when so evyr he begynnythe. / and also I trustyd
not hym so well but that I provyded for hym ryghte well. / and
*tha*t shall he well knowe. / and he to somon me now beyng here
for my ryghte and enerytaunce. / hyt wold myche bett*er* agreed
w*ith* hys honowr to haue somonyd me being at home for he
knewe well before my comyng hether. that he*ther* wold I come. /
and now to send me somons. Tell hym there shalle nevyr Scotte
cawse me to retorne my fase. & where he leyethe the frenshe
kyng to be hys alye. / hyt wold myche bett*er* agreed and beco*m*
hym. beynge maryd to the kyng of ynglonde*s* syst*er*. to reconte
the kyng of ynglond hys alye. And now for a conclusyon. //
reco*m*mend me to yo*u*r mast*er*. and tell hym yf he be so hardy to
envade my realme or cawse to entyr on fote of my grownde. / I
shall make hym as wery of hys p*ar*te as evyr was man. that began ony suche besynes. // and on thynge I ensure hym by the
faythe that I haue to the crowne of ynglond. and by the worde

of a kynge there shall nev*er* kyng nor prynce make peas w*ith* me
*tha*t ev*er* hys p*ar*te shalbe in hyt. // more ov*er* felow I care for no
thyng. but for mysse entretyng of my syst*er* that wolde god she
were in ynglond on a condycyon she coste the Schotte*s* kyng not
a peny. / The harawlde anssweryd and seyd. / yff yo*ur* grace
wolde geve hyr yo*ur* hole realme. / she wold forsake hyt to be
entretyd as she ys. The kyng seyd I knowe the contrarye &
knowe whate all thys matyr meanythe. / The kyng yo*ur* mast*er*
has anoynted w*ith* the crowns of the son.[24] / But I truste or hyt
be longe. / the ffrenshe kyng shall haue enowgh to do to kepe
hys crowns for hym selffe.

V. SKELTON'S HANDWRITING

IT IS PROBABLE that both Skelton's dedication to Henry VIII of
the *Chronique de Rains* (Corpus Christi College, Cambridge, MS
432) and the manuscript of "A Laud and Praise Made for Our
Sovereign Lord the King" (Public Record Office MS E. 36-228,
pp. 67-69) are written in Skelton's hand. M. R. James first ob-
served that the dedicatory pages of the *Chronique* manuscript are
holograph.[25] The fact that the hand which wrote the dedication
to Henry VIII also annotated the margins of the gift volume
makes James's conclusion extremely likely.

The close similarity between the "Bien men souient" devices
in the *Chronique* and in the "Laud and Praise" (see the illustra-

[24] In somewhat the same terms, Skelton accuses Wolsey of accepting bribes from
foreign nations:

> They shote at him with crownes;
> With crownes of golde enblased
> They make him so amased,
> And his eyen so dased,
> That he ne se can
> To know God nor man.
> —*Why Come Ye Not to Court*, ll. 175-80

[25] *A Descriptive Catalogue of the Manuscripts in the Library of Corpus Christi College,
Cambridge* (Cambridge, 1912), II, 338. In his recent book, *John Skelton* (Oxford,
1938), p. 141, L. J. Lloyd, referring to the manuscript of Skelton's translation of
Diodorus Siculus (Corpus Christi College MS 357), asserts, "Dr. M. R. James
speaks of 'the first three leaves written by Skelton in a large Gothic hand.' This
is on the whole unlikely, but the opinion of so great a paleographer cannot be
summarily dismissed." Mr. Lloyd has confused two Corpus Christi College manuscripts. James's statement concerns not the *Diodorus* (MS 357) but the first leaves
of the *Chronique* (MS 432).

tions on pp. 164, 174) suggests that the coronation poem, too, is a holograph. Furthermore, the scrawled "Deo gratias" below the "Bien men souient" of the "Laud and Praise" is matched by a precisely similar scrawl in the *Chronique* manuscript (fol. 3v). (Unfortunately, I find it impossible to reproduce the *Chronique* "Deo gratias" from the photograph in my possession.) The dedication to the *Chronique* is written chiefly in book script, while the "Laud and Praise" is in major part cursive (see the illustrations on pp. 116, 164). Nevertheless, comparison of the reproductions here presented will, I think, support the conclusion that both manuscripts were written by the same person, and it is no more than reasonable to suppose that the person who wrote both the dedication and the marginal annotations in Skelton's gift volume to Henry VIII was none other than Skelton himself.

VI. CHRONOLOGY OF SKELTON'S WORKS[26]

c. 1488.   Translation of the *Historical Library* of Diodorus Siculus (Corpus Christi College, Cambridge, MS 357). This is mentioned as "late translated" in Caxton's dedication to the *Boke of Eneydos* (1489).

c. 1488.   Translation of Cicero's *Familiar Letters* (lost, but see *Garland of Laurel*, l. 1185). A translation of "the epistles of Tully" is coupled with the *Diodorus* in Caxton's dedication of *Eneydos*.

c. 1488.   *Achademios* (lost, but see *Garland*, l. 1184). For the date assigned see above, p. 49.

1489 (after April 28).   Elegy on the death of the Earl of Northumberland. For the date see Skelton, *Works*, II, 89.

1489 (October 1).   "Prince Arthur's Creation" (lost, but see *Garland*, l. 1178). For the date see *Works*, II, 327.

1489-90.   "Recule against Gaguin" (lost, but see *Garland*, l. 1187). For the date see above, p. 26.

1494 (November 1).   "Ad tanti principis maiestatem in sua puericia" (*Speculum*, IX, 36-37). For the date see above, p. 74.

c. 1499.   *The Bowge of Court*. For the date see H. S. Sale, in *Modern Language Notes*, LII, 572-74.

---

[26] The list includes only those of Skelton's works for which some definite indication of date may be found.

1501 (August 28). *Speculum principis* (*Speculum*, IX, 33–36). For the date see *Speculum*, IX, 36.

Before 1504. *The Nigramansir* (lost, but see Warton, *The History of English Poetry* [London, 1840], pp. 508–11). According to Warton, the play was printed by Wynken de Worde in 1504.

1504–8. *Philip Sparrow*. This poem was apparently written during Skelton's Norfolk residence. See above, p. 107. It is mentioned in Barclay's *Ship of Fools* (1508).

1504–12. *Ware the Hawk!* This poem was certainly written while Skelton resided at Diss.

1506–7. "Two Knaves Sometime of Diss." For the date see above, p. 103, and *Works*, I, 173.

1507 (after April 25). "Lamentatio urbis Norvicen." For the date see *Works*, II, 214.

1509 (after June 24). "A Laud and Praise Made for Our Sovereign Lord the King." For the date see above, p. 106.

1509 (after June 24). "Pallinodium" (*Speculum*, IX, 37). For the date see Salter, in *Speculum*, IX, 30.

1509–12. Dedication of *Speculum principis* and "Complaint" (*Speculum*, IX, 37). This must postdate the coronation of Henry VIII and predate Skelton's assumption of the title *orator regius* (*c.* May, 1512).

1511 (November)–1512 (May). Dedication of *Chronique de Rains* (Corpus Christi College, Cambridge, MS 432). For the date see above, p. 164.

1512 (after April). "Eulogium pro suorum temporum conditione." For the date see Edwards, in *PMLA*, LIII, 602–3.

1512 (after April). "Calliope." For the date see Edwards, in *PMLA*, LIII, 602–3.

1512 (November 30). "Henrici septimi epitaphium." For the date see *Works*, I, 178.

1513 (August 28). "Elogium contra Gallos." For the date see above, p. 126.

1513 (between September 15 and 22). *A Ballad of the Scottish King* (ed. by Ashton, London, 1882). For the date see above, pp. 127–28.

1513 (after September 19). *Against the Scots*. For the date see above, pp. 127–28.

1513 (September 22). "Epitoma contra Scottos." For the date see above, p. 128.

1513–14. Poems against Garnesche. For the date see H. Stearns, in *Modern Language Notes*, XLIII, 518–23.

1515–16. "Against Venemous Tongues." For the date see R. L. Ramsay in "Early English Text Society [Publications]," E. S., XCVIII, cxviii.

1515–16. *Magnificence.* For the date see Ramsay, *op. cit.*, p. xxv.

1516 (August 16). "Elegia in Margaretæ nuper comitissæ de Derby." For the date see *Works*, I, 195.

1518. "In Bedel." For the date see above, p. 119.

1521. *Speak, Parrot.* For the date see above, pp. 161 ff.

1522. *Colin Clout.* For the date see above, pp. 188–90.

1522 (before November 17). *Why Come Ye Not to Court.* For the date see above, pp. 161–63.

1523 (*c.* January 1). *Garland of Laurel.* For the date see above, pp. 190–92.

1523 (autumn). *The Duke of Albany.* For the date see *Works*, II, 375–76.

1528. *Replication against Certain Young Scholars.* For the date see Mullinger, *The University of Cambridge* (1873), I, 607–8. Since the poem was not written until after Bilney had relapsed (see above, p. 213), it probably followed his trial (December 8, 1527) by several months at least.

Skelton's catalogue of his works in the *Garland of Laurel* provides a little additional information. Since the *Garland* was written in 1523, *Elinor Rumming* and the lyrics to Mistress Anne and to Mistress Margery Milk and Ale, which are mentioned in the catalogue, must have been composed before that date. Of the lost works listed in the *Garland*, it seems probable that "Royal Demeanance," "Book of Honorous Estate," and "New Grammar in English" were written while Skelton was tutor to Prince Henry, that is, 1494–1502 (see above, p. 74). Skelton's translation of the *Pilgrimage of the Life of Man* was written "Of my lady's grace at the contemplation" (*Garland*, l. 1219). If "my lady" means Margaret Beaufort, as Dyce supposes, the translation must predate 1509, the year of Margaret's death.

Bibliography

I. MODERN EDITIONS OF SKELTON'S WORKS

A. COMPLETE WORKS

The Poetical Works of John Skelton, edited with an introduction and notes by the Rev. Alexander Dyce, London, 1843.

The Poetical Works of John Skelton, "principally according to the edition of the Rev. Alexander Dyce," Cambridge, Mass., 1855; Boston, 1856, 1864, 1866, 1871, 1887.

The Complete Poems of John Skelton, edited by Philip Henderson, London, 1931. Based on Dyce.

The Poetical Works of Skelton and Donne, Boston, 188-. Reprinted from Dyce.

B. SELECTED WORKS

A Selection from the Poetical Works of John Skelton, edited by W. H. Williams, London, 1902. Based on Dyce.

Poems by John Skelton, selected and edited by Richard Hughes, London, 1924. Based on Dyce.

John Skelton, London, 1927. "The Augustan Books of English Poetry," Series 2, No. 12, Poems selected by Robert Graves.

A list of anthologies which contain one or more of Skelton's longer poems is in English Verse between Chaucer and Surrey, edited by E. P. Hammond (Duke University Press, 1927), p. 341.

C. SINGLE WORKS

A Ballade of the Scottysshe Kynge, edited by John Ashton, London, 1882, from the edition of Pynson (n. d.). Reprinted in A Century of Ballads, edited by John Ashton (Boston, 1888), pp. xiii ff.

Elynour Rumming, decorations by Pearl Binder, London, 1928.
——— with decorations by Claire Jones, San Francisco, 1930.

Garland of Laurel (MS Cotton Vitellius E x), edited with introduction and notes by E. P. Hammond in English Verse between Chaucer and Surrey (Duke University Press, 1927), pp. 336–67.

Magnyfycence (Rastell, n. d.), edited with an introduction and notes by R. L. Ramsay, "[Publications] Early English Text Society," E. S., XCVIII (1908 [for 1906]).

Speculum principis (MS Additional 26, 787), edited with an introduction by F. M. Salter, in Speculum, IX (1934), 25–37.

Why Come Ye Nat to Court? (from the fragmentary copy in MS Rawlinson C 813), edited by J. Zupitza, Archiv, LXXXV (1890), 429–36.

D. FACSIMILES

A Ballade of the Scottysshe Kynge (Pynson, n. d.), London, 1882.

The Historical Library of Diodorus Siculus, translated by Skelton from the Latin of Poggio (Corpus Christi College, Cambridge, MS 357, Vol. I), Modern Language Association of America. "Collection of Photographic Facsimiles," No. 29.

Magnyfycence (Rastell, n. d.), printed for the Roxburghe Club, London, 1821.

—— (Rastell, n. d.), "Tudor Facsimile Texts," London (?), 1910.

—— (Rastell, n. d.), "Students' Facsimile Edition," Amersham, England, 1914 (?).

Speculum principis (MS Additional, 26, 787), Modern Language Association of America. "Collection of Photographic Facsimiles," No. 27 (1925).

II. MODERN CRITICAL AND SCHOLARLY CONTRIBUTIONS

Auden, W. H. "John Skelton," in The Great Tudors, edited by K. Garvin, London, 1935.

Berdan, J. M. Early Tudor Poetry, New York, 1920.

—— "The Poetry of Skelton: a Renaissance Survival of Medieval Latin Influence," Romanic Review, VI (1915), 364–77.

—— "The Dating of Skelton's Satires," PMLA, XXIX (1914), 499–516.

—— " 'Speke, Parrot,' an Interpretation of Skelton's Satire," Modern Language Notes, XXX (1915), 140–44.

Bischoffsberger, E. Einfluss John Skeltons auf die englische Literatur, Freiburg, 1914.

Blunden, E. Votive Tablets, London, 1932 (the essay on Skelton is reprinted from London Times Literary Supplement, June 20, 1929).

Bradley, H. "Two Puzzles in Skelton," Academy, August 1, 1896.

Brie, F. "Skelton-Studien," Englische Studien, XXXVII (1907), 1–86.

———— "Zwei verlorene Dichtungen von John Skelton," Archiv, N. S., XXXVIII (1919), 226–28.

Cook, A. S. "Skelton's 'Garland of Laurel' and Chaucer's 'House of Fame,' " Modern Language Review, XI (1916), 9–14.

Dunbabin, R. L. "Skelton's Relation to Humanism," "Skelton's Birthplace," and "Notes and Emendations," Modern Language Review, XII (1917), 129–37, 137–39, 257–65.

Edwards, H. L. R. "John Skelton: a Genealogical Study," The Review of English Studies, XI (1934), 406–20.

———— and W. Nelson. "The Dating of Skelton's Later Poems," PMLA, LIII (1938), 601–22.

———— "Syr Capten of Catywade," London Times Literary Supplement, August 9, 1934; cf. B. Redstone, ibid., August 16, 1934; H. L. R. Edwards, ibid., August 30, 1934.

———— "Pereles Pomegarnet," London Times Literary Supplement, December 27, 1934.

———— "Pleris cum musco," London Times Literary Supplement, September 12, 1936; cf. G. P. C. Sutton and E. A. Bunyard, ibid., September 19, 1936; P. Abrahams, ibid., October 3, 1936.

———— "Hermoniake," London Times Literary Supplement, October 24, 1936.

———— "A Skelton Emendation," London Times Literary Supplement, December 19, 1936.

———— "Skelton at Diss," London Times Literary Supplement, May 22, 1937.

Golding, L. "Merie Skelton," Saturday Review, CXXXIII (1922), 30–31.

Gordon, I. A. "Skelton's 'Philip Sparrow' and the Roman Service-Book," Modern Language Review, XXIX (1934), 389–96.

———— "Skelton's 'Speke Parrot,' " London Times Literary Supplement, February 1, 1934.

———— "New Light on Skelton," London Times Literary Supplement, September 20, 1934; cf. J. Lloyd, H. L. R. Edwards, and E. Ellam, ibid., September 27, 1934; F. M. Salter, ibid., January 17, 1935.

———— "A Skelton Query," London Times Literary Supplement, November 15, 1934.

Graves, R. "English Epigrams," London Times Literary Supplement, July 19, 1934; cf. E. Bensly, *ibid.*, August 2, 1934.

Hall, W. C. "John Skelton," Papers of the Manchester Literary Club, LIX (1933), 119–38.

Hooper, E. S. "Skelton's 'Magnyfycence' and Cardinal Wolsey," Modern Language Notes, XVI (1901), 213–15.

Kerr, W. "Skelton and Politian," London Times Literary Supplement, December 20, 1934.

Koelbing, A. "Barclay and Skelton, Early German Influences on English Literature," Cambridge History of English Literature, Vol. III, chap. iv.

—— Zur Charakteristik John Skelton's, Stuttgart, 1904.

Krumpholz, H. John Skelton und sein Morality Play "Magnyfycence," Prossnitz, 1881.

Levin, H. "Skelton and Oxford," London Times Literary Supplement, May 9, 1936; cf. H. E. Salter, *ibid.*, May 16, 1936.

Lloyd, L. J. "John Skelton; a Forgotten Poet," English Review, XL (1925), 659–65.

—— "John Skelton and the New Learning," Modern Language Review, XXIV (1929), 445–46.

—— "A Note on Skelton," The Review of English Studies, V (1929), 302–6.

—— John Skelton, Oxford, 1938.

Nelson, W. "Skelton's 'Speak, Parrot,' " PMLA, LI (1936), 59–82.

—— "Skelton's Quarrel with Wolsey," PMLA, LI (1936), 377–98.

—— and H. L. R. Edwards, "The Dating of Skelton's Later Poems," PMLA, LIII (1938), 601–22.

Pyle, F. "The Origins of the Skeltonic," Notes and Queries, CLXXXI (1936), 362–64.

Rey, A. Skelton's Satirical Poems in Their Relation to Lydgate's Order of Fools, Cocke Lorell's Bote, and Barclay's Ship of Fools, Berne, 1899.

Sale, H. S. "The Date of Skelton's 'Bowge of Court,' " Modern Language Notes, LII (1937), 572–74.

—— "The Date of the 'Garlande of Laurell,' " Modern Language Notes, XLIII (1928), 314–16.

—— "John Skelton and Christopher Garnesche," Modern Language Notes, XLIII (1928), 518–23.

Salter, F. M. "Skelton's 'Speculum Principis,' " Speculum, IX (1934), 25–37.

Schöneberg, G. Die Sprache John Skeltons in seinen kleineren Werken, Marburg, 1888.

SeBoyar, G. E. "Skelton's 'Replycacion,' " Modern Language Notes, XXVIII (1913), 244-45.

Stearns, H. See Sale, H. S.

Thümmel, A. Studien über John Skelton, Leipzig, 1905.

Weitzmann, F. "Philip Sparrow's 'Elegy,' " London Times Literary Supplement, December 13, 1934.

Westlake, H. F. "Skelton in Westminster," London Times Literary Supplement, October 27, 1921.

Index